James Hogg is a ghostwriter and biographer specialising in sport and entertainment. His works include the biography of actor and explorer Brian Blessed, Formula One legend Johnny Herbert and comedian Ernie Wise of Morecambe and Wise fame. James lives in Yorkshire with his wife and two children.

MORE THAN JUST A GOOD LIFE

The Authorised Biography of Richard Briers

JAMES HOGG

CONSTABLE

CONSTABLE

First published in Great Britain in 2018 by Constable
This paperback edition published in 2019 by Constable

1 3 5 7 9 10 8 6 4 2

A CIP catalogue record for this book
is available from the British Library.

ISBN: 978-1-47212-923-9

Typeset in Bembo by Hewer Text UK Ltd, Edinburgh
Printed and bound in Great Britain by Clays Ltd, Elcograf S.p.A.

Papers used by Constable are from well-managed
forests and other responsible sources.

Constable
An imprint of
Little, Brown Book Group
Carmelite House
50 Victoria Embankment
London EC4Y 0DZ

An Hachette UK Company
www.hachette.co.uk

www.littlebrown.co.uk

CONTENTS

INTRODUCTION

In March 1998 the actor, Olivia Williams, was in New York having recently made the film *Rushmore*, alongside Bill Murray and Jason Schwartzman. Shortly before filming ended Olivia had received a text message from a friend of hers back in England.

'Dad opens on 2 April at the Golden Theatre on West 45th St,' the message read.

The friend was Lucy Briers, Richard's youngest daughter. She and Olivia had studied drama together at the Bristol Old Vic and, as well as the two of them becoming close friends, their families had become close and often socialised. Olivia's father had recently been to see Lucy in *The Rivals* at the Nottingham Playhouse and the message went on to say that if Olivia was still in New York when he opened, Richard hoped that she would do the same. All she had to do was inform Lucy how many tickets she wanted, and when she wanted to go.

The play in question was *The Chairs* by Eugène Ionesco, an absurdist comedy from 1952 that also starred Geraldine McEwan. As well as a sell-out tour, it had already enjoyed a successful run in London's West End, and the producers and stars alike were all thrilled at the prospect of taking it across the pond.

As she planned to still be in town, Olivia accepted the offer of tickets and requested two. All she had to do now was find somebody to accompany her. The obvious choice was her co-star and host in New York, Bill Murray. She had been staying with him and his family Upstate and thought it would be an ideal way to say thank you. In hindsight, this might not have been a good idea. Ionesco, it's safe to say, isn't everyone's cup of tea and she wasn't quite sure of Bill's taste in absurdist theatre. The moment Murray accepted her invitation Olivia began catastrophising about what could go wrong. She now admits that she was still going through her, 'Hey, wouldn't it be great if . . .' period, where questionable ideas would be vocalised without any thought of the consequences.

The fact that the play, and, in particular, Richard, received unanimously favourable reviews in New York, just as they had in England, failed to dissipate Olivia's sense of foreboding. When she and Murray arrived at the John Golden Theatre she had no idea what to expect.

On curtain up Murray had been quiet and impassive but, despite her fears, Olivia still managed to focus most of her attentions on the play. She too was thrilled by the production and agreed with the magazine, *Variety*, which had said, 'There's a lot of fussing about seats in "The Chairs," [a reference to the set] the revival of Eugène Ionesco's 1952 absurdist landmark, but the true fuss is likely to take place at the box office once word spreads about Richard Briers' performance.'

Once or twice Olivia sneaked a glance at her famous guest to see if he was laughing, restless, intrigued or sleeping, but he remained entirely inscrutable, watching, but barely moving. He was giving nothing away.

As you would expect, Olivia had planned to visit Richard in

his dressing room after the show. She was aware that he hated being away from home, so a familiar face with a few words of congratulation would be just what he needed. What she hadn't bargained for, however, was the fact that she would have a famous friend in tow who may not have enjoyed the show. When Olivia suggested to Bill that they should go and see Richard, he replied with a characteristically unreadable 'Oh, OK, we could do that'.

When, finally, they reached Richard's dressing room, Olivia was still nervous. She could already hear Richard's voice from the other side of the door and he sounded his usual cheerful self. Whether Murray had enjoyed the show or not, it was going to be a bizarre pairing and no mistake. *The Good Life* meets *Ghostbusters*.

Buoyed somewhat by hearing Richard's voice, Olivia knocked on his door and a second or so later the door was flung open and there, in his dressing gown, was Richard. All smiles, he gave her the standard Dickie Briers greeting, which was delivered at a rate of knots.

'Hello, love, how are you? Do come on in. Come on, come on, in you come, in you come. Who's this then? Who's your friend? Isn't that Bill Murray? Good heavens!'

As soon as Olivia was able to get a word in she said her hellos and then cleared the way so the two actors could see each other.

'Bill,' said Olivia. 'This is Richard Briers. Richard, this is Bill Murray.'

The next few seconds were going to be pivotal. Not only to Olivia's friendship with the Briers family, which was very dear to her, but also to her accommodation for the next couple of days. As soon as she finished speaking, Bill held out a hand, fell to his knees, and proceeded to worship at the feet of the aston-ished Dickie, who stood there, for once, completely dumbstruck.

Thank fuck for that, Olivia thought.

Richard eventually found his words again.

'I don't deserve this,' he said. 'Good heavens, Mr Murray, please get up! I don't know what to say. Come and sit down. It's so lovely to meet you. I'm a huge fan, you know. Please though, you must get up!'

Since opening night, Richard and Geraldine, who had also received fantastic notices, had received a steady stream of Hollywood stars, including Meryl Streep and Al Pacino, who had come backstage to congratulate them. None had fallen to their knees though.

Despite feeling embarrassed, Richard was thrilled to bits at Murray's gesture and over the next hour they sat on his dress-ing-room sofa, had a few drinks and chatted. The star of *Saturday Night Live* and *Groundhog Day* grilled Richard about rehearsing this unperformable absurdist play, after which they compared notes on playing Polonius. A year previously Richard had played Polonius in Kenneth Branagh's film adaptation of *Hamlet*, a role that Murray himself had recently been offered for a new adaptation starring Ethan Hawke. The juxtaposition of these two actors was nothing less than glorious.

This, more than any other anecdote that's been recalled during the research of this book, encapsulates the story you are about to read. It would be unwise to divulge the reasons why, as you might not read on. Suffice to say that the elements that make up Olivia's story – friendship, generosity, loyalty, travel anxiety, unease, concern, theatres, film stars, anticipation, reviews, swear words and alcohol – are prevalent throughout. What makes her anecdote especially pertinent, however, is that it proves, in the most amusing way, that anyone who had Richard Briers down as being a middle-class sitcom actor who drank tea, enjoyed gardening and went on daytrips to Eastbourne with Dame Thora Hird should reconsider their supposition immediately. After all, there aren't many sitcom actors who have appeared on Broadway, been nominated for a Tony Award and who have been worshipped – literally – by Bill Murray.

CHAPTER ONE

'That's not my baby!'

Richard David Briers was born on 14 January 1934 in Nelson Hospital in Merton, south-west London. His mother, Morna Phyllis (née Richardson), endured a difficult labour and after finally giving birth to Richard, he was immediately taken away so that she could rest. When Morna awoke a few hours later she asked a nurse if she could at last see her newborn baby.

'Certainly,' said the nurse. 'I'll fetch him now.'

After about ten minutes the nurse hadn't returned and Morna was becoming anxious. She was about to ask what on earth was going on when suddenly the nurse appeared carrying a tiny baby.

'He's absolutely beautiful,' said the nurse as she arrived at the side of the bed. 'Your husband has called, by the way. He'll be here in about an hour.'

As the nurse went to hand Morna her bundle of joy she instinctively held out her arms. The labour had lasted a good eight hours – 'eight hours' hard labour', she later called it – and to finally see the fruit of said labour was already becoming an emotional experience.

'There we are,' said the nurse as Morna took the baby. 'Remember to support his head.'

As the nurse was speaking Morna took a first look at her newborn child, and let out a piercing scream.

'What on earth's wrong?' said the nurse.

'That's not my baby!' yelled Morna. 'That's not my baby!'

'Now now, Mrs Briers,' cooed the nurse. 'Of course he's your baby. Look at him. Isn't he gorgeous? He's definitely got your eyes. Don't you worry. You're just a little bit emotional. Most mothers are at this stage.'

'I'm telling you now,' declared Morna, who was becoming annoyed, 'that is not my baby. Now, would you please take him away?'

Obviously believing that Morna was having some kind of breakdown, the nurse left her with the child and ran off to consult a higher authority. She returned presently with a doctor and the sister of the maternity ward. Morna, although still cradling the unwanted child, wasted no time in repeating her concerns.

'She's given me the wrong baby!' cried Morna. 'Now would somebody please take him away from me and find my baby!'

'Come along, Mrs Briers,' began the doctor, in his most patronising bedside manner. 'What on earth makes you think he isn't yours? Remember, you have been through rather a lot today. You're probably still a bit tired.'

'Never mind tired,' snapped Morna. 'He's got red hair. Look!'

With that Morna pulled back the blanket to reveal a sleeping newborn with a shock of bright red hair.

The doctor, who was still in full-on patronising mode, continued, 'Come, come. There's nothing strange about your baby having red hair, Mrs Briers. Lots of babies have red hair.'

'Actually, doctor, there is! Neither I nor my husband have red hair. None of my family have red hair, and unless my husband has been hiding red-haired relatives from me, neither does he. I'm telling you now, this is NOT my baby.'

With that, the doctor, who was now becoming nervous, asked to have a word with the nurse and the ward sister privately. When they returned, the ward sister, who appeared even more nervous, instructed the nurse, who was terrified, to take the baby back to the hospital nursery.

'What's happening?' asked Morna. 'Has anything happened to my baby?'

Without giving her an answer, the ward sister followed the nurse and a few minutes later the same nurse appeared, carrying a different bundle of joy.

'I'm so sorry,' she said, handing the bundle to Morna. 'It's never happened before. How can you ever forgive me?'

Uninterested in recriminations, Morna simply smiled at the nurse and gratefully took the bundle from her.

'*That's* my baby!' she cried once she had set eyes on him. 'Thank you, nurse. Thank you!'

Years later Richard claimed, quite legitimately, that he must have been the world's youngest ever farceur. Well, he and the red-haired imposter.

When Richard's father, Joseph Benjamin – or Joe, to all who knew him – came to collect Morna and Richard, the address to which he took them back was a one-bedroom flat at 12 Thornton Hill, Wimbledon. These days the road is chock-a-block full of millionaires, but in 1934 it was anything but and, although it wasn't a poor area exactly, it was a far cry from that to which his mother had been accustomed.

Morna, who was five feet tall, had blue eyes, long fair hair and, according to Richard's younger sister Jane, was feminine but feisty. She had been born in 1913 in the Indian city of Allahabad in the province of Uttar Pradesh, as had Morna's mother, Lillian. Morna's father, Frederick, had moved to Allahabad from London at the end of the nineteenth century and had carved out a successful career as a civil servant. As well as owning a large six-bedroom house with an acre or so of garden, the family had several servants and they enjoyed a rich and varied social life.

It seems that the acting gene, certainly with regards to the Richardson side of the family, might well have been passed down to Richard from Morna's father, Frederick – or Fred, as he was usually known.

'The operas of Gilbert and Sullivan were very, very popular back then,' says Richard's sister Jane, who must also have caught the gene as she too has spent her entire adult life as an actor. 'And my grandfather Fred, and my grandmother, come to think of it, were absolutely wild about them. They all were.'

Amateur dramatics was absolutely huge during the Raj, and because of their popularity the works of Gilbert and Sullivan were much performed. Not always very well, according to some sources, but what the actors lacked in talent they more than made up for in enthusiasm.

'Fred was actually quite good,' says Jane. 'And he specialised in playing the comedy character roles. It's all he did outside of work. He was obsessed!'

In the Allahabad *Saturday Gazette*, dated 11 February 1922, an extensive two-page review appeared for a performance of Gilbert and Sullivan's *The Gondoliers*, which had taken place the previous Tuesday. Produced by an amateur dramatics company bearing the same name as the opera itself, it was played over three nights at the Allahabad Coral Club and attracted a combined, and it appears appreciative, audience of well over 4000 people. The review (which goes on at some length and misspells the word cast as 'caste') pays tribute to everyone and everything concerned, from the costumes – 'the creation of Madame Dagmar's artistic brain' – to the gentlemen of the Government Carpentry School who designed and built the gondola. Not forgetting, of course, Messrs Youd et Cie, 'the famous Calcutta hairdressers', who supplied the wigs.

As one would expect, each member of the cast receives their own mini appraisal, including Richard and Jane's grandfather, Fred, who played the Duke of Plaza-Toro, a popular comic baritone part. 'Nonetheless deserving,' says the uncredited journalist, 'was Mr Richardson as the Duke who made an apt aristocrat, his facial contortions being at times excruciatingly funny.'

Morna too dabbled in acting – she played, among other roles, Jingles the Court Jester in a production of *Zurika, the Gypsy Maid*, causing, much to her father's satisfaction, 'considerable amusement' – and later went on to teach drama, as did Jane. Her real talents, however, lay as a concert pianist and by the time she became a teenager she was already being tipped for a place at the Royal College of Music in London.

'That was our mother's passion,' says Jane. 'And although she wasn't the first member of my family to be musical, she was the first who had the talent to do it professionally.'

Proof of Morna's early promise can be found in a copy of the *Naini Tal Gazette* dated Thursday 23 April 1925. Inside are the results of the theoretical music examinations that had been held the previous November. They state that 'Miss Mona [*sic*] Richardson, pupil of Miss L Pease, gained the Senior Exhibition Prize of nine guineas for scoring the highest marks in India at the Practical Music Examination held in the Naini Tal.'

Naturally proud of their talented daughter, Fred and Lillian Richardson eventually contacted the Royal College of Music and informed them of their daughter's prowess. Obviously impressed, they invited her for an interview and in June 1930, having been offered a place at the college, Morna and her family relocated to London so that she could begin her studies. While at the college, Morna would be taught to play the organ by a young Malcolm Sargent and receive lectures on conducting from a slightly older Adrian Boult.

By the time Morna and her family had arrived at Southampton docks, her future husband Joe had already been married a year, had a young son and was working as an estate agent's clerk in Harrow.

Born in 1907, Joe's family had been tenant farmers in Middlesex for much of the nineteenth century although his own father, Ben, had taken against agriculture from an early age and managed to plough his own furrow by making a career in finance. Compared to Morna, Joe's childhood had been fairly unremarkable and, as opposed to continuing his education after leaving school or at least following a particular ambition, he had simply flitted from job to job while suffering from an acutely short attention span.

In 1926 he had married a local girl called Vivienne Knott and in 1929 she had given birth to a son called Francis George. Other than that, little is known about Joe's early life or about his first marriage. Indeed, according to Jane, their father wasn't keen on discussing the past, full stop – 'Very few people were from that generation,' says Jane – and when Richard eventually contacted Francis, who then went by the name of Gordon, sometime in the 1960s, they developed a cordial relationship but were never close.

One thing Joe did have in common with Morna was a love of music and a talent for performing, although his ability was probably more aligned to that of her parents than it was hers. That said, Joe attended classes at the Guildhall School of Music occasionally and, by all accounts, he was a gifted singer. Subsequently, to supplement his sometimes erratic income, Joe would often perform with a pianist at masonic events and other gatherings in the City of London. While at the Royal College of Music, which she attended from 1930 to 1933, Morna would also earn a few extra pounds by performing at such events and, sometime in 1932, she received an urgent enquiry from a singer by the name of Joseph Briers. His usual pianist was ill, and he wondered if she could fill in for him at an event he had booked in the City of London. Morna accepted without hesitation and six months later Joe had left Vivienne and had set up home with Morna. Joe's relationship with Vivienne had been on the decline since Francis's birth and there was little outcry from their families at the separation as it was generally accepted as being a fait accompli.

Not that this made much of a difference to Joe and Morna's new life together. With a young child and a soon-to-be ex-wife to support, not to mention a propensity to move from job to job, Joe had even less money than usual and when Morna discovered that she was pregnant in the spring of 1933, it's fair to say that there were mixed feelings at 12 Thornton Hill. Morna, who was about to leave the Royal College of Music, had, according to one of her tutors, a potentially brilliant career as a concert pianist ahead of her and although the new arrival wouldn't necessarily prevent her from working, it would certainly make a difference. Fortunately for the expectant couple, Morna's parents were thrilled at the news of the pregnancy and offered to help them physically, as in babysitting, and financially. Fred and Lillian Richardson certainly weren't wealthy, not by any means, and for several years they had been living in slightly reduced circumstances in India. This had continued after their relocation, but they were still able to relieve some of the pressure from their daughter's young shoulders, and their joy at the occasion of the birth was palpable.

By the time Richard arrived his father was working as a bookmaker; something he enjoyed and was apparently rather good at. Joe, who was tall and had green eyes and dark brown hair, was quite a gregarious character, which helped to oil the wheels in many of the jobs he took. Conversely, he was also prone to bouts of nervousness and this is something he most definitely passed on to his new son.

'He was a good sort, but his attitude was "live for today",' Richard said in 2010. 'He was a bookmaker most of his life, but he never saved. He wanted to be popular in the pub, which he was. He was a rolling stone who liked life to be pleasant, but money was always short.'

The nervous energy that Richard inherited from his father manifested itself via the speed at which he spoke; something he eventually managed to turn to his advantage.

'He was five when I was born in 1939,' says Jane, 'and that's one of the first things I remember. He could talk incredibly fast.'

It appears that the source of all this nervousness was actually Joe's father.

'My paternal grandfather was a stockbroker with a very big personality,' remembered Richard. 'He was six-feet-two-inches, eighteen stone and quite overpowering and my father was frightened of him. He was always being told off as a boy and it gave him a complex that he wasn't really very good at anything, which was a shame.'

By the time Jane arrived the Briers family had moved from Wimbledon into a block of flats called Pepys Court just up the road in Raynes Park.

'The fact that the block was completely white didn't improve our chances much when London was being bombed,' remembers Jane. 'In fact, we seemed to spend our entire lives in the entrance hall. That's where we all congregated if there was an air raid, although I have no idea why.'

CHAPTER TWO

A Talent to Amuse

The first four years of Richard's life were spent either in the care of his mother, who had worked steadily since Richard was born and was gaining a fine reputation as a pianist, or with her parents, who lived in Wimbledon. As the Richardsons' first grandchild he was doted on and it was a sad day when they finally had to hand him over to the education system. Unfortunately for Morna, she wasn't able to utilise all the spare time she had once Richard had gone to school: after the war effort had taken hold, many orchestras, which were obviously affected by financial constraints and by conscription, had to close or at least take an indefinite sabbatical.

'I'm afraid that the war completely put paid to her career,' says Jane. 'She did find some work, but they were sporadic jobs for money as opposed to actual positions in orchestras. She wasn't the only one, of course. The war changed everything for everyone.'

For the young Richard, who from September 1938 attended Rokeby Preparatory School in Kingston upon Thames, the war presented two opportunities: collecting ironmongery, which he did from the ammunitions dump down the road from Pepys Court, and impersonating an Austrian-born homicidal maniac. Jane remembers Morna telling her about the allure of the ammunitions dump.

'According to her, Richard used to collect everything from that dump. He was fascinated by it and would arrive home with dead bullets, shells and pieces of shrapnel. I think all boys were into that.'

The impersonations are something that Jane remembers first hand.

'I'd have been about three or four at the time, but I remember Richard standing on a large bin one day while some children gathered around him. All of a sudden, he started shouting in a funny accent and waving one of his arms in the air. He carried on doing this for some time and I eventually realised he was impersonating Hitler!'

Richard's performance went down a storm with the children of Raynes Park and 'Briers does Hitler' became a long-running hit.

'We all used to fall about laughing,' remembers Jane. 'And the more we laughed, the longer he went on. He was far more engaging than the odious little man he was impersonating.'

Not surprisingly, Richard's passion for making people laugh wasn't always left at the school gates and it had been getting him into trouble right from day one.

'When our mother went to collect him from school on his first day she saw through the windows a child sitting at his desk *outside* the classroom. The desks and chairs, which were adjoined, had wheels on the bottom which meant that if a child was misbehaving they could be wheeled into the corridor.'

On closer inspection, Morna realised that the child who had been banished to the corridor was none other than Richard, and when she spoke to the woman who had wheeled him there, a teacher called Kate Walton-Smith, and asked her what his crime had been, she simply smiled at Morna and gave her a knowing but slightly frustrated look.

'It appears we have a bit of an entertainer on our hands here, Mrs Briers,' said the exasperated educator. 'He's very good at impressions, I'll give him that. His attention span needs work, however.'

Funnily enough, Richard's underdeveloped attention span had recently started becoming an issue at home too as it interfered with one of his chores.

'Mother had started sending Richard down to the shops whenever she needed something,' says Jane. 'And, after giving him the money and telling him what she wanted, off he'd trot. Fifteen minutes later he'd wander back in and when Mother asked him where the shopping was he'd say, "Oh, sorry, I forgot." He never changed really and our poor mother used to tear her hair out.'

Kate Walton-Smith had been teaching at Rokeby for over a decade when Richard arrived and, during that time, she had needed to cope with all kinds of testing behaviour.

Richard's older daughter Kate remembers Miss Walton-Smith explaining why she used to wheel her father into the corridor, and it wasn't quite the reason one might expect.

'Kate Walton-Smith had a real soft spot for Dad and they kept in touch until the day she died. We used to go to her house sometimes for tea and quite often the conversation would veer on to Dad's behaviour at school. Apparently, the main reason for her wheeling him into the corridor wasn't just because he was making his classmates laugh, it was because he made her laugh, so he actually managed to distract his own teacher! I think the attention span also played a part, or lack of, but I think the fact that his teacher had to remove him because he was making her laugh is wonderful.'

About three years later, which is when Jane remembers accompanying Morna on the school run, the situation hadn't changed.

'It didn't happen every time we picked him up,' says Jane, 'but I'd say he was in the corridor at least a third of the time. Mother used to go spare, but it didn't make any difference. We thought it was because he was being naughty.'

Richard later confirmed that he had no interest in school whatsoever and, when he wasn't trying to make his teachers or his fellow pupils laugh to relieve the boredom, he was simply daydreaming.

'It's not that Richard didn't want to learn,' says Jane. 'He just wanted to learn about subjects that interested him. In that respect he became a great self-educator. In fact, my one abiding memory of my brother is seeing him in the corner of our living room reading a book. He was always a voracious little reader.'

But there was another reason why the young Richard Briers wasted little time in becoming the class comedian, and it was all to do with self-preservation.

'According to Dad there were quite a lot of bullies at his school,' says Lucy. 'And early on I think he was picked on quite a bit.'

Although he was never short for his age, Richard was terribly thin as a child and as well as being, as he put it, 'a little bit of a softie,' he had absolutely no time for sports. He had realised soon after starting school that this rendered him as bully fodder and it seemed the only way of deterring the potential perpetrators was by impersonating the Führer and playing everything for laughs.

'Unfortunately, I think this merely intensified all that natural nervous energy he had,' says Kate. 'And because he was so busy making people laugh and keeping the bullies at bay he became a walking distraction; not only to those around him, but also to himself.'

At home, things were a little bit easier for Richard and by the time he was five he had already developed a keen passion for cinema.

'I had the back bedroom at Pepys Court, which overlooked a small car park and the Rialto Cinema,' he said in 2010. 'I think it's a funeral parlour now, which is a shame, but when I was in bed, I couldn't quite decipher the dialogue, but I could hear Humphrey Bogart's and James Cagney's voices.'

Trips to the cinema were a common occurrence for most households back in the 1930s and Richard would go as often as he could find a sponsor.

'I remember seeing Laurel and Hardy for the very first time,' he said in 1982. 'And that's something you don't forget in a hurry. I think I was about four or five years old and they were the first people I'd seen who I knew were being funny on purpose. It actually felt like they were being funny just for me. They taught me how to laugh.'

When he was about eight or nine years old, and after spending hours on end trying to persuade somebody – anybody – to take him to either the Rialto or one of the four other cinemas in nearby Wimbledon, his parents finally relented, and the budding film buff was allowed to go to the cinema without an adult, but there was one small condition.

'That condition was me, I'm afraid,' remembers Jane. 'And until we became close when I was five or six years old, he probably saw me as a bit of a burden. In fact, I'm absolutely sure he did.'

When Jane had first arrived at Pepys Court, Richard had been fairly attentive. Until the first bath time, that is. Then, when it became clear that his parents had brought him a sister and not a brother like he had wished for, he made his feelings known.

'Look, it hasn't got a willy,' he complained to his mother as she bathed Jane. 'You'll have to take it back right away and fetch me a new one!'

Richard's disapproval of his new sister persisted and as time went on the ways in which he demonstrated this became more and more creative. One day, shortly after an air-raid siren had sounded, Morna was leaving Pepys Court in a hurry with Richard and Jane when she suddenly realised she had forgotten something. 'Stay here, and I'll be back in a minute,' said Morna.

'I think this is probably my earliest memory,' says Jane, 'as I must have been about eighteen months old. I had lots of lovely blonde curls when I was very young and when my mother disappeared back to the flat, Richard took out a small pair of scissors that he must have pinched from school and chopped them all off! The thing is, I actually remember him doing it. I didn't mind one bit though. In fact, I think I just giggled. I thought it was fun. Mother didn't!'

It wasn't just Hitler's bombs that were a danger to children during the war. Disease was rife, especially in the cities, and child mortality was still frighteningly high.

One day at school, when Richard was eight years old, he suddenly started complaining of having earache. He was never a sickly child so his teacher, Miss Walton-Smith, sent him straight to the school nurse. Within an hour Richard had also come down with a fever and, as well as feeling extremely dizzy, he could barely stand up. Fearing he may have the mumps and even the dreaded meningitis, the nurse immediately took him to the local hospital where he was examined by a doctor.

'I'm afraid he had mastoiditis,' remembers Jane, 'which at that time was a major cause of child mortality in Britain. We were all desperately worried.'

Mastoiditis is a bacterial infection of the mastoid air cells that surround the inner and middle ear. Often the result of an untreated middle-ear infection, until penicillin came along it was very often fatal and even by the 1940s survival was not guaranteed.

'Antibiotics were still being developed,' remembers Jane, 'and for a few days it was feared we might lose him. I was only three at the time, but I remember visiting him in hospital. Mother was in floods of tears.'

Fortunately, the antibiotics he had been prescribed gradually started having an effect and within a week or so he was back to his old self again. Much to the relief of his family, of course, and even his long-suffering teacher.

'Miss Walton-Smith actually went to visit Richard in hospital. Isn't that nice? I know he could drive her crazy sometimes but there was obviously a bond between them.'

CHAPTER THREE

'If this attitude persists, one of us will have to leave.'

Growing up in London during the Second World War was obviously a different experience for children than it was for adults, providing they were not personally affected. Not surprisingly, some children found air aids and the like quite exciting and it was only when an explosion was actually felt that emotions such as fear made an appearance.

'Richard and I only experienced fear very occasionally,' remembers Jane. 'In fact, the only time I remember us being scared during the war was when we thought my parents were. That could be quite terrifying as you felt vulnerable.'

By far the most disturbing thing Richard and Jane ever saw during the war was the look on their father's face one evening after he had driven an ambulance to a house that had been hit by a bomb.

'Mother worked for the ARP [Air Raid Precautions] during the war,' says Jane, 'as did Fred and Lillian, and Father worked for the ambulances. Until this happened I don't think I'd realised what the consequences of war actually were. I was just too young.'

Richard went on to say something similar in an interview with the *Telegraph* many years later.

'When the sirens sounded we had to run like hell down to

the cement shelter under our block of flats. There'd be about forty of us down there, sometimes for hours on end, so we ended up getting very matey. It was so boring down there, particularly if you didn't have a comic to read. I know it sounds wrong, but I was always quite glad when there was a bang outside as at least something was happening.'

Jane remembers sitting with Richard in the living room on that fateful evening when suddenly their father opened the front door.

'As always, we ran to greet him but as we did I could see that his face was as white as a sheet. He was also on the verge of tears and the expression he wore was one of pure, unadulterated sorrow. I'd never seen anything like it before in my life. I don't think either of us had.'

About an hour earlier, Joe and his colleague had been called to a house in Wimbledon, which had been hit by a doodlebug. On sifting through the aftermath, they had found the bodies of five small children, assumedly siblings.

'I don't think my father had meant for Richard and me to hear about what he'd seen, but when Mother asked him what the matter was he just told her. I remember Richard and I were devastated and after that everything changed. All of a sudden, the war felt real and from then on, the moment we heard an air-raid siren we'd cling to each other like glue. It's funny, but before that night I don't think either of us had ever had to worry about anything in our lives. Well, nothing really important. After that we rarely stopped worrying, at least for the duration of the war.'

For the previous year or so Joe had been working for an air-filter manufacturer called Vokes. The factory, which was based in Guildford, Surrey, had a tannoy system installed and from time to time people's names would be called out and they would be asked to report to the manager's office right away. It didn't take Joe very long to realise that the reason for them being summoned was not because they were getting a promotion, or even a ticking off. It was to break the news that their families had been either killed or injured during an air raid and because of what he had seen at the bomb site, it was starting to turn an already nervous Joe into an absolute wreck. Unable to cope with the anxiety, he decided to take drastic action and within a couple of weeks he had managed to find his family some alternative accommodation in a village called Worplesdon, near Guildford.

'We were actually sharing a house with another family,' remembers Jane. 'But because of his schooling, it was decided that Richard would stay behind during the week and live with our grandparents in Wimbledon. I don't think my father was very happy, but life had to go on.'

With hindsight, and given Richard's scholarly instincts, or lack of them, staying on in Wimbledon was something of a waste of time. Fred and Lillian, who were paying for his education, still had high hopes for their first-born grandchild and at least wanted to get their money's worth. Richard, although happier being in Wimbledon surrounded by cinemas than he would have been in Worplesdon surrounded by sheep, still found the whole education thing a terrible bore and, unable to escape the confines of Rokeby Preparatory School from the hours of 8.45 a.m. until 3.15 p.m. (he would find that slightly easier at secondary school), he was eventually forced to branch out from just telling jokes, daydreaming and impersonating despots.

'I'm afraid he became a kind of junior spiv,' says Lucy. 'It's one of quite a few paradoxes surrounding my father as people tend to assume that as a child he was probably bright, studious, middle-class, well-behaved and politely spoken, and as an adult somebody who never swore, never smoked, drank tea, went to church and watched *Songs of Praise* all the time. If only they knew!'

Although it would come into its own in secondary school, Richard's career as a wheeler and dealer started at the age of ten when, after being asked one day by several fellow pupils if they could have one of his sweets, he discovered the economic model of supply and demand: Briers has sweets – Kids want sweets – Kids give Briers money – Briers gives them sweets – Briers buys more sweets – Kids buy more sweets. By the following day Richard had procured about ten bags of assorted sweets and, during playtime and lunchtime, he sold the lot.

'He was always the last one to eat his sweets,' says Jane. 'Most children would wolf them down immediately but not Richard. I remember eating mine one day after we'd each been given a bag by our grandparents and two days later – two days! – he pulled his out. I couldn't believe it. "Can I have one?" I begged, but he just looked at me with this rather smug grin on his face. He was like a very young Bond villain!'

By the time Richard had started attending the Ridgeway School in Wimbledon in September 1945, having unfortunately failed the entrance exam for King's College Wimbledon, he had extended his product range somewhat and in addition to assorted sweeties he was now peddling comics, including the *Beano*, *Dandy* and *Hotspur*, several brands of cigarette, including Woodbines and Park Drive, and even alcohol. A friend of his, whose parents owned a particularly well-occupied drinks cabinet, used to invite Richard around when his parents were out and after syphoning off a noggin or two for themselves he would then allow Richard to syphon some more and sell it at school.

'You see what I mean about paradoxes?' says Lucy. 'My dad became a byword for convention and decency in the 1960s, 1970s and 1980s, yet at the age of just eleven he was selling cigarettes and alcohol to his peers!'

So prolific did Richard's business interests become at Ridgeway School that at the end of 1947 the headmaster wrote in his annual report, 'It would seem that Richard Briers thinks he is running the school and not me. If this attitude persists one of us will have to leave.'

Joking apart, Richard always believed that had he not become an actor he would have made a career out of petty crime.

'The fact is, he was good at it,' says Lucy. 'In fact, at the time it was probably the only thing he felt he could succeed at.'

Indeed, when the television programme *Minder* (in which Richard later appeared in a feature-length episode called 'An Officer and a Car Salesman') started in the late 1970s, he commented immediately that the character of Arthur Daley, which was played by his old friend, George Cole, was actually him had he not become an actor.

'It may sound funny, but he really wasn't joking,' says Lucy. 'You see, this was before Dad had taken a serious interest in acting, and I think it was becoming addictive. He could feel himself being attracted to a ducker and diver type lifestyle.'

With money always being so scarce in the Briers household, Richard would shun any feelings of guilt and responsibility in favour of the notion that his 'commercial interests' were simply an antidote to being poor. Pretty soon, the antidote became a preoccupation and even when his sense of enterprise had shifted from his childhood black-market caper to the potentially fame-inducing acting profession, his desire to remain solvent persisted and merely strengthened as time went on.

'It's fair to say it became an obsession with him,' says Annie, Richard's widow. 'Ever since we met he was terrified about not having money in the bank and his work ethic reflected that. Once he'd found his niche, of course.'

When Richard wasn't flogging things at school he was playing truant from it, and if someone ever wanted to find him during school hours when he wasn't on the premises, there was only one place to look, and that was Raynes Park Station.

'He used to go to the waiting room there and read P. G. Wodehouse,' says Lucy, 'sometimes for hours on end. Even if he had an exam to do, he'd just write his name at the top of the paper, sneak out as soon as the teacher wasn't looking, and go straight there. It was his reading room.'

No one can remember who first introduced Richard to P. G. Wodehouse, but the celebrated Guildford-born author who had moved to America in 1946 became one of three passions that began during his early teenage years and would last the rest of his life; the other two being the American entertainer, Danny Kaye, whom he had first seen in the 1946 musical film, *Wonder Man*, and the Victorian actor-manager, Sir Henry Irving.

'Even at that age Dad was quite anachronistic,' says Lucy. 'And he was definitely a bit of an oddball. In fact, the only thing that rescued him from drawing his pension at thirteen and walking with a stick was his love of Danny Kaye. I think the other two aged him somewhat.'

The difference between P. G. Wodehouse, Sir Henry Irving and Danny Kaye, with regards to Richard's perusal of their work during his childhood, was that he read Wodehouse avidly, studied Irving devotedly, and impersonated Kaye badly.

'He was so fond of Danny Kaye,' says Jane. 'You see, Richard couldn't sing or dance, nor could he play an instrument. In fact, he had an absolutely terrible singing voice. That didn't matter, though. He'd seen all the films dozens of times and as well as knowing all the words to Danny Kaye's songs he knew all his moves and mannerisms. As long as there was one of Danny Kaye's seventy-eight records playing on the gramophone, he was very convincing.'

Richard's impressions of Danny Kaye always took place in the family home on either a Friday or Saturday evening. Towards the end of the war, Jane, Morna and Joe had moved back to London from Worplesdon and, with Pepys Court now re-let and with very little money coming in, they had been forced to move in with Richard, Fred and Lillian in Wimbledon. A piano was a mainstay in the Richardson home, and, after kicking off the proceedings by playing a piece by either Chopin or Mozart, Morna would then accompany young Jane as she sang a song by Shirley Temple. Third on the bill would always be Richard doing his Danny Kaye impression, after which Fred and Lillian, if they felt up to it, might sing something by Gilbert and Sullivan. Topping the bill at the 'Briers/Richardson Front Room Theatre' would be Morna and Joe, recreating the night they had first met back in 1932 playing, among others, the songs they had performed in the City of London.

'Those evenings were such a treat,' remembers Jane. 'Mother would play Chopin and make everybody cry, and then Father would sing a ballad and do the same. We were all performers, I suppose. All six of us. Although Richard and I didn't know it yet.'

Despite never training to be an actor, Morna had always been slightly obsessed by the acting industry and Jane believes that she, together with the aforementioned evenings and regular visits to the cinema, sparked Richard's interest.

'He'd actually started acting about three years previously,' remembers Jane, 'but that was just for fun. Our grandfather, Fred, ever the theatrical, used to make up stories based on two unnamed members of Hitler's government who he called the Fat Man and the Thin Man. I wish I'd asked him who the characters were based on, but I'm afraid I never did.'

After Fred had finished entertaining his grandchildren, Richard and Jane would retire to her bedroom where they would improvise stories featuring these two characters, usually for hours on end.

'We always used to do it on my bed, which meant we could push each other over,' remembers Jane. 'And it would usually go on either until we made too much noise or until I got hurt! After a while it would sometimes morph into us doing an impression of Laurel and Hardy, who every child in the land used to love watching at the cinema. In that respect there were probably millions of children all around the world doing exactly the same thing.'

Despite being close, Richard and Jane would often fight like cat and dog and, until she was about five years old, her older, taller and heavier brother would invariably come out on top.

'Then, I discovered his shins!' says Jane. 'One day he had me up against a wall after a fight and almost by accident I kicked him right on his shin. Suddenly, he started hopping around the room like a mad thing. *Got him!* I thought. From that moment on I actually stood a chance. I'd discovered his Achilles shin!'

With the balance shifting slightly, Richard decided to change tack and, as well as shifting the position of his legs, he also started issuing threats.

'Once again, he'd get me against the wall after beating me in a fight,' says Jane. 'But this time, he'd make sure I couldn't reach his shins. Then, once he knew he was safe, he'd say something like, "You tell Mum and I'll duff you up again! Got it?" To which I would reply, "I promise I won't say anything! Let me go, let me go!" Then, the moment he let me go, I'd run to the top of the stairs and shout, "MUUUUUUUUUUUUUMMY!" His face was an absolute picture!'

Jane's least favourite experience due to her brother's behaviour was the night he told her there was no Father Christmas.

'It was Christmas Eve one year and I was talking up the chimney to Father Christmas. I forget what I was saying exactly – probably asking for presents – but all of a sudden Richard walked in and said, "What on earth are you doing?" to which I replied, "I'm talking to Father Christmas, silly." Richard then sat down and said, "Ha! There is no Father Christmas."'

The scene that followed Richard's cruel revelation is one that has probably been played out in millions of households all over the world: the older, more enlightened sibling informing the younger innocent sibling that Father Christmas is actually their own father dressed up. Even so, Morna was far from happy with her son and tried desperately to reverse the situation.

'It was no good,' explains Jane. 'You see, for some reason I used to believe everything Richard said. Everything! It didn't matter what it was, if it came out of my brother's mouth, I considered it to be gospel. That was obviously the actor in him. Even then, he was incredibly plausible.'

But Richard's role as a typical older brother – one that rules with a rod of iron and beats up his younger siblings – was always more of a cameo part. Like most children in that situation, he was quite protective towards his sister, especially after hearing about what Joe had witnessed in Wimbledon.

'He was never a nasty little boy,' says Jane. 'But after that awful night in the war we became concerned with each other's wellbeing. In fact, I don't think we ever stopped worrying about each other after that.'

The best example of Richard's early concern and subsequent generosity took place shortly before the end of the war.

'I'd lost my panda,' says Jane. 'It sounds awfully trivial now but at the time of me losing it I was absolutely inconsolable. I think I'd lost it somewhere on Wimbledon Common and I was so upset that my parents spent an entire day scouring every inch of the common trying to find it.'

By the following day there was still no sign of Jane's panda and, just as she was beginning to resign herself to a life of panda-less misery and bedtime loneliness, Richard appeared.

'I remember sitting in my bedroom the day after my parents had tried to find my little panda and I was still crying. Then, all of a sudden, Richard came in carrying his teddy bear. "This is for you," he said, handing me the bear. "You will look after him, won't you?" I remember looking up at him thinking, *What a lovely thing to do*. I was so incredibly grateful.'

As well as impersonating Laurel and Hardy and improvising situations featuring two of Hitler's henchmen, Richard and Jane would also create news reports like the ones they had heard on the BBC Home Service. Read by the likes of John Snagge and Alvar Lidell, these would always start, 'Here is the news, and this is John Snagge/Alvar Lidell reading it', so as to distinguish the newsreaders from enemy propagandists. This is when Jane first noticed her brother's extraordinary verbal delivery, something for which he later became famous – and, for a time, infamous.

'He'd always been a quick talker,' says Jane, 'but not so as you'd really notice. Also, because it went with his personality – in that he always had the gift of the gab and could talk his way out of most situations – it didn't seem that strange. It was just part of Richard. Then, when he started improvising these news reports, which seemed to come out of nowhere, it was like hearing him for the first time. He just went on, and on, and on, at a hundred miles an hour. He was like a machine gun! He'd simply sit down, pretend to shuffle some papers, and then begin. "Here is the news, and this is Richard Briers reading it. Today, the Fat Man and the Thin Man, two of Hitler's most feared henchmen, were captured by two brave children in the west London area. Richard and Jane Briers, who live with their parents and grandparents in a nice house, intend to show these two varmints no mercy whatsoever and have asked Winston Churchill himself to come and collect them in his car."

'Looking back, he was incredibly creative,' continues Jane, 'And although we were just playing games there was obviously something there. He was incredibly talented.'

But it was Richard's anachronistic fascination with the actor Sir Henry Irving that sparked his ambition to become an actor.

'I forget who it was, but somebody once gave me a copy of a book about Sir Henry Irving called *The Actor and His World*,' Richard said in 1997. 'It was written by his grandson, Laurence Irving, and it was huge, about five hundred pages. It completely changed my life.'

The 'big red book' that was handed to Richard at the end of his first appearance on *This Is Your Life* in 1972 (he was the subject again in 1994) reveals that the person who thought Richard might benefit from owning a copy of Laurence Irving's homage to his revered grandfather was a Mrs Constance McDonnell, a friend of the family who had emigrated to Australia with her family in the 1950s. So significant was her gift, even in the eyes of the producers at ITV, that she was flown over as a surprise guest.

Until reading that book, Richard had been a show-off with a quick mouth who liked films, and despite his mother's interest in performers and performing, which Richard undoubtedly shared, that's all it ever had been – an interest. It was Irving who brought it all to life.

Born in Somerset in 1838, the year of Queen Victoria's coronation, Sir Henry Irving had become the first-ever theatrical knight and is credited with making the acting profession respectable. Despite passing away in 1905, his myriad achievements influenced countless twentieth-century actors including luminaries such as Sir Donald Wolfit, Sir Laurence Olivier, Dame Edith Evans and Sir John Gielgud (all of whom were early heroes of Richard's), and they continue to do so to this day. Known as 'The Guvnor', Irving spent much of his career at the Lyceum Theatre in London where he built around him a talented and devoted company of artists, designers and staff. From 1878, Irving's business manager, and the secretary and director of the Lyceum, was one Bram Stoker, later the author of *Dracula*, who began writing novels while working for Irving. It is widely acknowledged that Bram Stoker's real-life inspiration for the mannerisms of Count Dracula was Irving, although he always refused to play the part despite Stoker's many appeals.

'What I liked was the romance of Irving's story,' said Richard. '"The Knight from Nowhere", is what Max Beerbohm dubbed him.'

The son of a commercial traveller, Sir Henry Irving, or John Henry Brodribb as he was christened, went to live with an aunt at the age of four and doggedly pursued his ambition to become an actor despite having a stammer.

'He went from playing an Ugly Sister in *Cinderella*, to Hamlet,' continued Richard, 'and as a young actor he was booed off stage for having stage fright but encouraged by Samuel Johnson to overcome his fear. There was also death in the arms of his dresser, a lost unforgotten first love, a disapproving Methodist mother, a wife he never spoke to again after she scorned his art – "Are you going on making a fool of yourself like this all your life?" she said – and a tantalisingly unclear friendship with his stage partner, Ellen Terry, another of those rare names that still resound in a world of passing fame.'

Reading about Irving's inspirational story obviously made the acting profession accessible to the young Richard Briers, but the ambition to one day follow in his hero's footsteps, while itself probably earnest, was still only a pipe dream.

'He was obviously just a child,' says Lucy. 'But what reading about Sir Henry Irving did do, apart from introducing him to Shakespeare and making him want to read about the history of theatre, was to give Dad an interest outside of selling comics and cigarettes.'

His sister Jane agrees.

'Because of Henry Irving he suddenly started reading lots and lots of Shakespeare,' says Jane. 'And that's what really hooked him. Between Sir Henry and old Bill, they gradually started diverting Richard's attentions away from flogging things to something more exciting and worthwhile. I think they actually saved him.'

Whether or not a knowledge of what Irving had saved him from was part of Richard's devotion, nobody's really sure. But his commitment to the memory of the famed Victorian actor never faltered and he became a trustee of the Actors' Benevolent Fund, which Irving helped found (Richard was also trustee of the Henry Irving Foundation), and Richard went on to have the possibly unique distinction of playing four roles that will forever be associated with the great man: Hamlet, Richard III, King Lear and Mathias in *The Bells*, which was one of Irving's greatest successes at the Lyceum. Strangely enough, each of these roles was played at a very different stage of Richard's career: one at drama school, one in rep, one as a young star with fifteen years' experience and one as an old pro. Two were a roaring success, but two weren't. All will be revealed.

CHAPTER FOUR

'Electric cables. Fascinating!'

By the time Richard was fifteen years old he had become obsessed by the works of Shakespeare. So much so that in addition to being able to recite every main speech from every play by the Bard, he could recite his two favourites works, *Henry V* and *Hamlet*, verbatim.

The confidence he required to recite this material had appeared when he was just eight years old.

'I once shouted something in the kitchen in our flat in Raynes Park in which there was an echo,' he told Kate. 'I thought this was marvellous and spent the next half an hour or so falling in love with my own voice and growing an ego. It created a monster!'

Galvanised by this sense of self-awareness, the following week Richard enrolled as a server at the local church.

'What I was actually doing, of course, was dressing up in a period costume while having one or two lines to say during the service. When I realised that it wasn't for the glory of God but the glory of myself, I packed it in.'

Slowly but surely Richard's confidence as a performer, or a potential performer, as he was then, grew until finally he was moved to join the local amateur dramatics society. Always on the lookout for new talent, he was readily accepted into the fold and immediately offered a small part in a forthcoming production.

'The society were based in a local church,' he said in an interview. 'And I remember turning up for rehearsals there feeling quite full of myself. The fact is though, I was only really full of Shakespeare and although I could recite it, I couldn't act it. Not yet, at least. Everyone was very kind though, I remember, and shortly after joining I was given a small part in a farce called *Candied Peel* by Falkland L. Cary.'

What Richard didn't mention during that interview was the fact that he played an eighty-five-year-old waiter in *Candied Peel* and, as well as having to whiten his hair, Richard had to walk with a stoop and talk very, very slowly.

'That was a struggle, I can tell you,' he said. 'Fortunately, I didn't have many lines. Otherwise I'd have been in trouble. It wasn't that I couldn't speak slowly. Of course I could. At the time it wasn't natural though, and when I was nervous I used to speed up.'

By this time Richard's family were obviously aware that he was interested in acting as not only had he joined the amateur dramatics society, but he had been reciting the works of Shakespeare for at least the last six months.

'That's all we ever heard him do in the house,' remembers Jane. 'And because my mother was basically a frustrated actor she naturally encouraged him. I was too young to know if he was any good or not, but in the end my parents, who probably thought he was marvellous, asked for a second opinion.'

That second opinion came from the actor and entertainer, Terry-Thomas, who, as well as being Joe's cousin, was also a family friend. Although not yet a household name, he had, until very recently been appearing alongside the great Sid Field in a show at the Prince of Wales Theatre called *Piccadilly Hayride*, and had also made an appearance at the extremely prestigious Royal Command Performance at the Palladium. As far as the family was concerned, Terry wasn't just a celebrity, he was a man in the know so he was asked to take a look at young Richard in action.

'And he was actually very happy to,' remembers Jane. 'I remember him coming to the house first and then we all went down to the church. When Richard came on none of us could believe it was him. Not even when he started speaking. I honestly thought it was a little old man.'

All Richard had said to his family was that he had a small part as a waiter so if that was an attempt to try and fool them, it had worked. It may only have been a very small role, but he certainly made his mark.

'I remember at one point he had to carry a very full tray of glasses from stage left to stage right – this was after we knew it was him – and just as he set off all the glasses began to shake. The joke was that you weren't sure whether he was going to make it to the other side without smashing everything and he had everyone in stitches.'

Just like his grandfather Fred in *The Gondoliers*, Richard received rave reviews for his performance in the farce and, although these were merely verbal appraisals instead of written ones, he was immediately offered a role in the company's next production. The name of the play remains a mystery, more's the pity. But the result was quite different. For Richard, at least.

'When we first met to rehearse, the moment I started reading the director said, "Stop! You're going too fast." I carried on but after a few lines he asked me to stop again. In the end I'm afraid I was sacked because nobody could understand me.'

At a party, years later when he was famous, Richard met the director who had fired him. It wasn't quite on the scale of Decca turning down the Beatles, but the director was embarrassed nonetheless. 'I'm awfully sorry, Richard,' he said. 'I didn't know you were going to be good!'

Despite being banished from the amateur dramatics society, never to be seen again, Richard continued reciting the Bard and, instead of hiding his light under a bushel, he recited his heart out whenever and wherever he could. This, and the small amount of confidence he had gleaned from appearing as the waiter – Terry-Thomas thought he was marvellous – led Richard to volunteer to perform at Ridgeway School's end-of-year assembly.

'This time he didn't tell the family anything,' says Jane, 'and so my parents never witnessed his performance. I did, though, as I was at the same school. It was astonishing.'

Richard also hadn't mentioned the fact that he had volunteered to his sister, so she hadn't been expecting to see her brother on the school stage. When he was introduced by the headmaster, she almost fell off her chair.

'I think he'd run the headmaster ragged over the years and so what he thought Richard was going to do I have absolutely no idea. Set up a stall and start selling ciggies and sweets, probably. I think it was a shock to everybody.'

As the headmaster called out his name Richard calmly rose to his feet and walked towards the stage.

'By this time, I was starting to panic,' remembers Jane. 'Richard could be wonderfully unpredictable, especially in his endeavours at making people laugh. Given his history with the headmaster, I'm afraid I was fearing the worst.'

As the long-suffering headmaster made way for Richard centre stage, the budding young actor turned to face his fellow pupils. Then, after clearing his throat, he delivered the St Crispin's Day speech from *Henry V* in its entirety, beginning:

> What's he that wishes so?
> My cousin Westmoreland? No, my fair cousin.
> If we are marked to die, we are enough
> To do our country loss; and if to live,
> The fewer men, the greater share of honour.

To this day just the thought of Richard's performance sends shivers down Jane's spine.

'You remember I said that I believed everything Richard told me? Well, never was my assertion more applicable. His delivery was fast, I remember, but what a voice! And what conviction. He received an immediate standing ovation.'

Over the next twelve months Richard avoided amateur dramatic societies like the plague but continued reciting Shakespeare and, at the same time, began immersing himself in the works of some of the world's other great dramatists. Anton Chekhov, Henrik Ibsen and Samuel Beckett were his next fields of study and enjoyment; yet to counter all the heavy drama he was consuming, and to prevent him from becoming too serious, he continued devouring the somewhat lighter works of his original literary hero, P. G. Wodehouse.

*   *   *

When Richard finally left Ridgeway School in July 1950 he did so with a burgeoning love of theatre but without a single qualification to his name.

A few weeks later, the family moved from Wimbledon up to Wembley and, with Richard no longer being in full-time education, he was expected to start earning his keep.

'I didn't really know what to do when I left school,' he later said. 'Drama schools were an unknown quantity and having failed so miserably at school what I needed was a job.'

By September Richard had been offered a clerical job with an electrical company based in High Holborn and spent the next two years being bored to death.

'It's a part of my life that I've almost forgotten about really,' he once said. 'Then again, there wasn't that much to remember.'

Despite it being the bottom rung of the professional ladder, the role of office clerk presented the opportunity, to those who hadn't shone academically (or even tried, in Richard's case), that if you worked hard and kept your nose clean there was every chance you could make your way up the corporate ladder and remain at the company for life. Although he would later become famous for his work ethic, Richard would always need at least a smidgen of interest in order to put in any effort. In the absence of said interest – 'Electric cables, fascinating!' – he remained on the bottom rung for two long years.

'As well as looking after the office filing system and making the tea, I had to frank all the letters and then post them on my way home. Do you know, that was the highlight of my day really, posting a load of beautifully franked letters!'

To be fair, Richard did once attempt to reach the next rung on the corporate ladder, but alas, it was never meant to be.

'Once I'd become bored of being a clerk-cum-tea-boy-cum-franking-machine, which had taken about a day, I decided I was going to become a salesman for the same firm. Those boys used to come and go as they pleased and so they had freedom. What's more, they were always very smartly dressed and so were obviously earning good money. Far more than my paltry two pounds ten shillings a week!'

At first, Richard's enthusiasm for his new career was akin to that which he had shown after discovering Shakespeare. After all, he had been selling cigarettes, sweets and comics for years at school and had done so very successfully. He was merely going legit. But in order for Richard to be able to sell electric cables to whoever wanted to buy them, he first had to get himself a qualification in electrical engineering. And, in order to get that qualification, he would have to go somewhere that he prayed he had seen the back of.

'In order to get your qualification, Briers, we'll have to send you to night school, they said. Night school, I said? But I don't want to go to night school! No night school, no qualification, they said. Fair enough, I said.'

He didn't know it then but Richard's burgeoning new career as a salesman had already ended. It was just a case of him attending one of the classes and being handed a textbook.

'As soon as I picked up this book I realised that I couldn't understand a single word. Not a single bloody word! It was like reading a foreign language. I only attended the one class.'

Richard found out the following week that he had attended the second-year class instead of the first, but by then it was too late.

'Going back to school had been a sobering experience and it wasn't one I wished to repeat,' he said. 'It was like visiting the scene of the crime.'

What finally put paid to Richard's time as an office clerk – and every other form of conventional employment – was the company pension scheme.

'After he'd been there for two years he was eligible to join the pension scheme,' says Lucy. 'When the forms were presented to him to sign the first thing Dad noticed was his date of retirement. I don't know what day or month it said, but the year was 1999. It was only 1952 at the time and I think that scared him half to death.'

The two previous years had felt like a lifetime to Richard and the prospect of another forty-nine doing something similar was just too much to bear. As well as refusing to sign the forms, Richard started thinking about acting again. It was going to be his escape. Or at least he hoped it was.

At this point, what Richard really needed, apart from a new and different occupation, was a kindred spirit; somebody of a similar age who shared his passion for theatre. Not to mention his ambition to tread the boards.

Fortunately, he was about to get lucky.

CHAPTER FIVE

'Don't worry, officer, it's
only a severed head.'

Shortly after being petrified by the pension scheme, Richard received a letter from the Ministry of Defence informing him that he would be required to serve two years' National Service at RAF Northwood, which, funnily enough, was just a mile away from where he would start filming *The Good Life* in twenty-three years' time. This was initially a godsend for two reasons. First, he could finally escape the electrical company. And second, Northwood was just a short bus ride from home. The only downside for Ordinary Aircraftsman Briers number 2560678 was the job itself, as despite being surrounded by dozens of planes and having the rank of ordinary aircraftsman, the role he was allocated at the base was, of course, as an office clerk.

'It was like going out of the frying pan and into the fire,' he later said. 'I was in tears at the start.'

Fortunately for Richard, salvation soon arrived in the form of a fellow ordinary aircraftsman named Brian Murphy, who would later go on to star alongside Yootha Joyce in the popular 1970s sitcom, *George and Mildred*.

'The thing I remember most about Richard Briers *circa* 1952 was that he was absolutely desperate to act,' remembers Brian. 'He was like a coiled spring in that respect.'

About eighteen months older than Richard, Brian too had been studying theatre and reciting the works of Shakespeare for as long as he could remember. After acquiring an old reel-to-reel tape recorder one day, he suggested to Richard that they might like to make some recordings.

'I think it was an old Grundig machine,' says Brian. 'And because Richard lived nearby we used to use his bedroom as a recording studio. You'll never believe this, but the first time we did it we were actually arrested.'

Just as they were boarding the bus from Northwood to Wembley, Brian, Richard and a friend of theirs called Bernard Dandridge were stopped by a policeman.

'The tape recorder came in this enormous case,' says Brian. 'And when the policeman saw us lugging it onto the bus he stopped us and asked what was inside. "Oh, don't worry, officer," said Richard cheerfully. "It's just a severed head."'

Unfortunately for the three ordinary aircraftsmen, the policeman seemed to have left his sense of humour back at the station and, instead of remaining on the bus, they were invited back there to help him look for it. Brian wasn't amused.

'Two hours we were in that bloody police station! I could have killed him if it wasn't so funny.'

The following night the three friends tried again and this time they managed to make it all the way to Wembley.

'We always tried to record scenes that would feature the three of us,' says Brian. 'Then later on we'd take it in turns to record speeches from all the parts we hoped to play at the Old Vic. That was our ambition. To play Shakespeare at the Old Vic.'

Whenever an additional actor was required for a particular scene, Richard would fetch his sister, Jane.

'He didn't need to go very far as I was usually sitting just outside the door. I was desperate to be involved but he only let me in if it was absolutely necessary.'

In an attempt to curry favour with the trio, Jane would make them tea and jam sandwiches. After delivering them to Richard's bedroom she would then loiter a while, in the hope of being allowed to stay. Fat chance.

'I remember Richard asking Jane to play Ophelia one evening,' says Brian, 'which was one of the few roles we couldn't impersonate. But the moment she'd delivered her lines he kicked her downstairs and said, "We'll call if we need you again." Poor Jane. She was actually very good.'

When he wasn't recording Shakespeare or being cruel to his sister, Richard was cocking things up merrily at RAF Northwood.

'I worked in the personnel department,' he said. 'And it was my job to inform people when they were due to be demobbed. The trouble was, I kept on forgetting!'

Richard's early inability to concentrate on things that didn't interest him had endured and anybody who was due to be demobbed from RAF Northwood between 1952 and 1954 was probably going to be in for a wait.

'On one occasion there was a marine craft unit attached to RAF Northwood that was based off the coast somewhere,' remembers Brian. 'That was one of the cushiest jobs in National Service as there was no drill, very little discipline, and basically you were just left there to get on with it. Because they weren't based at camp the crew of these craft would often get forgotten about, certainly by Richard, and one day he received a plea from about six of them complaining that they should have been demobbed weeks ago!'

Try as he might (although it's doubtful as to whether he ever did), Richard just couldn't get to grips with the filing system and would put active personnel in what was called the 'dead file', which was for people who had been demobbed, and vice versa.

'Why I wasn't demobbed early or court-martialled I'll never know,' he once said to Kate. 'They probably couldn't find my file!'

What kept Richard going through this period (and probably helped to distract him, if truth be known) wasn't just the promise of recording some Shakespeare at the end of the working day, it was the prospect of at last being able to tread the boards. Once again, Brian was the fixer.

'A few years previously I'd joined an amateur dramatics society called the Borough Polytechnic Players. We were based at a place called the Edric Hall Theatre, which was part of the polytechnic, and one day I suggested to Richard that he should join us.'

Although enthusiastic about the suggestion, Richard was naturally quite nervous about reprising his association with an amateur dramatics society but, after a little bit of assurance from Brian, he agreed to tag along.

'The show we were putting on at the time was *The Ghost Train* by Arnold Ridley,' says Brian, 'who later went on to play Private Godfrey in *Dad's Army*. It was still a very popular play back then and had been adapted for the screen four times: two for cinema and two for television. Fortunately for Richard there was one small part that hadn't been cast yet and after talking to the director he was offered it. Richard was so enthusiastic at Borough, and I think he loved every moment of it. I was thrilled when he joined us.'

In addition to playing smaller roles, Richard also gained some experience backstage. During *The Ghost Train*, which is set inside a station waiting room, it was his job to start the fire and keep it going. Although this was sixty-five years ago, Brian still remembers it vividly. 'I remember watching him trying to light the fire on the set one day. He was blowing on the sparks like you wouldn't believe and there was smoke going everywhere!'

The two actors Richard and Brian emulated while appearing with the Borough Polytechnic Players were John Neville and Richard Burton, who then were the Old Vic's two leading male actors.

'The company within the Old Vic was the precursor to what eventually became the National Theatre,' says Brian. 'So, if theatre was your thing, which it was for us, that was obviously the pinnacle. We even considered changing our names at one point in order to make us sound more interesting, although I can't remember what we came up with.'

Richard would later 'blame' Brian for kickstarting his career as an actor and, in his words, 'inflicting me on an unsuspecting public!'

' "You do realise it's all your fucking fault," he once said to me. My God, that man could swear.'

Indeed, it's fair to say that unless you knew Richard personally you could be forgiven for assuming that if there was any vulgar language within his idiolect it would be confined to words such as 'heck', 'blast' and 'damn it'. Brian Murphy, and, it has to be said, 95 per cent of people who have been interviewed for this book, would disagree.

'When I first got to know Richard he hardly swore at all. Then, once he was at drama school, he started prefacing certain sentences with words like "fucking". By the time he started in television there was no stopping him!'

Richard's first leading role was as Jack Absolute in Richard Brinsley Sheridan's comedy, *The Rivals*. Jack's father, Sir Anthony Absolute, was played by Brian. As well as Richard's immediate family coming along to support him, his cousin, Terry-Thomas, whose career was now marching on apace, once again did the same.

During a television interview in 1990 Richard recalled his famous cousin pulling him to one side after seeing him in *The Rivals* and offering him some advice.

'He said to me, "I think you've got something, you know, but you really ought to get yourself trained at a proper drama school. You've got an awful lot of speech mannerisms."' Richard's impression of Terry, including his cousin's own speech mannerisms, was wonderfully accurate.

Richard had no idea what he was going to do after he had been demobbed, and his cousin's advice planted a seed in his head that, over the next year or so, would steadily grow into a bona fide objective. One that, providing he continued performing regularly, had every chance of becoming a reality.

'The more he acted the more he wanted to act,' says Brian. 'And of course, the more experience he got, the better he became. Seeing him progress was a joy to watch, and, bearing in mind what he achieved, it was also a privilege.'

As time went on, Richard's attributes as an actor steadily came to the fore, as did the aspects that needed work.

'His comic timing was impeccable right from day one,' remembers Brian. 'And that's something he quite rightly became famous for. It's the kind of thing you can't really learn, though. It's instinctive.'

When it came to weaknesses, things hadn't changed since Richard was ousted from his first amateur dramatics company four or five years previously for speaking too fast, although Brian and the Borough Polytechnic Players were sure that, with help, he could turn it into an advantage.

'We were always adamant that, providing he learned how to control it, Richard could use this to his benefit. He just lacked a bit of clarity.'

'Dad had been quite nervous as a child,' says Lucy. 'He had a tendency to focus on the negatives in life. Perhaps that was down to the war? He was also extremely self-deprecating, and although that's seen as being a trait of the English it was always very earnest with Dad; partly because he didn't take himself too seriously, but also because he didn't have much confidence.'

He may not have been an especially confident twenty-one-year-old, but what the young Richard Briers did have at the time, and what had enabled him to recite the St Crispin's Day speech at the school assembly and perform with the Borough Polytechnic Players (in addition to his talent, of course), was a seemingly boundless and extremely steely determination. This would ultimately become his trump card as an actor, and would enable him to deal with any issues that life might throw at him.

CHAPTER SIX

'No, no, no. You're trying too hard, love!'

Since his chat with Terry-Thomas, Richard had thought about little else other than attending drama school. His family were thrilled at the idea, especially his mother, and so, in 1954, on the suggestion of his famous cousin and with the blessing of everyone who knew him, Richard applied to audition for drama schools. Up until April 2018, everyone who knew Richard had always been under the impression that he only ever auditioned for the Royal Academy of Dramatic Art (RADA), but after recently discovering a letter in her father's study from the principal of the Webber Douglas Academy, a Mr Walter Johnstone Douglas, to Richard's commanding officer, asking if he could be excused his final few weeks of National Service, his daughter Lucy believes otherwise.

'Dad auditioned for the Webber Douglas Academy at least a couple of months before RADA and was accepted immediately. The principal wanted him to start at the beginning of the summer term on 3 May, but Dad didn't get his release until the 19th. The letter said it would be a pity to make him wait until the autumn term which started in September and would be grateful if he would give the matter his consideration. He actually finishes the letter by saying, "The boy is talented, and I think should do well," which is nice.'

It seems that Richard may well have already planned to audition for RADA, and so instead of accepting Webber Douglas's offer, he ploughed ahead with his application to the Royal Academy, which is ultimately where he ended up.

Founded in 1904 by the actor-manager, Sir Herbert Beerbohm Tree, RADA had produced some of the world's most respected actors, including two of Richard's current idols: the recently knighted Sir John Gielgud, and Flora Robson, who would become a dame in 1960. Both had featured much in the material that had inspired Richard to become an actor, and the prospect of following in their footsteps, although a few years afterwards, was drool-inducing to say the least.

The audition 'bloody well terrified me', he said in 1996. 'I did a speech from *Hamlet*, of course, and something more modern, I think a Chekhov. I only just scraped in.'

Luckily, Richard kept a great deal of paraphernalia from his time at RADA; from his audition sheet to some vocal exercises he had written down in a red notebook. His wife Annie has a theory as to why he did this: 'He was so happy to be there,' says Annie. 'And so proud. That's why he kept everything.'

The audition sheet, on which Richard has fortunately marked his chosen piece, states that it was to be held at 62 Gower Street on Friday 9 April at 11.15 a.m., and goes on to say that, 'The candidate must learn and speak in character one of the following passages and when a passage has been selected the whole play should be obtained and read through.'

The passages from which he had to choose, and their opening lines, are as follows:

Romeo and Juliet – Act V, Scene III – Romeo. 'How oft
  when men are at the point of death have they been
  merry.'

King Henry IV, Part 1 – Act I, Scene III – Hotspur. 'My
  liege, I did deny no prisoners.'

Hamlet – Act II, Scene II – Hamlet. 'I have of late – but
  wherefore I know not – lost all my mirth.'

Good Friday by John Masefield – Longinus. 'We nailed him
  there, aloft between the thieves, in the bright air.'

His House in Order by Arthur W. Pinero – Act III – Hilary.
  'Well, here was this woman, we will suppose, entertaining the idea of eloping with her companion in sin and
  branding her innocent child with illegitimacy.'

Three Sisters by Anton Chekhov – Act VI – Tuzenbach.
  'What trifles, what little things, suddenly à propos of
  nothing, acquire importance in life!'

A Bill of Divorcement by Clemence Dane – Act II – Hilary.
  'What was I calling you for, eh? Oh yes, a riddle. I've got
  a riddle for you.'

Pygmalion by G. Bernard Shaw – Act II – Higgins.
  'There! That's all you get out of Eliza. Ah-ah-ow-oo!
  No use explaining. As a military man you ought to
  know that.'

A Hundred Years Old by Serafin and Joaquin Alvarez
  Quintero – Act I – Trino. 'I have an idea for a book,
  which will be most diverting . . . the most extraordinary
  book ever written.'

The Skin Game by John Galsworthy – Act I – *Hornblower*.
  'And how have ye tried bein' neighbourly with me? If I
  haven't a wife, I've got a daughter-in-law.'

Richard had marked *Hamlet* as his first choice, which tallies with the interview, and *Pygmalion* as a backup. If his second piece was a Chekhov, the chances are it would have been from *Uncle Vanya* as it was, and always remained, his favourite Chekhovian play.

The vocal exercises are quite amusing as one of them was meant to aid the tone of Richard's voice and the other – his rapidity!

For the vocal exercise to aid tone, Richard has written down the opening stanza from Arthur O'Shaughnessy's poem, 'Ode':

> We are the music makers,
> And we are the dreamers of dreams,
> Wandering by lone sea-breakers,
> And sitting by desolate streams; —
> World-losers and world-forsakers,
> On whom the pale moon gleams:
> Yet we are the movers and shakers
> Of the world for ever, it seems.

And for rapidity we have Zara's solo from the Act 1 finale of Gilbert and Sullivan's *Utopia, Limited*; something with which his grandfather Fred would have been thrilled.

> A complicated gentleman allow me to present
> Of all the arts and faculties the terse embodiment;
> He's a great Arithmetician who can demonstrate with ease
> That two and two are three or five or anything you please:
> An eminent Logician who can make it clear to you
> That black is white – when look'd at from the proper point
> of view;

A marvellous Philologist who'll undertake to show
That 'yes' is but another and a neater form of 'no'.

It's easy to imagine Richard practising these exercises of an evening, although why anybody thought he needed to improve the rapidity of his voice is beyond reckoning. Perhaps it was meant as a joke.

Despite his habit of being overtly modest in interviews, Richard's assessment of how he fared at his audition is right on the button, as he achieved 62 per cent with the minimum required pass mark being 60. Albert Finney and Peter O'Toole, who auditioned on the same day as Richard, achieved 89 per cent and 91 per cent respectively. It was always Richard's belief, although perhaps not the belief of O'Toole and Finney who undoubtedly had to work at becoming successful, that they were the more natural actors.

'Finney, O'Toole and Alan Bates, who was also in my class, were the new wave and they got the leading roles. I was the slightly prissy boy from Wimbledon, destined to play the silly ass walking in and out of French windows carrying a tennis racket and saying, "I'm terribly sorry I'm late!" I had to work at it. They didn't. To them it was natural.'

But that wasn't Richard's only issue with this new wave of northern powerhouses.

'They made me feel quite old fashioned,' he said in 2003. 'I hadn't even started in the business and I felt redundant. They were so fit and good looking. The exact opposite of me.'

Whether or not Richard's assessments regarding the kitchen-sink boys are accurate is open to debate, but it certainly wasn't a lack of natural talent that prevented him from achieving a higher pass mark at the audition. Once again, it was down to nerves.

'I was very, very nervous,' he once said in an interview. 'But when I found out I'd passed I was elated because it felt like I'd found my natural home. It was where I wanted to be.'

Brian Murphy and the Borough Polytechnic Players had obviously whetted Richard's appetite for a life in acting, but this was the real thing. There was no monotonous day job to consider now. No more clockwatching, staring into space or failing to demob half a dozen or so desperate servicemen. For the next two years, Richard would be able to live and breathe acting, and if he didn't have to talk about anything else for the entire twenty-four months, he would be a happy man.

'Dad was always at his most comfortable around actors,' remembers Kate. 'Acting was his first language and so to suddenly be surrounded by so many like-minded people must have been a huge thrill for him. And a relief, I suppose.'

Indeed, it was, and it's fair to say that the class of 1954 had plenty of interesting and talented people for Richard to befriend. In addition to Albert Finney, Peter O'Toole and Alan Bates, he studied alongside the likes of Tom Courtenay, Roy Kinnear, Frank Finlay, Rosemary Leach and Peter Bowles. Not a bad cast.

'It was certainly a bumper crop,' Richard said. 'I think RADA had always been seen as being quite establishment, and when all these northern actors suddenly arrived talking in their own dialects and refusing to conform, the powers that be got an almighty shock!'

Which brings us on to something that not even a steely determination could help fix.

Despite him going on to become one of the most versatile and prolific actors of his generation, Richard Briers was, perhaps surprisingly, terrible at accents.

'He was dreadful,' remembers Peter Bowles. 'Really, really bad, which is one of the reasons why, early on at least, he specialised in playing rather nervy, upbeat middle-class types.'

Richard himself would almost echo Peter's assessment whenever it came up in conversation.

'I couldn't do a northern accent to save my life,' he once said. 'It was RP or nothing at all!'

Grange Calveley, who wrote and created the incredibly popular 1970s cartoon, *Roobarb* (also known as *Roobarb and Custard*), for which Richard provided the voices, remembers Richard's wariness at being asked to come out of his comfort zone, some seventeen years after graduating from RADA.

'In series one of *Roobarb and Custard* there is a story entitled "When the Pipes Call the Tune",' remembers Grange. 'In it, Custard says something along the lines of, "Ye teck the high road an I'll teck the low road, an' I'll be in Scotland afore ye." At the recording, Richard did the line several times and eventually became quite agitated. "OK, Richard," we said. "Let's go again. TAKE FIVE!" "Ye teck the ... Oh, for fuck's sake, Grange," cried Richard. "I cannot do a fuckin' Scottish accent – especially while being a fuckin' cat!" "OK," I said, and I walked into the booth and took the script as Richard muttered a low "sorry".'

A few minutes later Grange opened the booth door and handed back the script to Richard without a word being said.

'The crew were on tenterhooks by then,' remembers Grange. 'Richard looked at the rewrite, beamed and said, "Ahhaaa!

Now we're on our way t' fuckin' Scotland . . . Thank you that man with the pencil!''

' "TAKE SIX."

' "Ye teck the high road an I'll teck the low road . . . an' I'll be in Scotland afore ye, said Custard in a dreadful Scottish accent."

' "Perfect, Richard!"

'It was a very funny afternoon and that line is still there.'

Peter Bowles, who remained friends with Richard until he died, claims that, had his friend not continued living at home while studying at RADA, he might have been able to escape the linguistic confines of received pronunciation.

'Being an aspiring actor when you're young can be a very lonely existence,' he says. 'Like Richard, I didn't enjoy school one bit and we found that when we went to RADA everybody was like us. It was wonderful. The problem for Richard was because he was living at home he was going back into his old environment in the evenings, and I think that took the edge off. It must have been terribly hard for him.'

Richard never claimed this to be an issue while he was at RADA – not publicly, at least – but had he been living in digs like the majority of his classmates, not only might he have learned how to do a northern accent – 'Finney would have seen to that,' says Peter Bowles – but his nerves may also have come to heel slightly.

Richard's daughter Kate believes that had her father become less nervous, things wouldn't necessarily have turned out for the better.

'At the end of the day, Dad was Dad, and once he'd learned how to relax a bit and control the speed of his voice, he suddenly had something unique. Nobody could match Dad for speed and clarity.'

Brian Murphy agrees.

'I said earlier that I thought he'd turn it into an advantage, and he did. Take *Brothers in Law* and *Marriage Lines* for instance, which are what made him a star. Both of those roles required Richard to play a very highly strung, nervous young gentleman, which is exactly what he was. The difference being – and it's a subtle one – that instead of it being in control of him, he was in control of it. Imagine if they'd cured him of that? He'd have been just like everyone else.'

The person Richard always credited with teaching him how to control his nerves and subsequently his voice was the then principal of RADA, John Fernald.

'He realised he had a student who was a bit odd, but funny and committed to learning,' Richard told the *Guardian* in 2008. 'And so, he helped me a great deal. I was in a class with Peter O'Toole and Albert Finney, who didn't need any lessons at all. I was painstakingly slow in my progress in comparison with them and as a result was always trying too hard.'

Funnily enough, John Fernald wasn't the only person at RADA to notice that Richard might be trying a bit too hard. In fact, one of the very first people to take him to task about this was the aforementioned Mr Finney, for whom his nervous fellow pupil had a great deal of time. Richard once recalled the conversation with Finney for a documentary.

'Albert Finney said to me in that broad Salford accent of his, "No, no, no, Richard. You're trying too hard, love. You're trying too hard! Let them come to you, love. Let them come to you. Don't keep on bashing them in the face!" He was absolutely right, of course.'

Funnily enough, despite Richard potentially appearing a bit old fashioned to the new wave of British actors, they all thought very highly of him.

'They liked Richard because he was different,' says Peter Bowles. 'He may have sounded a bit old fashioned but the way he acted was anything but. He had a lot of raw talent and despite the obvious differences they treated him as one of them. He was also funny, of course, which helped. Richard could make anybody laugh. Anybody!'

The actor Dudley Sutton, who is perhaps best known for playing Tinker in the BBC's long-running series, *Lovejoy*, was at RADA with Richard for about a year before being, as he puts it, 'chucked out!' He remembers the hard-nosed kitchen-sink boys being fascinated by this nine-stone southern softie.

'When we first saw him, I think we all thought, *Here we go, another member of the blooming establishment. This one's proper old-school!* He won us round, though, partly because he wasn't at all stuck up, but also because he was bloody good. There was obviously still a demand for those parts he played, although a diminishing one, and we all assumed he was like that in real life. We were wrong.'

Perhaps John Fernald went out of his way to help Richard's confidence because he saw some of himself in the young actor.

'John instilled a great confidence in me which allowed me to relax,' said Richard. 'He was a sweet man and, funnily enough, very highly strung and intense himself. I kept in touch with him for a long time; he died when he was quite young but knew that I had made a name for myself and was very pleased for me.'

One early attempt by Fernald to boost Richard's confidence had the young actor in stitches.

'He said to me, "Well, I don't think you should worry too much about your nerves, Briers, because you've got very eloquent eyes." I found that very funny, but I was flattered by the compliment and from that moment on I began to progress.'

Fernald may well have made the difference with regards to moulding Richard, building his confidence and helping him to grasp and control his talents, but there was one other person attached to RADA who, once Richard's confidence had emerged, enabled him to fuse it with his dogged determination, and, ultimately, prepare him for life as a professional actor. The mentor in question was Flora Robson.

'It's hard to believe really, but Richard used to spend some of his weekends with her at her home in Buckinghamshire,' says Peter Bowles. 'He met her at the academy, where she would do talks occasionally on her experiences in the theatre.'

So, while Peter Bowles and Albert Finney were in their digs drinking beer and talking about the noble profession, Richard would sometimes be in Buckinghamshire spending time with an Oscar-nominated actor who was regarded as being one of the finest theatrical actors alive.

Born in 1902, Flora Robson had graduated from RADA in 1921 having won that year's Bronze Medal. She too had been reciting Shakespeare long before she ever took to a stage but, because her looks weren't considered to be conventional, she had wondered how she would fare after graduating. Like Richard, Flora Robson had been encouraged to make her differences work for her and, bolstered by an inordinate amount of talent, she had made herself almost indispensable in the eyes of film and theatre producers, taking character and leading roles alike. In that respect she was what Richard hoped to be: somebody who was continuously paid to act.

The late actor Roger Moore, who also attended RADA, mentioned one of Flora's talks in his autobiography *My Word Is My Bond* and as well as referring to her character he also recalled a wonderful tale regarding her looks.

We students were all gathered for what were generally very interesting and informative talks. I recall one in particular – Dame Flora Robson. She was both a splendid actor and a very warm human being.

At the end of her fascinating address, in which she talked of the many great actors and directors with whom she had shared the stage and screen, she invited questions from the students. One dim young thing raised her hand.

'Dame Flora, why is it on screen you don't look half bad and yet you are quite ugly today?' Dame Flora gazed down at the girl with a beatific smile. 'If you are ever fortunate enough to get a job in the cinema,' she said, 'you'll find there is such a thing as make-up and lighting.' There were no more questions.

It is unknown whether Flora Robson made a habit of inviting students to the home in Buckinghamshire, which she shared with her two sisters, but the romantic surely hopes that, like the inspirational John Fernald, she had aligned Richard's struggles and his potential with her own and had taken him under her wing.

When it came to gaining experience in front of an audience while at RADA, Richard had the upper hand on the vast

majority of his fellow students, as whenever he wasn't performing with the academy, he was helping out some old friends.

'Fortunately for us, Richard agreed to carry on appearing in
our productions, both when he was at RADA and even afterwards,' remembers Brian. 'I'd signed up to do three years'
National Service instead of two which meant that I was just as
involved as ever, and when Richard arrived in the evenings all
we wanted to hear about was what life was like at RADA.'

In 1955 Brian would finish his National Service and start
attending Joan Littlewood's Theatre Workshop, which is where
he first met his future *George and Mildred* co-star, Yootha Joyce.
But before Brian and Richard finally called time on their tenure
with the Borough Polytechnic Players they appeared in several
more plays together, including *Othello*, in which Richard played
the Duke of Venice – 'He was appearing in something at RADA
at the time,' says Brian, 'so he could only take a small role' – and
the ever-popular *Charley's Aunt*, in which Richard played Lord
Fancourt Babberley, a role that he would reprise for a television
production in 1965 playing alongside Frank Pettingell, Colin
Gordon and Edwin Apps.

But it was Richard's performances with RADA that were
winning him the most amount of attention and in his final two
terms he gained a reputation for being, as one journalist put it,
'a bit of a bright young thing', and was considered among many
as being a potential medal winner.

His most talked-about outing while at RADA was undoubtedly the time he tackled Hamlet for a production that was part
of the then annual Shakespeare festival at Southwark Cathedral.
Southwark was the Bard's own parish and he had worshipped at
the cathedral while living close to the Globe Theatre. This

made Richard's performance almost a pilgrimage, and despite John Fernald's successes in helping him to remain calm and confident while on stage, the sheer gravitas of the situation helped resurrect his pesky nerves. He subsequently rattled off what is widely considered to be one of the fastest Hamlets in history.

Several critics were in the audience that evening, including the revered William Aubrey Darlington, or W. A. Darlington as he was better known to the readers of the *Daily Telegraph*. He claimed in the following morning's edition that, 'Richard Briers played Hamlet like a demented typewriter', a quote that Richard himself found most amusing and one that he would recall regularly for the rest of his days.

Dudley Sutton played the poisoner in that production of *Hamlet* and he believes W. A. Darlington was, in his words, 'talking utter crap'.

'Richard was absolutely fine as Hamlet,' remembers Dudley. 'I mean, what do they expect? For a student to get through Hamlet in such a large venue was astonishing. It was Richard who made that quote from Darlington famous, and that was typical him. Always putting himself down.'

Like Dudley, the industry newspaper, the *Stage*, was slightly more complimentary, and although the critic makes a reference to Richard's delivery, it's less barefaced.

'Richard Briers as Hamlet is careful with the part, which he treats like some priceless antique likely to shatter at a touch. His performance, apart from being very studied, lacks a line of definition. He is at best in the closet scene with Annie Aris, and beside Ophelia's grave where he is helped by Robert Cooke's admirable Gravedigger.'

On the whole, Richard agreed with the overall assessment of his efforts but as opposed to concentrating on the negatives therein – something to which he had always been prone – he decided to rest on his laurels (just for the time being), regroup and continue his ascent within a profession that he now considered his own.

'I may not have been the best Hamlet of my generation,' he said of his performance, 'but I was certainly the fastest. On the opening night I took twenty-four minutes off the running time and I think it must have been the only *Hamlet* in recent times where people were able to get out to the pub afterwards for a drink.'

According to Brian Murphy, who saw Richard's performance, people were indeed going for a drink, but they were under the impression that they would be coming back for more.

'There were people in the audience who obviously didn't know the play and when the curtain came down at the end, one or two audience members ran to the bar believing it to be the interval! I'd certainly never seen that before.'

In January 1956, RADA announced details of what were then referred to as the Matinee Awards; a showcase, basically, at which the end-of-year awards would be bestowed, with two, the Gold and Silver Medals, being decided on the day by a judging panel featuring some famous alumni. In order for this to happen the outgoing students would all appear in a programme of short plays and scenes; in addition to the judging panel and the tutors, they would be watched by a multitude of hopefully enthralled theatrical agents and producers, who, afterwards, would be invited to register any interests. That year's theatrical cattle market, as it was once described, would take place at Her Majesty's Theatre in London (which had originally been constructed for RADA's founder, Sir Herbert Beerbohm Tree), on Tuesday 26 March at 2 p.m. While it wasn't exactly make or break, Richard was well aware of the opportunity that lay before him, but he had the advantage of not knowing the identity of the most important members of the audience.

'I have to say they all seemed very grand,' he said. 'It was a mixture of theatrical agents, tutors, producers and people who'd been invited by the students. You know, friends and family. There were hundreds of them! Had I known where the producers and agents were sitting it might have put me off and the chances are I'd have fluffed it.'

Despite his erratic Hamlet, Richard was being touted to win the Gold or Silver Medal. John Fernald, Flora Robson and the teaching staff at the academy had worked wonders with him, but it was talent, hard work and determination that had got him this far. They had helped, of course, but Richard had given it his all.

'One thing Dad never skimped on was effort,' says Lucy, 'providing, as ever, he was interested in the subject. At RADA he was creating a future for himself and so he gave it everything. He had some amazing support, but because of his nerves and lack of confidence he had to work really hard.'

Once again, some of Richard's modesty when he refers to his endeavours at RADA has to be discounted, as there were few at the academy who were as dedicated as he was.

'Richard worked incredibly hard,' says Peter Bowles. 'But he had to. The Albert Finneys and the Peter O'Tooles of this world were the more natural actors, there's no denying it. But that certainly didn't make them better, not once Richard had found his feet, and I think that's one of the reasons why they all respected him.'

The judging panel that evening again featured several of Richard's idols, although this time he managed to thwart his nerves from speeding up his tongue. The panel was comprised of the novelist and playwright Clemence Dane, the actor-manager John Clements, and the actors Margaret Leighton, who just a few weeks after the ceremony would win a Tony Award for her appearance in *Separate Tables*, Eric Portman and Laurence Naismith. Richard admired Clements and, in particular, Laurence Naismith.

The two plays Richard appeared in that evening were a one-act farce by Chekhov called *The Proposal* and a one-act farce in verse by Molière entitled *The Imaginary Cuckold*. These were undoubtedly the highlights from the night's proceedings, and, in addition to winning Richard a coveted Silver Medal, his performances also prompted a journalist from the *Stage* to write, 'Richard Briers, who played Lomov [in *The Proposal*], was awarded the academy Silver Medal, but the judges were probably more influenced by Mr. Briers' irascible and disconsolate Sganarelle in a spirited and well-mannered performance of the Molière farce.'

The following month *The Proposal* was televised for the BBC and, in an edition dated 18 April 1956, the *Lancashire Evening Post* commented, 'In a somewhat dim night's session, the 67-year-old Chekhov play, *The Proposal* came out brightest. This was a sharp snippet of drama, expertly played by a beautifully balanced cast in which Gillian Martell and Richard Briers showed how they won their RADA awards.'

As if any further motivation were needed for Richard to go

on and make a successful career for himself, one of his tutors at RADA, a female instructor who for some reason disliked Richard intensely, said to him after he had collected the Silver Medal that, regardless of his success on the evening, in her opinion he would amount to nothing within the industry. Like his unorthodox delivery, it would be something that Richard would endeavour to use to his advantage.

'Dad didn't talk about his time at RADA much,' says Lucy. 'But that's one of the few things he told me. He didn't name the tutor. He had far too much class for that. What he did do, however, was tell me that it made him more determined than ever to succeed.'

Rather ironically, one of the few awards that was not left to the panel to judge but was still to be announced and awarded on the day was the academy's 1956 prize for diction, or the Lurgan Prize, as it was known. Had somebody suggested two years previously that Richard Briers might be awarded the Lurgan – or even a Silver Medal, for that matter – they would doubtless have received a bigger laugh than the one Richard got on falling off the arm of his sofa after drunkenly complimenting Penelope Keith on her neck in an episode of *The Good Life*. Even so, that's exactly what happened, and when John Fernald handed Richard the award towards the end of the evening you would have been hard pushed to decide who was prouder – the master or the pupil.

CHAPTER SEVEN

'Anything but the bloody Prince!'

Also in the audience at RADA's 1956 Matinee Awards was the director of Liverpool Repertory Company, Willard Stoker. Each year he would travel down to London for the ceremony and after watching the outgoing students' performances he would then offer one of them a one-year contract with the company, which was based at the Liverpool Playhouse. Although the standard of repertory theatre was generally high in the major towns and cities, there were three companies in particular from whom an offer of work would be considered an ideal conclusion to their endeavours as a student. They were the Bristol Old Vic, Birmingham Rep and Liverpool Rep. Albert Finney had already been offered a contract at Birmingham, Peter O'Toole was going to Bristol, where he would cause absolute mayhem, so that just left Liverpool. Fortunately, like the panel, Willard Stoker had been incredibly impressed by Richard's performances that day and was left in no doubt as to who he would be offering a contract.

'It was the perfect end to a perfect day,' remembered Richard. 'Everybody was desperate to be offered work in rep, but if Bristol, Birmingham or Liverpool came in for you, that really was something else. The cherry on the cake.'

The following morning, when Richard arrived at the academy, he was handed a letter that, right until his death, took pride of place in his RADA folder.

Dear Richard,

I am so delighted to read of your success yesterday. Laurie and I were there to see you and were thrilled. Both your parts were excellently played, and you had the advantage of being in the best production by Miles M. He wrote me a fan letter, my first one, when I was just out of RADA! You have the very best prize in going to Liverpool and I hope to see you if I tour that way. An excellent place to stay will be with Miss D. Kelly, 126, Bedford Street South, Liverpool 7. She is the best cook in England, and you need some good feeding when you work hard. We both send you our love and hearty congratulations.

Yours sincerely,

Flora

Formed in 1911, Liverpool Repertory Theatre's original producer had been Basil Dean, co-founder of the Entertainments National Service Association, or ENSA as it was better known. Its alumni of actors was, again, something that stirred Richard's enthusiasm as by performing there he would be attaching his name to the likes of Noël Coward and Gertrude Lawrence, who had appeared with the company as children. Not to mention more contemporary performers such as Michael Redgrave, Richard Burton, Diana Wynyard and Rex Harrison.

Richard's future wife, Annie, had already been with Liverpool Rep for three years when he was offered the contract and she remembers Willard Stoker waxing lyrical about him on his return from London.

'Bill used to go down every year to RADA and since I'd been there he'd hired some very talented people. This time, though, it was different, as he kept going on about how talented this year's student was. "You really should see him," he said. "He's great in comedy and has amazing timing. I believe he can play anything." He was actually in danger of putting him on a pedestal.'

Despite Willard Stoker's claim that his new charge could tackle any role that was asked of him, Richard's own ambitions were slightly narrower. Nonetheless, just like his occasional mentor, Flora Robson, he would find himself playing a variety of different roles.

'To be honest, I was expecting to play leading roles and nothing else at Liverpool,' he once said. 'But I ended up being cast as all kinds of individuals – old people, mainly. It was like being back in am dram at that old church hall!'

Annie says, 'It was quite good for him as he had time to settle down and learn his craft and become a real part of the company.'

Years later, while looking through photo albums from that period, Richard would joke to Lucy and Kate that while Annie was centre-stage playing a young attractive lead opposite one of the leading actors, he would be at the back of the stage somewhere playing an octogenarian with white frizzy hair and a bladder problem.

'I remember looking through an album of photos of their time at Liverpool Rep one day,' remembers Lucy, 'and there was this one photo in particular that interested me. Mum was in the foreground playing a lead and, in the background, there was this rather strange-looking white-haired character wearing some really bad five-and-nine make-up. "Who on earth's that?" I asked, after which there was a pause while Dad examined the photo. "Good God, that's me!" he said finally. "I look bloody terrible!" Despite that, he was definitely the go-to actor for butlers or doddery old pensioners at Liverpool.'

Before moving lock-stock from London up to Liverpool, which he was due to do in August 1956, Richard was asked by Willard Stoker if he would like to appear in two of the company's end-of-season productions that were taking place that May, thus bumping up his contract to fifteen months in total.

The two end-of-season plays were *Theme and Variations*, a romantic drama written by Stoker himself, set in Russia and featuring the music of Tchaikovsky, and, before that, a Shakespearean play set in Denmark with which Richard was already rather familiar.

'I couldn't believe it when Willard Stoker told me they were putting on *Hamlet*. Bloody *Hamlet*! "What part do you want me to play?" I asked him. "Not the Prince," I cried. "Anything but the bloody Prince!"'

Fortunately for Richard the part of the Prince had been given to a friend of his called Brian Bedford. Already a respected and quite experienced Shakespearean actor, Brian Bedford had left RADA in 1955, a year into Richard's tenure, and he would go on to play Ariel in *The Tempest* opposite John Gielgud's Prospero just a year or so later. Having such a talented Shakespearean scholar and performer in the company made the prospect of joining it even more attractive to the enthusiastic Richard. He returned to London at the end of the season, and by the time August came along he was desperate to start work in earnest.

'It was probably the longest two months of my entire life,' he once said, 'and I couldn't wait. All that talent and history. I was incredibly excited.'

Richard's first part as a full-time member of Liverpool Rep was in George Bernard Shaw's political extravaganza, *The Apple Cart*, which was being staged to celebrate the Irish playwright's centenary. Opening on 5 September 1956, it starred William Roderick as King Magnus and Helen Lindsay as, in the words of the *Stage*, 'a ravishing Orinthia'. As always, the members of the press were out in force for the first play of the esteemed company's new season and despite only having a small role – 'They started small, and pretty much remained so!' he once said – his contribution didn't go unnoticed.

Like the esteemed alumni who had first attracted Richard to Liverpool Rep, the current crop of actors were doing a splendid job in upholding the company's reputation as being one of the finest in the country. In addition to the aforementioned Brian Bedford, who, as well as being nominated for seven Tony Awards and winning one, would provide the voice of Robin Hood in Disney's 1973 film of the same name, they included the actors Pauline Yates, who went on to appear as Elizabeth Perrin alongside Leonard Rossiter in *The Fall and Rise of Reginald Perrin*, Thelma Barlow, an already experienced stage actor who would spend over a quarter of a century playing Mavis Wilton in *Coronation Street*, Alan Pickford, who became one of the country's most prolific leading actors during the 1960s and 1970s, Mona Bruce, who played, among countless other roles, Catherine Gardiner in the 1980s series, *Gems*, and her husband, Robert James, who became a stalwart of British stage and television drama. A sociable group, it seemed, and Richard was accepted by the company immediately. Although money was rather tight, his social life had never been healthier.

But out of the fifteen or so people who made up the Liverpool Repertory Company there was one in particular with whom he was especially keen on spending time – a small, dark-haired and rather pretty young lady from Chester called Ann Davies, or Annie to all who knew her at the theatre. Hailing originally from Plaistow in the East End of London, Annie and her family had moved up to Chester when she was a small child, and, thanks to her maternal grandmother who often took her to the theatre, Annie had become passionate about the industry from an early age. Unlike Richard, who was ten months her senior, Annie didn't really know about drama schools and wanted to go straight into a working environment. The best way to achieve this was to try and join a repertory company as a dogsbody, which is Annie's own description, and, in spring 1953, she had done just that. Since then Annie had worked her way up to be the company's assistant stage manager and by the time Richard arrived on the scene she had also played a variety of roles.

Although she rather liked the look of Willard Stoker's new RADA scholarship student, Annie had a rather unnerving hunch that the feeling might not be mutual.

'To tell you the truth, I thought he was gay!' says Annie. 'A lot of the leading actors were, which sometimes used to break our hearts. He was quite a lively sort of a chap and I'm afraid I just assumed he was too.'

Fortunately for both parties, Richard sat on the same side of the church and while not being at all experienced in that department, he was no shrinking violet. Within a matter of days, he had registered his interest by asking Annie if she would like to join him in doing something all young virile couples did back then – taking tea.

'It all sounds quite boring, doesn't it?' says Annie. 'But that's what people did in those days. I think we were both a bit lonely at the time. I certainly was. And I got the feeling right away that Richard needed somebody. He was a determined young man, but he was also vulnerable.'

The way relationships were formed and how they progressed was obviously very different in the 1950s and people often got engaged or even married within just a few weeks of knowing each other – companionship perhaps being a chief motivator.

'Dad always described Mum as being his best friend,' says Lucy. 'And I think relationships that have that kind of friendship at the core are ultimately the ones that sustain. I don't think Mum and Dad had fallen madly in love with each other in Liverpool – that came later – but there was definitely a bond between them. As Mum said, I also think they were lonely.'

What perhaps soldered that bond and helped them maintain an interest in each other's lives was a mutual respect as actors but also a shared interest in theatre.

'That's what really bonded us,' remembers Annie, 'and because it kept the conversation flowing we covered all kinds of different subjects and we got to know each other very quickly. Richard knew a lot about theatre – a lot more than I did – and, what's more, he enjoyed talking about it! Fortunately for him I was always a grateful and interested audience, so it worked.'

Again, as was the custom in those days, finding yourself a husband or wife was as much an expectation as it was a dream and, had Richard and Annie got together ten or twenty years later, they might have had a longer courtship. As it was, Richard decided that, like his swift delivery, over which he now had some control, courtships should be swifter still and after just two months of taking tea together and talking about the theatre, Richard popped the question.

'You're going to ask me if he got down on one knee, aren't you?' says Annie, smiling. 'Well, if you're hoping he did, I'm afraid you're going to be disappointed. We were having a cup of tea one day and he just asked me if I'd like to marry him. I said yes, and that was that. It was all over in a flash.'

Just two weeks after becoming engaged to Annie over tea, Richard invited his fiancée out for yet more tea, over which he was to deliver quite a nasty shock.

'He came into the theatre one afternoon and said he'd like a chat,' remembers Annie. 'He looked quite nervous and that made me nervous too. "Is anything the matter?" I asked, but he didn't answer.'

After leaving the theatre and finding a quiet table in the café across the road, Richard nervously delivered his news.

'I think it's all happened a bit too soon,' he said.

'What's happened a bit too soon?' replied Annie.

'Us becoming engaged.'

Annie was obviously surprised by Richard's announcement, but she managed to remain calm.

'Do you want to become unengaged then?' she asked helpfully.

'Well, if you wouldn't mind,' said Richard. 'I think it's for the best.'

'All right. If that's what you want,' said Annie. 'What happens now?'

Richard obviously hadn't thought this far ahead and, after considering Annie's question for a moment, he made a request. A bit of a cheeky one, under the circumstances.

'Couldn't we just carry on as we were?' he asked.

Now it was Annie's turn to pause and consider.

'Well, yes, I suppose so,' she finally said.

Nobody knows for sure what made him call off the engagement, but Kate has a good idea.

'I think it was because he didn't have any money,' she says. 'He definitely wanted to marry Mum, but without two ha'pennies to rub together he probably thought he should wait until he had some financial security. It was, in some ways, an honourable gesture.'

Fortunately for all concerned, Richard eventually allowed his burgeoning ardour to get the better of his desire for fiscal solvency and, about a month after calling off the engagement, he asked his ex-fiancée if she would like to slip across the road for yet another cup of tea.

'While we'd been engaged my mother had started sorting out the wedding,' says Annie. 'She'd been terribly disappointed when it was called off and so when he took me to the café, instead of asking me to marry him again, he said, "Do you know what, Annie? I've had a change of heart. You can tell your mother to get the wedding ready." I didn't know whether to hug him or hit him!'

Richard's proposal may have been lacking in romance somewhat, but he made up for this slightly by announcing their engagement, or rather their re-engagement, where else, but in the *Stage*. In the issue dated 29 November 1956, under the headline, ROMANCE AT LIVERPOOL, the newspaper printed the following:

Annie Davies, Stage Manager at Liverpool Playhouse, and Richard Briers, this year's RADA Playhouse Scholarship winner, have announced their engagement. They are both 22-years-old.

Miss Davies joined the resident company as a student four years ago and has played several parts. This season she took over, at short notice, the stage management.

Mr. Briers went to Liverpool straight from RADA towards the end of last season to appear in two productions and joined the company this autumn.

Even after becoming engaged, Annie was under no illusions as to what was Richard's main priority. More importantly, though, she understood exactly why.

'I knew that all the time, really and truly, it was his work that came first, and that's what he concentrated on. Had I not been able to share that with him by talking about theatre, appearing in plays with him and helping each other learn our lines, it would never have worked.'

One could be forgiven for believing that Richard's focus and drive were the result of the young actor wanting to make it big in the profession and become respected or famous, and hopefully both. But, in truth, there was a very different motive behind Richard's yearning for success; one that undoubtedly stemmed from his childhood.

'Dad was very, very ambitious,' says Lucy. 'Not in a "Oh, I want to be famous" kind of way. He was just focused on the fact that he did not want to have the same money troubles as his parents. That's what drove him initially.'

Richard was never backward in coming forward about the

lack of money during his childhood. Indeed, had it not been for Morna's parents and a wealthy relative on his father's side who used to send the family a cheque for £100 at Christmas – 'I remember my dad told me he used to sit by the letterbox waiting for it to arrive' – things would have been a lot worse. As it was, the family had always struggled on in what he often described as 'genteel poverty'. But Richard didn't want to struggle on. He'd seen enough of that – and, come hell or high water, he was going to make sure that he and Annie never had to endure the same kind of worry or ignominy that his parents often did.

Strangely enough, a hundred years previously in 1856, Sir Henry Irving, or just Henry Irving as he was then, had made his first appearance as an actor at the Sunderland Empire playing Gaston, Duke of Orleans, in Edward Bulwer-Lytton's play, *Richelieu*, which portrays the life of the famous French statesman, Cardinal Richelieu. Not an especially famous play (at least, not these days), it is probably best known for including the line, 'The pen is mightier than the sword', which Cardinal Richelieu delivers in Act II. Henry Irving's first line as the Duke of Orleans was the first line of Act I and has gone down in theatrical history. As Gaston reclines on a fauteuil, he takes a glug of wine and shouts, 'Here's to our enterprise!'

Richard loved that line and, for as long as Annie can remember, he used to recite the line like some kind of professional maxim.

'"Here's to our enterprise!" he'd shout whenever he was offered a job,' says Annie. 'It was always said humorously, but there was a steely intent underneath.'

Richard's fellow thespians at Liverpool were not quite as enthusiastic about 'The Guvnor', as Richard had now started referring to him. They preferred their champions to be slightly more contemporary and, in some cases, even alive.

'The rest of the company used to tease Richard mercilessly,' remembers Annie. 'Whenever he turned up for rehearsals they'd all shout, "Hello Richard. Have you brought Henry with you today? Is he behind you?" To be fair to Richard he would often howl with laughter at this and in order to play along he would immediately start doing an impression of Irving playing Hamlet or something. It was always great fun.'

Before he left Liverpool, Richard managed to talk Willard Stoker into putting on a double bill of Victorian dramas that his deceased hero had made famous; the aforementioned play, *The Bells*, and another called *Lady Audley's Secret*, which was based on a novel of the same name by Mary Elizabeth Braddon.

The Bells, in particular, is not a barrel of laughs. Set in Alsace on the French–German border, it tells the story of a family man named Mathias who, fifteen years earlier, had robbed a Polish man in order to pay a debt, and who then kills the Pole after his victim has managed to track him down. Wracked with guilt, Mathias eventually suffers a heart attack while imagining himself being executed for what he has done, at which point the play ends. *The Good Life* it was not.

Undeterred by the doom-laden subject matter, and by the fact that nobody had bothered to revive the play in decades, Richard and Willard Stoker plodded on regardless and, while the director got on with rehearsals, Richard began studying Irving's portrayal of Mathias, which he fully intended to imitate.

'Richard used to imitate Irving all the time,' remembers Brian Murphy. 'And he used to joke sometimes that he was the reincarnation of him. Or, at least, I think it was a joke! The only time this made me wonder was when Richard had a problem with his spine while he was doing National Service. He had a slight curvature, I think, which they managed to put right, but I later read somewhere that Irving had suffered a similar problem. It was very strange.'

The press, far from being put off by the relative obscurity of the two plays (compared to their usual fare), were intrigued at the prospect of a young unknown impersonating one of history's most respected actors, and, while not quite making the headlines, it appeared to capture their imagination.

Even one of the broadsheets, believed to be *The Times*, thought it necessary to report on the production and printed a photo of Richard in full Irving regalia. Beneath the photo it reads, '23-year-old unknown actor Richard Briers, who claims he is Sir Henry Irving's reincarnation, is shown rehearsing the lead role of Mathias in the Liverpool Playhouse's revival of *The Bells*. Irving also had his first success in *The Bells* when he was 33.'

Despite the glaring mistake regarding the similarity of their ages, it was refreshing for one of the nationals to dedicate a photo and a column inch or two to the goings on at one of the regional repertory companies, although they stopped short of printing a review. Those were still the preserve of the West End so it was left to the *Stage*, once again, and to the local and regional press to cover Richard and Willard's revival. The *Stage*, in particular, was impressed by Richard's efforts, although it also highlighted his rawness and inexperience as an actor.

The grim story of the Polish Jew murdered and flung into a lime kiln for his money is played with straight intensity, with 23-year-old Richard Briers as Mathias – a part which carried Irving to the top of the Victorian theatrical tree and with whom it will always be remembered. Young Briers, naturally, could not have seen Irving, but he has moulded his study of the part on Irving's by steeping himself in written accounts of his performances, studying his portraits, and copying, to some extent, his makeup. It is an excellent portrayal, especially for so young an actor who only left RADA some eighteen months ago. He is not so horrific, nor does he chill the bones as older generations of playgoers related Irving did. Nevertheless, he is very convincing and enacts the dream scene admirably.

Although it wasn't the most praiseworthy review Richard ever received, there were few that gave him as much satisfaction. Partly because it compared him to Irving, of course, but also because it acted as a kind of barometer for the progress he had made and the obstacles he had yet to scale.

The enterprise was starting to take shape, but there were still an awful lot of boards to tread.

CHAPTER EIGHT

'This is so sudden – etc, etc.'

For as long as he was ensconced in the Liverpool Playhouse, Richard's earning potential would be limited to the eight pounds a week he was earning from the company (Annie was earning two pounds more as she was doing stage management). This meant he had no choice other than to knuckle down, immerse himself in the company and its work, and acquire as much experience as he possibly could. Actors who have performed in repertory theatre often speak warmly about their experiences and Richard was no different.

'You learn so much doing rep,' he later said. 'It's the variety, I suppose, and the sheer speed at which everything moves. At the same time you have to maintain quality, and that's the tricky part. We did all kinds of stuff at Liverpool and I played all kinds of parts. It was where I honed my craft, don't you know. If you can call it a craft. I'd call it a paid hobby!'

With less than a tenner a week being handed to him, Richard's coffers, such as they were, were never going to stretch to much of a wedding, and so, when tradition intervened in the shape of Annie's parents, Ronald and Sally, Richard was mightily relieved.

'I don't think my mother and father would have allowed Richard to pay for the wedding,' says Annie. 'Even if he'd had the money. It was something they wanted to do.'

Richard's relationship with Annie's parents had been warm and convivial right from day one. This meant that when he needed to borrow five pounds for an engagement ring and a wedding ring, he knew exactly where to go.

'I went straight to my future mother-in-law, Sally,' he said in 1996. 'She was thrilled that the wedding was back on and she didn't hesitate in saying yes. That was the mark of our relationship. She was simply a marvellous human being, and I had no problem asking her.'

In truth, Annie had been quite surprised at how well Sally and Ron had taken to Richard.

'I think they were relieved I was marrying another actor as we'd have something in common. Richard didn't have to charm them deliberately, by the way. Although I'm sure he could have. They genuinely liked him.'

So, on Sunday 17 February 1957, just six months after meeting Annie (and proposing twice), Richard David Briers married Ann Cuerton Davies at St Nicholas Parish Church in Liverpool. There were roughly thirty guests in all – fifteen members of family and about fifteen members of the company – and because the company was in the middle of rehearsals at the time, everything had to fit around that. Fellow company member, Thelma Barlow, remembers the day well.

'Because we were rehearsing a new play everybody was hard at it, and so in order for us all to be able to attend both the wedding service and the reception, they ended up holding the reception in a Chinese restaurant that used to be just across the road from the theatre. It was a lovely day, I remember, and Annie looked absolutely stunning. Richard scrubbed up rather nicely too, and they seemed incredibly happy together. They were obviously a perfect match.'

What Thelma remembers most about the reception wasn't the rather unorthodox venue or even the speeches. It was the side orders of food.

'Even though it was held in a Chinese restaurant – with Chinese food, of course – everything was served with chips! I think all Chinese restaurants did in those days as the British weren't quite ready for rice. As for Richard's speech, I'm afraid I can't remember – although it was probably very quick!'

One person who sadly couldn't attend the wedding was Terry-Thomas, but he did write Richard a note after receiving his invitation. Written on a personalised notecard with a crest underneath his name featuring a drawing of a cow and the words, 'I shall not be cowed' underneath, the note is pure Terry-Thomas and evokes his distinctive voice.

'Congrats Richard! And thanks for the invitation. Who is she? Where did you meet her? This is so sudden – etc, etc. Oddly enough, I am coming to Liverpool on Tuesday 19th February – in fact, next week for the trade show of "Brothers in Law." Could we not have a get together afterwards? Oh, I almost forgot to tell you – it's a blow – but I can't make the wedding as am on T.V. that day here in London. Curses!! Cheers, Terry'.

A few weeks after the wedding had taken place Richard received a follow-up note from his cousin.

'Dear Richard! How did it go? Well, I hope. I've been too busy to write to you before. I am enclosing a slip of paper (which shouldn't bounce) so please buy yourself something that both of you can enjoy – like a bottle of brandy – or a hair dryer for you both! Cheers, Terry'.

As a wedding present, one of Richard's relatives had offered to pay for a honeymoon for the happy couple; a gesture that unfortunately they weren't able to utilise fully.

'We had a night in a hotel,' remembers Annie. 'That was our honeymoon! We'd actually been lucky to get a full day off rehearsals really, so had to think ourselves lucky. The hotel in question also had to be local to the theatre as the following day we were straight back to work, so the wedding, the reception and the honeymoon all took place within two miles of the Liverpool Playhouse. That must be a first!'

So, less than twenty-four hours after tying the knot, Mr and Mrs Briers were back at the Liverpool Playhouse, living the dream.

Richard's digs were slightly more spacious than Annie's so they decided that his would become their new home. Although the arrangement worked reasonably well, there were a few, slightly predictable teething troubles.

'He was so untidy!' remembers Annie. 'In fact, the only things he ever used to tidy up were his books. He was so proud of his books, so they were looked after. Unlike his clothes!'

The only genuine downside to Richard and Annie's new life together was a chest complaint that had been bothering Richard on and off ever since he was a child. As he had started smoking at the age of fourteen and had never smoked a cigarette with a filter on, one might assume that when the complaint became troublesome again a few months after getting married, he might have been advised by his doctor to give them up immediately. Not a bit of it, which is a fact Kate still finds incredibly hard to believe.

Butter wouldn't melt. Richard aged one. Who'd have thought that in just a few years' time he'd be climbing on dustbins and impersonating Adolf Hitler.

Richard as a baby with Mum and Dad.

With his father, Joe, at London Zoo in the late 1930s.

Spot the Briers competition. First prize: a copy of the *Beano* and twenty Woodbines. Richard at Rokeby School in July 1945 (third row, second left).

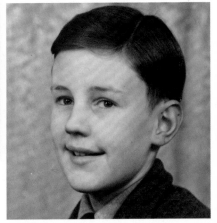

(above) Joe, Jane and Richard enjoying a day out in the mid-1940s.

(right) Would you buy cigarettes from this child? Of course you would! Richard aged 12.

As flattering as this was, Richard had already set his heart on RADA.

THE
WEBBER-DOUGLAS SCHOOL OF SINGING
AND DRAMATIC ART LTD.

Managing Director
and Principal:
W. JOHNSTONE-DOUGLAS

Directors:
D. E. Brown
H. F. Mathews, F.C.A.
C. M. Peache
C. G. Thornhill

32/34 CLAREVILLE STREET
S.W.7

Telephone: FREmantle 2988

Dear Sir,

RICHARD BRIERS

I gave the above an audition this morning, and I have accepted him as a full time dramatic student at this School. Our next term starts on May 3rd, and I understand he does not receive his release until the 19th.

I wonder whether it would be possible to put this forward so that he could begin here on May 3rd, otherwise it will mean his waiting until the Autumn Term, which does not start until September 20th. It seems a pity that he should hang about for four months.

I should be most grateful if you would give this matter your consideration. The boy is talented and I think should do well.

Yours faithfully,

Principal.

Sqdn./ Ldr. MERRICK,
H.Q. (U) C.C.,
Northwood,
Middlesex.

Richard's scrapbook covering his time at RADA and with the Borough Polytechnic Players. The 'terrible three', as Richard referred to them, are Richard, Bernard Dandridge and Brian Murphy (far left, middle).

'The best thing I ever did' was how Richard described his marriage to Annie. Outside St Nicholas Parish Church, Liverpool on Sunday 17 February 1957.

Richard and Annie at Liverpool Playhouse just a few days after their wedding.

One of the few occasions Richard wasn't cast as an 'old duffer' while at Liverpool Rep. Here playing Crichton in J. M. Barrie's *The Admirable Crichton*, June 1957.

Living the dream. Sir Henry Irving was Richard's one true obsession and playing Mathias in *The Bells* was almost a rite of passage.

Harold French wasn't Richard's first mentor, but he was certainly the most influential.

'You've got an awful lot of speech mannerisms.' With helpful cousin Terry-Thomas in the film *A Matter of WHO.*

An early film appearance as Eustace Hignett in the disastrous *Girl on the Boat*, 1962.

Richard with Anna Massey in *Double Yolk*, which featured two separate plays. This one, *Special Providence*, was directed by Celia Johnson.

With Annie and Kate in 1965.

With Prunella Scales in the immensely popular *Marriage Lines*, which ran from 1963 until 1966. After this, nothing would ever be the same again. *(© Trinity Mirror / Mirrorpix / Alamy Stock Photo)*

Richard with Michael Hordern in the original production of *Relatively Speaking* at the Duke of York's Theatre.

Richard either voiced or starred in hundreds of commercials during his career. The emoluments saved his bacon on one occasion and enabled him to take risks.

On the set of *Fathom* which was made in the summer and autumn of 1966. Richard had every right to look confused as nobody knew what the heck was going on!

On holiday in St Just, Cornwall. The Briers rented the same cottage every summer for four years.

At Richard's parents' house in Hatch End. From left, Richard's father Joe, a family friend, Richard's mother Morna, Richard, Annie, another family friend, and Sheila who was married to Richard's Uncle George (Joe's brother). Lucy and Kate are at the front.

Hello Dick! On tour as Richard III with
Derek Jacobi (left, obviously) as Buckingham.

With Michael Gambon during a recording
of the popular (among the cast and crew, at
least) *The Other One*.

'Nobody made me laugh harder on set. Not even
Ronnie Fraser.' With Julie Ege during the making
of *Rentadick*, 1972.

'Dad had started smoking literally behind the bike sheds and because he'd also been selling cigarettes to his fellow pupils, they'd always been available to him. By 1957 he'd been smoking for thirteen years solid so it's incredible that, when he finally went to the doctor, it wasn't even mentioned.'

This was still a good few years before the dangers of smoking had been made public and, in 1957, both doctors and dentists alike were still endorsing cigarettes. Doctors were even prescribing them for ailments such as throat infections. Perhaps the most shocking example of this was when the cigarette company Camel declared that, 'More Doctors Smoke Camels than any other Cigarette'. A bold claim, but one that was probably true, bearing in mind the number of free cigarettes doctors used to receive.

Richard's own doctor did at least diagnose a secondary cause of his complaint, and suggested a remedy that fitted in perfectly with the married couple's plans.

'Back then Liverpool was very badly polluted,' says Kate. 'And the doctor told Dad that this was the cause of his complaint. Not the twenty Woodbines a day, obviously! Anyway, he or she recommended that Dad didn't spend any more time in Liverpool than they had to.'

Richard and Annie's tenure with Liverpool Rep finally came to an end in August 1957, just in time for Richard to be introduced to his next mentor – the film and stage director, Harold French. Born in London in 1897, French had worked as an actor first, training at the Italia Conti School, and had also spent a short amount of time working as a screenwriter for Douglas Fairbanks Jr's production company, Criterion Films. But it was as a director that French was always happiest and, in June 1957, he had been hired by the producer, Jack Waller, to direct a promising new farce by Earle Couttie called *There's Something About a Sailor*. It would tour first, followed hopefully by a transfer into the West End.

After two months trying to cast the play, French still hadn't been able to find his lead actor and he was starting to worry. Luckily for Richard, the lead-less director was visiting Liverpool shortly before Richard was due to leave and had caught him playing Lucentio in *The Taming of the Shrew*. Just as Willard Stoker had done fifteen months previously, Harold collared Richard after the show and offered him the lead role there and then.

'There was something very, very special about Richard,' French later said. 'He had a great energy about him, and an innate ability to make people laugh.'

Richard, who went on to cite French as one of his best friends and biggest inspirations, was just as complimentary.

'It was the stage-director Harold French who gave me my break in a play called *There's Something About a Sailor*. I didn't have looks or a great physique, but what I had was comedy timing and a rather funny face . . . He had been an actor himself but was advised to direct and that was his gift – he went for truth rather than cheap effects. He once said to me: "If you ever get big headed I'll kill you," which was typical of his bluntness. He was marvellously supportive, and it was a great journey we went on together.'

The plot of *There's Something About a Sailor*, such as it is, centres on the mistaken destruction of a set of plans for a new naval weapon by a bungling National Serviceman named Ordinary Seaman Blissworth (Richard). Mingled within the usual misunderstandings is a rather tepid love affair, again involving Blissworth, and despite it being quite a vapid tale it proved popular with the public and was later filmed by the *Carry On* team under the title, *Watch Your Stern*, with the then more established actor, Kenneth Connor, playing the part of Blissworth.

The tour started at the New Theatre Oxford on 16 October 1957 and finished at the King's Theatre Southsea about a month later. As is often the way, the members of the press were slightly at odds with the provincial theatregoing public, but one thing they all agreed on was the talent displayed by the young man playing the lead. The *Stage* said, 'Some of the situations are promising but they are not sufficiently developed by the author, and the weakness of the play is its failure to give more than barely adequate material to the very promising artist, Richard Briers, a comedian of obvious talent.'

In the end, what prevented *There's Something About a Sailor* from transferring to the West End was the lack of available theatres. And so, after just a month on the road, Richard went back to Chester where Annie had been staying with her parents. Naturally, he was disappointed. After all, he had come within a cat's whisker of having his name in lights in the West End and just weeks after leaving rep. On the plus side, he had been working! That was what mattered most. And he had made a new friend. A friend who knew an awful lot of influential people – 'Harold knew everybody in the business and he kept talking about me at all these VIP parties he went to,' Richard said.

It would be three months before Richard found work again, but it would be the longest stretch of unemployment he would ever have to endure. This, perhaps more than anything else bar his family, made Richard Briers feel grateful, especially as the vast majority of actors were, at best, employed irregularly and on very little money. This unwanted breather was more down to the time of year than a dip in popularity. Richard's agent was Philip Pearman from MCA who, as well as looking after Peter Bowles, Albert Finney and Alan Bates, was married to the actor Coral Browne. He had snapped up Richard at RADA's Matinee Awards in 1956 and, in late February 1958, finally started earning his 10 per cent.

'He said I'd been offered six months at Coventry Rep, and at first I have to admit that I was somewhat underwhelmed, for the simple reason it felt like a step backwards.'

Philip Pearman assured Richard that six months at Coventry was anything but a step backwards, especially now he had a tour under his belt. It was important that he maintained momentum.

The first play Richard was due to appear in at the Belgrade Theatre was Peter Ustinov's *Romanoff and Juliet*; a spoof set during the Cold War that had been loosely based on *Romeo and Juliet*.

Shortly after arriving in Coventry, Richard wrote a letter to Annie, who was living in London and appearing in rep at Guildford.

Darling Annie. Arrived safely to absolutely smashing digs with loads of food. Plenty of good trains back and forward so should be ok for coming home. No Sunday dress rehearsals! One only on a Monday – 3 cheers! Am playing the spy in Romanoff & Juliet. They sent me a script which arrived yesterday at Number 1 which is a lot of use! If you could collect it and post it to me at digs. Hope everything went well with you and flat ok. Will close now as want to post this before rehearsal starts. Really fantastic theatre. Haven't seen stage yet. Wish you were here with me. Lots of ex RADA types here. Elaine Usher [a friend of Annie's] is in 'Picnic'. All my love darling, Richard.

He followed this up a few days later with the following:

Darling Annie. Many thanks for the script. I am very pleased with the part as it is something I have never done before (with a very bad Russian accent!) and we have an incredibly good producer so am learning a lot. The Bishop would have been good, but I would only have been repeating myself. I can't tell you how beautiful the theatre is. It is without doubt the finest one in the country. I have given your love to Elaine Usher. A very clever young lady that one. She is aiming for films I should think. My digs are terrific, and I get four meals a day. I am determined to put on weight during this season. Met Pearman at second night of 'Picnic'. Saw Val May but he didn't see me. I will write to him as soon as possible. Do hope you can get a radio by the week-end. I will be able to get to Guildford ok and should just about make it by about 7.30 p.m. on Saturday night. I should get a train about 5–5.30 p.m. I felt awful about taking our tape recorder to Coventry as I haven't even played it once and have left you with a funereal silence at Number 25. Still, it won't be long before I see you again. I love you so much and I don't like this wretched totting about. Maybe it won't be so bad when I start working really hard. See you on Saturday after the show at the glorious Guildford Civic Theatre. All my love darling. Take care of yourself, Richard

If the company Willard Stoker had assembled up at Liverpool was considered big on talent – and it was – the troupe of players Bryan Bailey had assembled at the newly built Belgrade Theatre positively oozed with it. Richard's second production at the theatre, which opened on 14 May 1958, was a revival of George Bernard Shaw's *Saint Joan*, in which he played Bertrand de Poulengy. The two most recent productions of Shaw's thirty-five-year-old play – a film adaptation written by Graham Greene that had been released in 1957 and a West End production two years before that had featured a young Kenneth Williams as the Dauphin – had each boasted a fine Joan of Arc: the American Jean Seberg in the film, and the Irish actor Siobhan McKenna in the play. Neither, however, could hold a torch to the young RADA graduate Richard had been cast alongside at Coventry.

Siân Phillips had entered the Royal Academy of Dramatic Art in 1955 after winning a scholarship and had studied alongside Glenda Jackson and Diana Rigg. Since graduating with the coveted Gold Medal for her performance as Hedda Gabler, Phillips had been offered the lead in three major Hollywood films, but had turned them down in favour of doing more stage work. What Richard would have made of this it's hard to say, but he would have winced when she told him the difference in pay. Even so, Hollywood's loss was definitely Coventry's gain – and Richard's – as the production gained national attention and immediately put Coventry Rep, and the brand-new Belgrade Theatre, well and truly on the theatrical map.

The rest of Bryan Bailey's twenty-strong cast for *Saint Joan* included David Kelly, Alfred Lynch, Alan Howard, Barbara Atkinson, Patsy Byrne and two of Richard's classmates from RADA, Patrick O'Connell and Frank Finlay. These names, together with those at Liverpool – not forgetting the esteemed alumni – help to demonstrate just how important and influential repertory theatre was at its peak. Indeed, the vast majority of 'national treasures' such as Richard who fall into the category of actor will have spent valuable time in at least one of the repertory theatres.

Richard was to take the lead in Coventry's next production, something he had been desperate to do since arriving. Noël Coward's *Nude with Violin*, which had premiered at the Globe Theatre on Shaftesbury Avenue on 8 November 1956, had originally starred Sir John Gielgud as the lead character Sebastian, with Michael Wilding and then Robert Helpmann taking over. The play had received merely polite notices on opening yet had done excellent business at the box office, making it a natural choice for the repertory company, especially as it was going to be the first time the play had been revived in the UK since its original run.

Despite experiencing a certain amount of joy and relief at being cast in a leading role, it was unfortunately to be short lived as the next four productions at the Belgrade Theatre had Richard cast as, perhaps slightly predictably, a load of old codgers. The problem Richard had – actually, there were three of them – came in the shape of Frank Finlay, Alfred Lynch and a young visiting actor named Michael Crawford.

All three were considered to be natural leading actors and, although Richard wasn't overly short or bad looking, he was far too quirky to be considered for the majority of parts on offer. Subsequently, Richard was relegated to playing cameos and, in some productions, he would even play two or sometimes three different roles. Had he been sixty-five years old and approaching the end of a hard-fought yet mediocre career appearing in this, that and the other, then he may have been grateful for the work. The fact was that he was over forty years younger than that, had recently completed a successful national tour playing the lead role after leaving one of the country's most prestigious repertory companies, and had a Silver Medal from RADA. This, contrary to what his agent might say, was not the reason Richard Briers had decided to chance all by becoming an actor, and the experience he was gaining playing older characters did not justify the fact that he was in danger of becoming typecast – as a senior citizen – in his early twenties. Something had to give and even Annie, who was now living down in London where she and Richard had taken a flat, was becoming worried.

'There was an article in the *Coventry Evening Telegraph* one day about the repertory company and it referred to Richard as the actor who played "all the old character roles". That, I think, was the last straw for him. He may not have been David Niven, but he wasn't A. E. Matthews either!'

With frustration beginning to take hold, Richard decided to call Harold French. They had got on incredibly well on the national tour and even at this early stage they had developed a kind of father/son relationship. Perhaps he would know what to do.

After Richard explained the situation to an attentive Harold, the director told him not to despair and said that he would drive up and see him the following week.

'By the way, I'll be bringing a friend of mine with me,' he said before hanging up. 'Somebody you already know.'

CHAPTER NINE

Blink and You'll Miss Him

To aptly illustrate Richard's problem, when Harold and his guest arrived at the Belgrade Theatre the following week, Richard and the company were rehearsing George Bernard Shaw's *Major Barbara*, in which Richard would be playing Peter Shirley, an older gentleman who has been sacked from his job for being – too old!

The guest in question was one of the people responsible for awarding Richard his Silver Medal, John Clements. He had achieved worldwide fame in 1939 appearing alongside Ralph Richardson in Alexander and Zoltan Korda's Oscar-nominated film, *The Four Feathers*, and was one of the country's most respected stage actors. He had become an actor-manager in the style of Henry Irving, and when Richard saw Clements with Harold, he was obviously thrilled but also curious.

After seeking permission from the director to whisk Richard away and have a word or two in his ear, Harold French and John Clements began setting out their stall.

'We've recently bought the rights to a new comedy called *It's Only Me* by Lionel Hale,' began Harold. 'John is going to produce, I'll direct, and John and Kay [the actor Kay Hammond, who was Clements's wife] will play the two leads. There is another lead, however.'

Bearing in mind what Richard had told Harold over the phone he was already praying that he would be the third.

'What's the play about?' asked Richard.

'It all centres around a wealthy stockbroker who loses everything,' began Clements. 'His wife dismisses her husband's worries and believes that he'll find a way of keeping her in the style to which she has become accustomed, and if he doesn't, there's another stockbroker waiting in the wings who will. This wakes the stockbroker up to what's happening and what's really important. It's all about self-awareness.'

Richard had enjoyed John Clements's synopsis, and when Harold confirmed that they would like him to play Joseph Field, a young mining engineer whose heart is in market gardening, he thought all his Christmases had come at once. Better still, French and Clements were hoping that they could take it on tour prior to it transferring into the West End. This time there would be no question-mark over it making it into London as the theatre, the Duke of York's on St Martin's Lane, had already been booked. The play would open there, barring any disasters, on 18 April 1959.

In its original form the play was almost three hours long – far too long for a run in the West End – and, in addition to chopping at least an hour off its running time, it was also decided that a change of name would be in order. By the time it went on tour, *It's Only Me* had become *Gilt and Gingerbread*.

The national tour, which took in eight cities from Brighton up to Newcastle between November 1958 and early April 1959, did excellent business and with two household names at the helm and some extremely complimentary notices – for Richard, the play and his fellow actors – things were looking up for the hitherto slightly forlorn Mr Briers.

John Clements and Kay Hammond were the first major stars Richard had worked with on the stage, and Clements in particular made an indelible mark on Richard.

'Like Harold, John Clements became a bit of a father figure and he taught me how to behave on stage. What I mean is, he was so utterly unselfish, which allowed me, as the junior lead, to focus on what I was doing and just relax. That's the way to behave on stage and it's something I've always tried to emulate.'

Indeed, the number of former colleagues who have mentioned Richard's onstage generosity is incredible. Take the Scottish actor, Jimmy Yuill, for example. He played the Earl of Kent to Richard's Lear in the late 1980s and says it's the thing he remembers most about his old friend.

'Richard's generosity to other actors on stage became legendary,' remembers Jimmy. 'He was playing the King and after making one of his many speeches he'd turn his back on the audience, walk down stage and say, "Go on, Jimmy. Off you go." He knew that if he stayed where he was all eyes would remain on him, and I'd say the majority of actors would understandably have done just that. Richard wasn't interested though. He was so incredibly unselfish.'

Clements, who was also a scholar of Henry Irving, had taken to Richard as Richard had to him, and when at work the two would talk about the business, and about you know who, for hours on end. Clements was a very close friend of Irving's grandson, the aforementioned Laurence Irving, who was an artist and set designer, and Clements had promised to try and get him along to one of the shows. This was almost too much for Richard to bear – a direct link to 'the Guvnor'. But, with a West End debut looming, he was going to have to put this to the back of his mind.

By the time *Gilt and Gingerbread* was ready to open at the Duke of York's, it had been on the road for almost five months and had developed a healthy reputation. Conversely, it was thought the long run-in may have cost the production some of its original spark and, while the notices in the nationals were generally positive, it was agreed that whoever was responsible for reducing the length of the play should probably have taken off another twenty minutes.

Even so, Richard's own notices were unanimously tremendous with *The Times* commenting that, 'Mr. Richard Briers is first rate as the vehemently apologetic young engineer who is a botanist at heart and obviously counts an expedition which has ruined his principal as a sort of botanical triumph, since it has put him on the track of a rare plant.'

As well as Richard receiving phone calls and telegrams from friends and family congratulating him on his triumphant West End debut, his agent was also receiving a welcome amount of attention.

'The day after the first night he was hardly off the phone,' remembered Richard, who had moved back to London to join Annie shortly after Christmas 1958. 'It was all about television this time, which was all very exciting.'

Apart from the bits and pieces he had done while at RADA, which, as well as a lead in *The Proposal*, included a bit part in *She Stoops to Conquer* in which Albert Finney played Mr Hardcastle, Richard had appeared in just one television programme and one film since starting in rep: an ITV Playhouse production called *Badger's Green*, starring Walter Hudd and George Benson, in which he had a few lines, and a low-budget naval comedy called *Girls at Sea*, which starred Ronald Shiner and Guy Rolfe.

In this Richard played a character called, 'Popeye' Lewis, but once again, it was a case of 'blink and you'll miss him'. One of the lead actors in *Girls at Sea* was the much-admired Shakespearean actor, Michael Hordern. It is not known whether he and Richard met on set, but in less than ten years' time they, together with Celia Johnson and a young actor called Jennifer Hilary, would make theatrical history by starring in the first hit play by a man currently believed to be the world's most performed living playwright.

Despite spending the start of 1958 worrying, the following twenty months were extremely promising for Richard. As well as appearing at one of the most talked about repertory theatres of the time, he had made his film debut and his West End debut – alongside two major stars – and had made a handful of small but valuable appearances on television; a medium that, while not possessing the same intimacy or immediacy as theatre, paid far, far better and was something he was keen to break into. Best of all, he and Annie had at last been able to live together in London, although Annie had already been there for six months. With Richard hailing from the west of the city originally and Annie the east, it was ultimately home for both of them.

'From a personal point of view, I'd been dying to get back to London for ages,' Richard said in 1990. 'It's where my family were, not to mention the majority of my friends. But from a professional point of view it's where you needed to be if you were an actor. Unless you were doing rep or a tour, of course.'

He may not have been doing rep any more, but another tour would be in the offing sooner than he thought as shortly after

Gilt and Gingerbread closed in September 1959, Richard was offered another junior lead role, this time in a new production called *Double Yolk* alongside the prolific stage and film actor, Judy Campbell, who is also the mother of Andrew and Jane Birkin, and Robert Flemyng, the hugely popular film star who, in 1941, had been awarded the Military Cross. Yet again, Richard had been cast alongside two significant stars and in a production that, despite sounding like a Whitehall farce, had the makings of a hit.

'I was incredibly lucky to be offered such a good part straight after *Gilt and Gingerbread*,' Richard said. 'The producers seemed to like all this high-energy stuff.'

Since Richard had wrestled control of his verbal delivery back from his nerves (at least most of the time), he had obviously been using it wisely and, although it's fair to say that his physical appearance wasn't exactly unique – white, thin, medium height with brown hair – the energy he possessed most certainly was. Where other actors would often just blend into the background, Richard stood out like a beacon and what made this so appealing to audiences was the fact that it was all so completely natural.

'That's definitely what set Dad apart from other actors,' says Lucy. 'That and his timing. Timing is something that's difficult to define and impossible to explain. It's also instinctive; so once he'd managed to combine his timing with his energy, he presented quite a unique combination.'

Written by Hugh and Margaret Williams, *Double Yolk* was an umbrella title for two linked plays, *A Sparrow Falls* and *Special Providence*. Lasting roughly an hour each their titles were rather ingeniously based on Hamlet's line, 'There is special providence in the fall of a sparrow.'

There are two interesting facts about *Double Yolk* (apart from the above). Firstly, the actor playing Richard's wife was a twenty-two-year-old, untrained but evidently talented performer named Anna Massey. Their chemistry on stage led the *Birmingham Evening Post* to comment that, 'In *Special Providence*, Richard Briers gives a remarkable, sustained performance, particularly in his naturalistic narrative as the distressed airman, and Anna Massey provides all the emotions at will in the magazine-story role of the devoted, worried young wife.' Secondly, the person directing *Special Providence* was the soon-to-be-familiar Celia Johnson, making the overall experience for Richard pivotal, to say the least.

'It was wall-to-wall luminaries at first,' said Richard. 'Something I'd dreamed about but wasn't at all expecting. Being directed by Celia Johnson, for instance, was a marvellous experience. A bit scary at first, but she was so patient with us.'

Just two weeks after *Double Yolk* opened on 10 February 1960 – this time at St Martin's Theatre, opposite the Ivy restaurant – Richard's second feature film was released to a fair-to-middling reception. *Bottoms Up* was a spin-off of the 1950s sitcom, *Whacko!*, starring the then immensely popular handlebar-moustachioed comedian, Jimmy Edwards, and had been co-written by two up-and-coming comedy writers, Frank Muir and Denis Norden, whose most popular work to date had been the Dick Bentley vehicle, *And so to Bentley*, which starred a young Peter Sellers. As far as Denis Norden can remember, he and Muir did not get to meet Richard during the filming of *Bottoms Up* as he wasn't on set for long. They did, however, receive an offer of two tickets for *Double Yolk*, and, fortunately, they accepted.

'Frank and I found the show itself quite forgettable, but not Richard. He looked and sounded different and we had an idea where we could use him.'

At the time Norden and Muir were writing a new comedy series for the BBC called *The Seven Faces of Jim*, again starring the in-vogue Jimmy Edwards.

'*The Seven Faces of Jim* was basically a series of seven parodies lampooning different film genres,' remembers Denis. 'And the one we had in mind for Richard was a wartime skit called "Angels 15".'

But it wasn't just Richard's acting skills that impressed Norden and Muir when they finally got Richard on set.

'Richard caught on to what we were trying to do immediately, and he also saw comic possibilities within the character he played that Frank and I hadn't. I must say we were both very pleasantly surprised.'

In all, Richard appeared in three episodes of the first series of *The Seven Faces of Jim*, which also starred June Whitfield and Ronnie Barker. Given that it was his first outing in television comedy, it is easy to see why Norden and Muir were impressed by Richard as his interplay with Jimmy Edwards is a joy, as is his timing. Series two and three were unfortunately wiped by the corporation, but the first series remains good viewing, not only as it marks the start of Richard's career in television comedy, but also for the scripts, which have aged well, and his three co-stars who are all at the top of their game.

Apart from some much-needed exposure and experience, what Richard gained from appearing in *The Seven Faces of Jim* was a lifelong friendship with Ronnie Barker.

'Richard and Ronnie hit it off immediately,' remembers Annie. 'They shared a similar sense of humour and they admired each other very much. Ronnie was a very private man, as was Richard, in a way, and I think they could relax in each other's company.'

It would be another eight years before Richard and Ronnie Barker got to know each other properly, but in the meantime Richard's esteemed second cousin was about to make another appearance, as was a potentially life-changing offer.

CHAPTER TEN

'Do you enjoy sitcom?'

By the spring of 1960, offers of work, especially in the West End, were lining up like taxis for Richard and, keen to capitalise on the exposure he received on *The Seven Faces of Jim*, he decided that his next theatrical adventure should be in comedy. *It's in the Bag*, which had been adapted by Robin Maugham from the French farce *Oscar*, by Claude Magnier, was a vehicle for the now immensely popular Terry-Thomas. As he had a say in casting, he had no hesitation in offering one of the three juvenile leading roles to his now in-demand talented second cousin. For this outing, which did only reasonable business despite some encouraging reviews, Richard was back at the Duke of York's Theatre and, as a thank you, he decided to invite the two writers who had given him a leg up the televisual ladder.

Once again, Norden and Muir were unimpressed by the play, but not by Richard's performance – which gave them an idea.

'Frank and I had recently been asked to adapt Henry Cecil's best-selling novel, *Brothers in Law*, for television, and would eventually have to find somebody to play the lead character, Roger Thursby. Ian Carmichael had played Thursby in the film and he'd been perfect, so ideally we wanted someone similar.'

Henry Cecil's novel, which tells of an idealistic young man entering the legal profession, had first been published in 1955 and had been made into a film by the Boulting brothers – the third of six institutional satires including *Private's Progress* (army), *Lucky Jim* (academia) and *Carlton-Browne of the FO* (diplomacy) – two years later in 1957. The three lead roles in the film had been played by the aforementioned Carmichael, Richard Attenborough and, would you believe it, Terry-Thomas. Thomas had stolen the show in *Private's Progress*, which was the first Boulting brothers satire, simply by referring to the men under him as being 'an absolute shower'. Sixty years on, people issuing reprimands in jest might still quote that line, together with Thomas's 'Ready now?' and 'Hard cheese' from the marvellous *School for Scoundrels*.

Sure enough, when it came to casting *Brothers in Law*, the BBC asked Norden and Muir if they had anyone in mind for Roger Thursby, and so Richard's name was immediately suggested. The book and the film had been so successful that it wasn't deemed necessary to cast a star in the role of the anxious lawyer, and so Richard was considered ideal, especially as there were similarities to his predecessor on the big screen, Ian Carmichael.

Thirteen episodes of *Brothers in Law* were made in all, with the first going to air on Tuesday 17 April 1962. 'Wonderful Land' by the Shadows was at number one, the French film, *Jules et Jim*, was causing a stir at the box office, and Richard Briers was having an attack of the nerves – again.

'It's a funny feeling knowing that sixteen or seventeen million people are about to watch you on television,' he said some time afterwards. 'That was probably half the population then, and there were only two channels. I'd been terribly nervous filming the show, but I was a damn sight worse watching it! That's what started to establish me in sitcom though, and Denis Norden and dear Frank Muir seemed to like me for some reason. They were very good to me.'

Alas, Richard's last-minute attack of the nerves wasn't about to be alleviated by the reception his new show received and, under the strangely written headline – PERHAPS THE BIG BBC-TV BUILD-UP PROMISED TOO MUCH FOR THE DEBUT BUT THE FIRST 'BROTHERS' EPISODE HAS THIN PLOT – the often complimentary *Stage* lamented the possibility of it not living up to expectations.

BBC-tv's new series 'Brothers in Law' seemed to have everything in its favour when it made its debut last week. It was developed from the very successful book of the same name by Henry Cecil, a book which later was made into a successful movie, it was scripted by Frank Muir and Denis Norden with additional material by Cecil and it appeared in the peak viewing BBC slot between 'Compact' and 'Z Cars'. With all these factors in its favour the programme promised to be first class. But it wasn't.

The *Aberdeen Evening Express* was in complete agreement with the *Stage*, but they at least saw promise in the show and gave Richard an honourable mention.

Perhaps one expected too much from the show, [and] although the first of the series was not above average it showed promise. The humour raised the odd laugh, but it was predictable and restricted to the light court room variety. The script was not one of Muir and Norden's best and the plot was thin. However, the script will no doubt improve in later programmes. Richard Briers gave a creditable performance as the green and nervous young barrister and was given good support by John Glyn-Jones and June Barry.

Fortunately for all concerned, the critic at the *Aberdeen Evening Express* had been correct in predicting an improvement in the show and as the weeks went on the viewing figures grew in number, as did the plaudits for Richard's performance.

'Television then was a very placid medium on the whole,' says Denis Norden, 'and it needed energy. Anybody who brought energy to the screen immediately stood out and that's why Richard himself was such a success. He was the difference television needed.'

While being a parody of the legal world, *Brothers in Law* did manage to fool its creator one day, much to the amusement of Richard.

'Henry Cecil, the chap who wrote the book *Brothers in Law*, was actually a county court judge for much of his adult life and one day, while he was presiding over things in Manchester or somewhere, he thought he recognised the man in the dock. "Haven't I seen you in this court before, young man?" asked the esteemed judge. "No, your honour," replied the accused. "Now, now, I'm sure I have, young man," retorted the judge. "You have definitely been up before this court in the past while I have been presiding." "I promise you I haven't," replied the accused, who by now was getting rather annoyed, as was the cause of his exasperation. "Why can't you just tell me the damn truth?" snapped the esteemed judge. "I have definitely seen you in this court before!" It turned out the judge *had* seen the man in court before, but it was a court that had been built by the set builders at Television Centre. The chap in the dock was an actor who'd appeared as a thief in an episode of *Brothers in Law* just a couple of weeks before and poor Henry had got a bit confused!'

The actor who played Henry Blagrove, who is Thursby's chief friend and ally in *Brothers in Law*, was Richard Waring, the brother of the character actor, Derek Waring. He too had appeared in *The Seven Faces of Jim*, although in a different episode, and *Brothers in Law* was also his big break as an actor. But the difference between the two Richards was that Richard Waring wasn't really interested in being an actor at all and had always been far happier writing. In fact, in addition to contributing some material to *Brothers in Law*, Waring had written extensively for the BBC, including several episodes of the ratings behemoth, *The Charlie Drake Show*.

Impressed by his younger, more theatrical co-star, Waring decided to devise and write a sitcom for Richard and in the spring of 1963 sent him ten scripts for a show entitled *The Marriage Lines*. Soon to have the definite article removed, *Marriage Lines* became a precursor to just about every British middle-class sitcom there has ever been and was one of two domestic situation comedies that captured the public's imaginations in the early 1960s – the other being Galton and Simpson's *Steptoe and Son*, which first aired in January 1962. Before that only a handful of television sitcoms had been produced. Indeed, the term 'situation comedy' had only been in existence since 1953 after *The Goon Show*'s producer, Peter Eton, had suggested it as a possible format for Tony Hancock's style of comedy. *Marriage Lines*, which was subtitled *A Quizzical Look at the Early Days of Married Life*, had none of the baggage or expectation that *Brothers in Law* had carried and, with a plot that was brilliant in its simplicity – just like *Steptoe and Son* – it allowed the characters to develop and ultimately shine. With scripts that certainly belied the deliberately simplistic plot – although nowhere near as much as Galton and Simpson's creation – it had all the makings of a hit show, and is generally considered to have aged quite well.

The plot centres on a newly married couple, George and Kate Starling, played by Richard and Prunella Scales, and the frustrations they face going about their everyday life. It really was that simple. When asked about his inspiration for writing *Marriage Lines*, Richard Waring said that he thought all marriages were founded on a mixture of mutual trust and suspicion and that each episode would examine one facet of those early days when anything short of perfect harmony raises grim thoughts of incompatibility in the mind of each partner.

When they first went to air, the main difference between *Marriage Lines* and *Steptoe and Son* was the 'sit', as in situation. *Marriage Lines* was, at least at first glance, far more pertinent to everyday life than the rag-and-bone men of *Steptoe and Son* and it was very easy to relate to the comedy. If the viewer wasn't in that situation themselves they undoubtedly knew somebody who was, and that level of association was something normally reserved for soap operas. Subsequently, as with the likes of *The Archers* and *Coronation Street*, *Marriage Lines* developed a very loyal audience and, after making an excellent debut in August 1963, the viewing figures rose for a few weeks as word got around and then barely wavered. *Steptoe and Son* would also become pertinent, of course, but only once the backstory had begun to unravel and the relationship between Harold and Albert had been laid bare. By then, pathos had become the main source of the 'com', which is something *Marriage Lines* rarely relied on.

Prunella Scales, who was about eighteen months older than Richard, had first appeared on television in 1952 when she played Lydia Bennet in a production of Jane Austen's *Pride and Prejudice* alongside Peter Cushing as Mr Darcy.

Since then Prunella had been making steady progress on this relatively new and unstoppable medium and at the time of meeting Richard she had recently played Martha in a successful adaptation of Frances Hodgson Burnett's *The Secret Garden*. Like Richard, Prunella was yet to star in a show that ran for more than a few episodes and while appearing as a barmaid one day for the BBC at Television Centre, she was approached by Richard who had a question for her.

' "Do you enjoy sitcom?" he asked me, and I thought, what a strange question. "Yes," I replied finally. "I suppose I do." I'm awfully glad I did because after that he invited me to read for the part of Kate Starling.'

According to Richard, his portrayal of the slightly hapless but well-meaning George Starling was quite easy to evoke. 'George Starling in *Marriage Lines* was just like Tom Good in *The Good Life*,' he said, 'in that I pretty much played myself – a highly strung, nervous and rather stupid person who was desperate to get things right but was forever getting them wrong!'

One of the reasons Richard approached Prunella Scales was that she seemed to possess the same kind of effortless energy he did, the kind Denis Norden thought was lacking in 1960s television.

'The truth is that I was one of the few female actors who could cope with his quick delivery,' admits Prunella. 'In fact, I welcomed it in a way as it kept me on my toes.'

Richard agreed.

'Once Pru and I had got used to each other everything just flowed and I think we were jolly good together. She's such a natural actor, and so providing the scripts were OK, and they were, we couldn't miss.'

After making *Fawlty Towers*, Prunella Scales would describe working with John Cleese as being like trying to keep a live machine gun pointing away from you. Without the experience of working with Richard in *Marriage Lines*, who could be likened to something slightly less dangerous, she may not have been able to cope.

'I was looking at an extract from *Marriage Lines* the other day,' says Prunella, 'and we still speak faster than anyone else in the business. The speed of us was staggering and I couldn't believe it. I was quite proud!'

When *Marriage Lines* first aired at 8.05 p.m. on 17 August 1963 Prunella was engaged to the actor Timothy West, whom she would marry just two months later. Funnily enough, Timothy had also been cast in Richard Waring's new sitcom, although the chances of him getting a second episode, let alone a second series, were slim at best.

'I played the chap called Bob from whom George and Kate Starling got their flat,' remembers Timothy. 'I have a telephone conversation with Richard at the start of my episode and at the end of it he puts the phone down and says, "Dear old Bob. He's had to go to South Africa for five years and says we can rent his flat." The moment I read that in the script I thought, that's the end of me then!'

Just like *Brothers in Law* (and *The Good Life*, as it turned out), *Marriage Lines* was greeted by an indifferent press and the *Birmingham Daily Post* seemed to speak for the majority of the media when, once again, it questioned the quality of the show but not its stars. This stance was at odds with the public, who took to the show immediately. It said, 'The return to the BBC of the reticent and perplexed young character which Richard Briers so successfully portrayed in last year's *Brothers in Law* series was something to welcome as a British antidote to the slick exaggerations of American comedy.'

Had Richard lived in Birmingham and popped out to buy the *Evening Post*, he would have been thrilled on reading that opening sentence but the 'devil' was in the one that followed.

'Whether, however, his return last night in the new BBC comedy *Marriage Lines* is going to be sufficiently attractive to tempt viewers to desert *Gunsmoke* on the other channel remains to be seen, and possibly is doubtful.'

The newspaper then goes on to admit that British TV series in any sphere seem to be slow starters and improve as they go along, before backtracking slightly and questioning the chances of *Marriage Lines* doing so. It's a confused review, which perhaps represents the dichotomy of having 'slow starters' on such a fast and seemingly disposable medium – something the general public seemed to grasp a lot easier than the press.

Marriage Lines would run for five series, finishing on 3 June 1966 after a total of forty-six episodes, including two ten-minute shorts that Richard and Prunella would perform on the

1963 and 1964 editions of *Christmas Night with the Stars*, the ridiculously popular BBC seasonal extravaganza that used to showcase the corporation's most popular television shows. Sadly, only series one and series three of *Marriage Lines* exist in their entirety, with series two, four and five falling victim to the BBC's scream-inducing wiping policy. The two existing series have been released on DVD, however, and the scripts hold up well, as does the interplay between Richard and Prunella, which became the show's main talking point.

As well as turning Richard and Prunella Scales into household names, *Marriage Lines* also improved their chances of getting theatrical work, albeit in plays of a similar ilk.

'To be involved in a popular television sitcom so early on in your acting life is a great piece of good fortune,' Prunella said in the television show *A Good Life* in 2000, 'as it means the general public will take the giant step from the pavement into the theatre as they're dying to see what you look like in real life.'

But before Richard could accept any more theatrical work he first had to get his head around something slightly more significant – an event that he and Annie had been hoping would happen for some years and had been looking forward to since the end of 1962. They were about to become parents.

CHAPTER ELEVEN

How To Get Ahead in Advertising

Richard and Annie had been trying for a baby since marrying at the start of 1957 and by the time *Brothers in Law* came along they were starting to worry.

'I've no idea what the matter was,' says Annie, 'but when I found out I was pregnant at the end of 1962 we were both very, very relieved. Richard was thrilled!'

Even so, Annie's first pregnancy was far from easy and while Richard was heading off to a rehearsal somewhere or to film an episode of *Brothers in Law*, Annie would be heading to the bathroom.

'My God, I had terrible sickness,' she says. 'Pregnancy was like acting, though: long periods of boredom followed by short bursts of excitement. I was glad when it was all over.'

Just six days before *Marriage Lines* had been due to premier on the BBC, Annie was taken to Queen Charlotte's Hospital where, at 6.30 a.m. on 10 August 1963, she gave birth to a daughter they named Katy Ann. Weighing in at a healthy seven pounds three, Kate was indeed the apple of her father's eye, although when it came to undertaking any fatherly duties it's safe to say that, just like his two hit shows, *Brothers in Law* and *Marriage Lines*, he was a proverbial 'slow starter'. Annie remembers this all too well.

'At first Richard was obviously just relieved that Kate and I were OK, but I think it took him time to come to terms with the whole family thing. You know what men are like. Before a baby arrives, they think the world revolves around them, *and* they get all the attention. Then, when they're finally pushed aside by something small and noisy they either sulk or take time to adjust. Richard didn't sulk, fortunately. In fact, he never really sulked about anything. But there was definitely a bedding-in period! He was also incredibly busy.'

In between first appearing in *Brothers in Law* and celebrating the birth of his daughter, Richard had been running around from studio to studio as well as fulfilling his ambition of having a starring role in a television series. He had also done the same on film, but with dramatically different results. *The Girl on the Boat*, which had been released in 1962, should have been the perfect vehicle for Richard, both personally and professionally. Based on the novel of the same name by Richard's favourite author, P. G. Wodehouse, it was directed by the television director Henry Kaplan, in what was thankfully his only big-screen outing, and starred Norman Wisdom, Millicent Martin, Bernard Cribbins, Athene Seyler and Sheila Hancock. Richard was third in the billing behind Wisdom and Martin – much higher than last time – but, as with so many of his vehicles thus far, the press said: 'you're quite good, unlike the end product'. Except this time the chances of them eventually warming to said end product, which they could only do by seeing it again, were less than zero.

As well as giving it two stars out of five, the *Radio Times* later said, 'Norman Wisdom tried something different from his usual slapstick with this seagoing comedy romance. It doesn't work for Wisdom, though it does for the less mannered professionals in support such as Richard Briers, Millicent Martin and Athene Seyler.'

Sheila Hancock, who appeared in several scenes with Richard, and actually picks him up and carries him in one of them, remembers Richard being about the only saving grace in what was a pretty dire experience.

'Thankfully the film sank without trace because it was probably one of the worst ever made, and all I really remember about shooting it was meeting Richard, who became a lifelong friend.'

But what charmed Sheila Hancock the most during their time together at Shepperton Studios in Surrey was Richard's devotion to his wife; something that, like his generosity on the stage, has been much mentioned by his friends and colleagues.

'At the time, Richard hadn't been married to Annie that long and I hadn't met her yet,' remembers Sheila. 'I remember being fascinated, though, as every night he couldn't wait to get home. He was so domesticated and loving!'

Despite him being a home bird (something that ultimately became stronger as he got older), Richard was conscious that all that hard work he had put in was beginning to pay off. After making *The Girl on the Boat*, which appeared just after *Brothers in Law* started, he made two more films in quick succession before Kate arrived – uncredited acknowledgments in *The V.I.P.s* starring Elizabeth Taylor and *Doctor in Distress* starring Dirk Bogarde – and accepted a further four roles on television, including one for an episode of *Dixon of Dock Green*.

'Somebody from the BBC put a script through my letterbox one day without even a letter,' he said in 2012. 'I wasn't playing a policeman, though. Oh no, I was playing a thief! And I remember the fee, funnily enough, which was £150. Not bad really. It was filmed live of course, with old Jack Warner as PC Dixon. Jack was a dear man I remember, and even though he had no idea who I was he still spoke to me. "Alright, son?" he asked.'

The theatre, too, was continuing to bear fruit for Richard and although the lion's share of the scripts being sent to him were either comedies or farces, with which he was fine – up to a point – he hadn't been discounted entirely by the directors and producers casting straighter fare. In the summer of 1964 he received an offer that, even if he had to turn down some television, he was determined to do. Richard recalled how it all came about for an interview in 1978.

'When I got the offer, the only bit of drama I'd done since *Brothers in Law* was a three-play production which started at the Arts Theatre Club and then moved to the Criterion called, rather imaginatively, *Three*. The plays in question, two of which had been conceived as radio plays, were *A Slight Ache*, by Harold Pinter, *The Form*, by N. F. Simpson and *Lunch Hour* by John Mortimer.'

Emlyn Williams and Alison Leggatt were Richard's co-stars in *Three*, and despite the *New Statesman* and several broadsheet newspapers raving about the production – '*Three* is an excellent idea of theatre, and a bouquet for the Arts. I hope it lives long in London' – it lasted but a few weeks, leaving Richard bound to nothing but comedy.

'Then, completely out of the blue, my agent called me up and asked me if I'd be interested in appearing in a new play called *Hamp*. I assumed it was yet another comedy but when I vocalised my assumption I was told to sit tight. "I think you might be pleasantly surprised," said my agent.'

Hamp, which is set during the First World War, tells the story of a young soldier (Private Hamp), who is to be court-martialled for desertion after crawling out of a shell hole at Passchendaele and then walking away from the scene. Hamp's senior officer believes that the court could insist on the death penalty, but the private disagrees, assuming, somewhat naively, that those passing sentence will have more important things to worry about. Finally, the court indeed decrees that Hamp must meet a death as unceremonious as the Army can make it, but after he survives the firing squad, it is left to the senior officer, Lieutenant Hargreaves, which was the role that had been offered to Richard, to finish him off with his revolver. This truly was the antithesis of everything that had made Richard a star.

On finishing the script, Richard called his agent and told him he would like to accept the role of Lieutenant Hargreaves. On this occasion the money, which was peanuts, didn't matter, and when *Hamp* had its world premiere at the Theatre Royal Newcastle on 10 August 1964, which was Kate's first birthday, Richard lined up for the curtain call alongside two of Britain's finest young actors: John Hurt, who played Hamp, and Leonard Rossiter, who played the prosecuting officer, Lieutenant Tom Webb. Their involvement had been payment enough for Richard and, although he knew full well that in order for his enterprise to flourish he would have to continue making comedy, appearing in *Hamp* had whetted his appetite for drama and had satisfied his growing urge to take a chance every so often.

The reviews for *Hamp* were glowing at Newcastle, especially for John Hurt, and that was despite him and his fellow actors almost falling off the stage.

'The director decided to build the stage up,' Richard said, 'thus increasing the rake six or seven times. The result was that the actors would enter from the wings, turn to face the audience, hurtle downhill to the footlights, brake sharply, and then turn to trudge up the slope in second gear. The sight of Leonard's face registering mock-exhaustion as he trudged upstage is something I shall treasure always. Ever after, the play was affectionately known as *Ramp*.'

After spending a week at the Theatre Royal Newcastle, which, despite the 'Ramp', Richard later claimed as being his favourite theatre, *Hamp* moved to the Edinburgh Festival where it played until the end of August. This was yet another new experience for Richard, and one that he would repeat twenty-six years later with a young Kenneth Branagh, this time playing one of the most demanding roles a senior actor, as he was then, can undertake. But as much as Richard enjoyed being part of the 1964 Edinburgh Festival, it was his Liverpudlian co-star who had impressed him the most.

'I remember saying to my wife, "there's this wonderful actor called Leonard Rossiter, but I don't think he'll ever become a star – he's too real".'

Just a month after *Hamp* had its premiere, a film adaptation of the play, called *King & Country*, opened in cinemas throughout the UK. It was directed by the American Joseph Losey, who had been making films in Europe after being blacklisted in the 1950s, and the parts played by Hurt, Briers and Rossiter had been given to Tom Courtenay, Dirk Bogarde and Leo McKern respectively. Although Richard would have loved to have appeared in the film, he managed to hide his jealousy. 'I think that's what stopped us going into the West End though,' he said in 2009, 'because the play and the film were virtually out at the same time.'

Interestingly, Richard claimed in the same interview that appearing in such a tragic tale was good for his ego and even made him imagine, although briefly, that he might have a future in tear-jerkers. 'But it was never going to be,' he said. 'In fact, I was looking at some production photos from *Hamp* the other day and I could see the first stirrings of the comic expressions that I would later use for Tom Good in *The Good Life*.'

The mind boggles.

As predicted, Richard's time as a tear-jerker was more of a weekend away than a departure. And, with *Marriage Lines* still going strong, it would be left to a new but nevertheless burgeoning side of his career to offer him anything other than comedy. Something that, paradoxically, would enable Richard to go back into serious theatre later on in life and on more than one occasion. Advertising.

By this time, Richard and his young family were living at 16 Pleydell Avenue, west London, which is roughly eight miles north of Pepys Court. Since moving back to the city he and Annie had been renting flats all over the place, but by 1962 they had saved up enough money to buy a house. With children on the cards, they had wanted to settle somewhere leafy and had finally decided on the Stamford Brook/Chiswick area.

The demand for Richard's services in the advertising industry had burst into life shortly after he appeared in *The Seven Faces of*

Jim and had pretty much grown with his career. Television advertising itself was just six years old at the time and, with the accepted technique often being to charm the viewers into buying products, the companies involved had to find somebody charming. And popular, if possible.

When Richard died in 2013 the words 'effortlessly charming' were omnipresent throughout the tributes and obituaries, and as tempting as it is to assume that 'effortlessly charming' is something you have to include when somebody of Richard's popularity dies, it was neither a cliché nor a truism. It was Richard. Add that to an instantly recognisable voice, a lovable and friendly face, if needed, and an innate ability to act, and you have the makings of an actor who, as more and more channels appeared – not to mention commercial radio – became ridiculously busy. Once *Marriage Lines* had become popular, the general public had started seeing Richard Briers as a friend. He was the neighbour everyone wanted, and this was long before *The Good Life* had started. Who better to tell the great British public what to buy? Richard obviously knew the value of this, which is one of the reasons why, certainly until the 1990s, he rarely played a baddie on television.

'I'm a very gregarious character and I enjoy being recognised,' he once said. 'In fact, I insist on it! If I played baddies all the time people might not want to talk to me, and that would never do.'

As a result of the upturn in their fortunes, 16 Pleydell Avenue wasn't the only house Richard and Annie bought in the early 1960s. In fact, according to Lucy, it was one of three.

'I think Dad had been doing really well since he started appearing on television and about the same time as buying

Pleydell Avenue he bought his mum and dad a bungalow in Hatch End and another bungalow for his dad's brother, Uncle George. This, I think, is how Dad measured his success: his ability to provide for his family. Ultimately – and again, this is down to them being strapped for cash when he was a child – that's all that really mattered to him. He didn't want any member of his family to be in that situation ever again.'

Strangely enough, had it not been for the offer of an advertisement in 1968 for the then newly formed bed manufacturer, Slumberland, Richard may well have ended up in penury.

'One day Dad received an unexpected tax bill from the HMRC,' says Kate. 'This terrified him half to death as we had just moved to a bigger house and it looked as if they were going to have to sell it to pay the bill. Then, literally a few days before a decision had to be made, Dad was asked to do a live action advert by Slumberland, which saved the day. From that moment on Mum and Dad always slept on Slumberland beds, partly out of loyalty, I think, but also out of superstition!'

CHAPTER TWELVE

Can You *Fathom* It?

In January 1965, shortly after his thirty-first birthday, Richard was contacted by the producer and director, John Gale, who was then one of the most successful theatrical producers in the country.

'Have you ever done any Coward?' he asked Richard.

'I did *Nude with Violin* at the Belgrade,' he replied. 'That was back in 1958 though.'

'How would you like to play Roland Maule in *Present Laughter*?' continued Gale. 'Nigel Patrick's directing, and he's playing the lead, Garry Essendine. He thinks you'll be perfect, and so do I.'

Although Richard sometimes claimed that he was afraid of being typecast during this period, the fact is the work he was being offered, by and large, was of the highest quality and as long as he allowed himself to deviate occasionally, à la *Hamp*, and remind the general public that there was more to his repertoire, then there was no point rocking the boat. Richard appreciated this, which is why his protestations were few and far between.

What *Present Laughter* had going for it, apart from a good part in a good play with a top cast and at least six months' work, was the writer. Noël Coward, while not quite in the same league as P. G. Wodehouse with regards to Richard's devotion, was nevertheless a talent who had been amusing Richard for many years, and ever since he had appeared as Sebastian in *Nude with Violin* he had been desperate to do more.

Also in the cast of *Present Laughter* were Phyllis Calvert, Maxine Audley, Avice Landone and Coward's long-time companion, Graham Payn; with just one production each, it was Richard and the lead actor and director, Nigel Patrick, who had the least amount of experience playing Coward, something that made Richard nervous, especially when it was rumoured that Coward himself might be dropping by during rehearsals. He later said to Lucy, 'The prospect of Coward himself walking through the door at any moment was distinctly off-putting and it did nothing for my performance. I was bloody terrified!'

By the time Noël Coward made it over from Jamaica, the cast were just about ready for their first run-through and when Richard was informed by somebody at the producer's office that Coward would be attending, it set him back years.

Shortly after Coward's death in 1973, Richard was asked to recall the experience for an interview.

'Noël came along to watch a run-through, but beforehand he came backstage to meet the cast. This probably wasn't the case, but everybody seemed to know him except me, and I'm sure he thought I was a bit strange – which I suppose I was! "I'll be giving notes," he said. Gulp! In the end Noël and I played the scene between Garry and Roland Maule, with Noël playing the part of Garry, and because I was so terribly nervous I went at about a hundred miles an hour. Afterwards Noël wagged his finger at me, which apparently, he was famous for, and said, "My God, you frighten me to death!" Later on, Noël demonstrated the part where Garry eagerly throws his arms around Joanna and says to her, "My darling," while looking at his watch behind her back.

It was a privilege to have seen the great man in action; he performed with such a light touch. But he became somewhat irritable with me, I think, as I was too nervous for him.'

Despite the rather erratic run-through, Noël Coward eventually warmed to the anxious actor and by the time the opening night came around on 21 April 1965 he was hailing Richard as 'one of our greatest farceurs'. Asked why he thought so, the Master replied, 'Simple. He doesn't hang about!'

Richard's wife Annie had her own encounter with Coward during the run of *Present Laughter* and ended up almost falling in love with him.

'There was a party one night after one of the performances of *Present Laughter* and Richard had invited me along. I'd already seen the show several times and so instead of watching it again I decided to go and see *The Killing of Sister George* at the Duke of York's with Beryl Reid and Eileen Atkins. Lo and behold, who was sitting just a few seats away from me but Noël. "Annie, my dear," he said. "How lovely to see you. Would you care to accompany me backstage afterwards to meet the cast?" Naturally I said yes and after the show he put his arm around my shoulder and escorted me backstage. By then I'd already fallen in love with him. He simply oozed star quality and charisma.'

After saying hello to Beryl Reid and Eileen Atkins, *et al.*, the Master offered Annie a lift to the Queen's Theatre where the party was taking place.

'He told me to stay where I was while he went to fetch the car and returned a few minutes later driving an Austin Princess – the sort of limousine fitted with rugs and seats that fold down that I always associate with grand people like mayors. "I suppose you expected a Rolls-Royce," said my chauffeur. "Well, I suppose I always think of you in a Rolls-Royce," I stumbled, to which Noël replied imperiously, "Very unfashionable, you know. Terribly non-U. Austin Princesses are now in." That told me!'

Over the next few years Richard stayed in touch with his famous admirer and, if Noël was ever in town while he was in a play, Richard would be sure to send tickets to wherever Coward was staying. But despite enjoying the respect of Noël Coward, which was obviously reciprocated tenfold, Richard always felt slightly intimidated in his presence and, when Richard wrote a short book about the Master in 1987 entitled *Coward & Company – A light-hearted and affectionate evocation of Noël Coward and his world* – he mentioned this fact more than once.

'To me,' said Richard, 'as to so many other people, he appeared to live in another stratosphere; for all we knew he could have been on Mars. As a result, when you did finally meet him, the aura that surrounded Noël Coward was quite overpowering.'

One of the last times Richard saw Coward was in 1968. He and Ronnie Barker had just opened in *The Real Inspector Hound*, Tom Stoppard's one-act play about two pretentious theatre critics who, while watching a murder mystery, become involved in the action thus triggering a series of unfortunate events that parallel the play they are watching. This time Coward said hello prior to curtain-up, which put Richard in a bit of a spin. He later recalled the episode in *Coward & Company*.

Coward came around and sat in the very dressing room [at the Criterion Theatre] that he'd occupied himself when he'd played *Design for Living* with Alfred Lunt and Lynn Fontanne. I'm still hopelessly star-struck today, and on that occasion in Coward's presence I was completely tongue-tied.

I tried offering him a drink.

'Vodka and tonic,' he replied. I hadn't any vodka.

I nipped next door to Ronnie Barker. 'I've only got half a bottle,' he warned – and that was a shade optimistic when I looked at the level. Then I found that I didn't have a decent glass, so Coward had to make do with an awful tooth mug of a tumbler. Dithering about in a lather of perspiration, I tried to be self-deprecating and said to him of the play, 'Of course, this is just a light romp, sir.'

'I really think it is a little more than that,' he replied crisply. And he was absolutely right: it's a very clever play. Again, I had been wrong-footed, neatly and precisely, as only the Master knew how.'

Fortunately for Richard, Coward must have been in a forgiving mood at the Criterion Theatre that evening as when the BBC approached him about making an adaptation of his play, *Hay Fever,* just several days later he agreed, with the recommendation that Richard should play the part of Sandy Tyrell.

For his part, Richard obviously felt a connection with Noël Coward; something that went far beyond a mutual admiration of Victorian actor-managers (Coward's first mentor had been Sir Charles Hawtrey, another of Richard's heroes) or dexterity of speech. It was to do with the fact that, despite his obvious talent, Noël Coward's journey from suburban Teddington to Las Vegas via Broadway and the West End had been fraught with difficulty and, as well as suffering a great many hardships along the way, he had also endured his fair share of failures. Richard's experiences had been different to Coward's but there were similarities. Coward's father, for instance, who was a piano salesman, had lacked drive or ambition and subsequently the family finances were often poor. More pertinent, perhaps, is the fact that Coward had received hardly any formal education as a child, yet he had been a voracious reader from an early age. The lack of schooling, however, as with Richard, to paraphrase an old adage, 'had never done him any harm'. This, not to mention the reading matter they both enjoyed, from Dickens to P. G. Wodehouse, bonded Richard to the Master, and so the fact that he became nervous in his presence and ended up writing a book about him are hardly surprising. Coward, like Richard, had been a self-starter and, with help, encouragement and some training, had formed his enterprise, worked bloody hard and had made a success of his life. Richard would use Coward's story, without drawing attention to any similarities to his own, as a way to motivate friends or colleagues who were perhaps lacking in confidence and would do so by presenting them with a copy of Coward's autobiography, *Present Indicative*.

'It made a big impression on me,' said Michael Frayn, to whom Richard presented a copy on the opening night of Frayn's play, *The Two of Us*, in which he starred in 1970 alongside Lynn Redgrave. 'Until then I had seen Coward's life as an unbroken success but when I read it I realised it wasn't like that at all. He'd had all kinds of disasters.'

One of Richard's own favourite Noël Coward stories can be found in *Coward & Company*, and refers to the arrival of some angry young men in the late 1950s.

'With the arrival of kitchen sink drama,' Richard wrote, 'the charm and the glamour of Coward's work was suddenly eclipsed by a greyer cloud of realism. "A terrible pall of significance," Coward once called it.'

Indeed. Almost overnight, Noël Coward's work had become unfashionable and he was regarded by critics as a has-been. This rapid reappraisal of his work naturally hurt the Master, yet his response to the mass denunciation was typical of the man and was something Richard would use as a maxim, just like, 'Here's to our enterprise!'

He simply said, 'Press on, dear boy, press on!'

In June 1966, approximately six months after he had finished appearing in *Present Laughter*, the forty-sixth and final episode of *Marriage Lines* was broadcast on BBC1, bringing to an end one of the most successful situation comedies of the 1960s. During its three-year run, Richard and Prunella Scales had both become household names, but as grateful as he was for having been in such a successful show so early on in his career, Richard breathed a huge sigh of relief when it ended.

'I was in danger of being typecast – on television, at least – as a kind of nervous idiot who means well,' he said in 1990, 'and so I had to try and put that character in a box for a while and move on. I had no problem making my living in comedy, if that was all that was offered to me, but it's such a broad genre, you see, and so if I was going to be known as a comedy actor, I wanted to explore it.'

Paradoxically, just a few days after *Marriage Lines* had ended Richard was invited to do a screentest at Shepperton Studios for a role that was so against type one could have been forgiven for believing that Richard had been invited by mistake – a belief that even Richard himself shared.

'I didn't know what the bloody hell was going on,' he told Kate. 'The film was a spy-spoof, which were all the rage back then, and the part I was up for was the assistant to some criminal mastermind.'

Richard came away from the screen test feeling like a prize plum and the moment he got home he picked up the phone to remonstrate with his agent and bemoan the fact that several hours of his time had obviously been completely wasted.

'But they've offered you the part,' pleaded the agent.

'What?' replied Richard, completely astounded. 'They can't have. That's just silly. It must be a mistake. Are you sure they don't mean another Richard?'

'Definitely not. They called shortly after the test. You start filming in August. Five months in southern Spain.'

Richard being offered a role that might have been better suited to several other 'Richards' is only half of the story, as the film in question, *Fathom*, has to be seen to be believed. While it's not the worst film ever made, it is undoubtedly one of the most ill-conceived. The film's star is none other than Raquel Welch who, at a little under twenty-six years of age, had just made two films back-to-back that would make her a huge worldwide star: *Fantastic Voyage*, which was released while *Fathom* was being filmed in October 1966, and *One Million Years B.C.*, which was released two months later in December. Both films grossed millions at the box office at a time when a million was still a lot. While *Fantastic Voyage* would obviously be classed as science fiction and *One Million Years B.C.* as fantasy/adventure, *Fathom* was a kind of weird aquatic/aeronautical spy-spoof hybrid that had more baddies than a gangsters' convention (the best being the monocle-wearing, moustache-tweaking Sergi Serapkin, played by a very over-the-top Clive Revill), a casting director who needed to lie down in a darkened room for a few years and an overly generous budget. The plot, which apparently changed several times while filming, centres on a beautiful American skydiver, Fathom Harvill (Raquel Welch), who gets wrapped up in international intrigue when Scottish spy, Douglas Campbell (Ronald Fraser), and his assistant, Flight Lt Timothy Webb (Richard), recruit her to help them on a secret mission. Before long, Fathom realises that no one around her can easily be trusted, leading to various adventures involving bullfights, beaches, speedboat chases, skydives and, of course, romance. Richard and Ronald Fraser turn out to be baddies, but you only find this out at the very end and while Fraser, who has obviously borrowed his Scottish accent from Richard, meets with a sticky end, Richard gets away by the skin of his teeth.

The script, which was written by Lorenzo Semple Jr, the man responsible for writing the original *Batman* television series, not to mention the 1980 film, *Flash Gordon*, is, as one might imagine, pretty OTT in places and, together with Revill's performance and some rather nice photography, is what makes the film watchable.

Even when Richard arrived in Miramar near Valencia, where much of *Fathom* was filmed, he was half expecting to be sent straight home.

'Dad had played against type before, but never like this,' says Lucy. 'He just did not understand why he had been given this part. He's constantly in scenes with Raquel Welch in her bikini, which I'm sure he enjoyed, and he's calling her "love" all the time. Not in a theatrical way, like he might a friend, but in a blokeish way. He's also driving a speedboat for much of the film which is wonderfully ridiculous! But I was really impressed that he was actually driving the speedboat – no stunt double required!'

Miscasting and speedboats notwithstanding, filming *Fathom* was, overall, an enjoyable experience for Richard and as well as getting on very well with Ronnie Fraser, he also struck up an unlikely friendship with his other, slightly more alluring, co-star.

'Dad said Raquel Welch was absolutely lovely,' says Lucy, 'and very easy to work with. She was just as confused as everyone else as to which direction the plot was going but she wasn't at all starry. Apparently, she, Dad, Ronnie and the others would meet on set every morning, stare at the script and say, "Does anyone have any idea what's going on?" Even the director would say, "Look, I don't really understand what's going on in this scene but let's shoot it anyway."'

At her home, Lucy has a photo of Richard, Ronnie and some of the other actors on the *Fathom* set and, as well as looking a bit bemused, they are all howling with laughter.

'Dad said it was indicative of the atmosphere,' says Lucy, 'and the film. Happy confusion!'

CHAPTER THIRTEEN

Relatively Alan

When Richard finally returned to London at the end of 1966, he already had a year's worth of work in the bag, with more to come should any adverts or bits of TV materialise. The work in question, a new play called *Relatively Speaking* by an up-and-coming playwright named Alan Ayckbourn, had been agreed over a year before and, in addition to one or two visits from Annie, together with regular letters from Kate, was part of what had enabled Richard to tolerate being away from home for the best part of half a year.

'Richard had only been abroad a few times before *Fathom*,' says Annie. 'It was also the longest he'd gone without performing in theatre since he was a teenager, I think. He was getting all kinds of withdrawal symptoms.'

For the rest of his days, it's probably fair to say that, unless Annie was with him, Richard Briers was what one would call an 'innocent abroad' when on his travels (even when filming *Monarch of the Glen* in the Scottish Highlands!) and so his homecoming after *Fathom* was obviously a happy one.

'Kate had missed him so, so much,' remembers Annie. 'She'd turned three in August and by the time it got to December we were literally counting down the days. "How many days till Daddy gets home, Mummy?" she'd say. "Only ten now, darling.

He'll be here soon." It was like waiting for the arrival of Father Christmas!'

What Richard was hoping for that Christmas was a nice new script for *Relatively Speaking*, which he was due to start rehearsing in early January 1967. *Relatively Speaking*, which is widely considered by critics to be Ayckbourn's most-crafted piece, concerns two couples – Greg and Ginny, who are in their twenties, and Philip and Sheila, who are middle-aged. Greg desperately wants to marry Ginny, who has only recently broken off an affair with her boss, Philip. Ginny goes down to Philip's country home to get back some love letters, after telling Greg that she is going to visit her parents. Greg follows her secretly, and for the rest of the afternoon we have the two couples assembled in Philip's garden, which is where the majority of the action takes place. Greg believes that Philip is Ginny's father and that Philip's wife, Sheila, is Ginny's mother. Philip mistakenly gets the idea that Greg is having an affair with Sheila, and Sheila is led to believe that Ginny is nothing more than her husband's secretary. As the afternoon goes on the situation becomes increasingly complicated and, as the critics claim, it is incredibly well-crafted and at times hilarious.

What excited Richard even more than the prospect of appearing in a brand-new play by a well-regarded young playwright were his not quite so young but extremely highly regarded co-stars: Michael Hordern and Celia Johnson. He had already worked with both of them, of course, and with the play being, as Richard described it, 'The best thing I've read in decades,' he was sure they were on course for a gigantic success.

What Richard didn't know at the time was the full story of

how he had been cast in *Relatively Speaking*, which is a good job as he might have been slightly put out.

Alan Ayckbourn had started writing the play, originally titled *Meet My Father*, in May 1965, with Joan Greenwood, Alec McCowan and Lynn Redgrave initially earmarked for the roles of Sheila, Greg and Ginny. The Scarborough-based playwright, who was knighted for services to theatre in 1997, had a contract with the BBC at the time and, despite some encouraging noises from the producer and the promise of a West End run, was reluctant to give it all up.

'The last play I had on in the West End had lasted a couple of weeks,' says Sir Alan, 'yet I'd been encouraged to leave the BBC, which I'd done. Fortunately, they had me back after the play flopped so there was no way I was going to leave again. Not until I knew it was a hit.'

After much toing and froing, the producer, Peter Bridge, finally settled on three of the four cast members, and Alan Ayckbourn was happy with all of them. 'He said he'd got Michael Hordern for the part of Philip, which was amazing, and Celia Johnson for Sheila, which was equally as impressive. He'd also cast a marvellous young actor named Jennifer Hilary for the role of Ginny and so the only one left was Greg.'

After compiling a list of possible candidates for the role of Greg, Ayckbourn and Peter Bridge duly handed it to the leading lady. 'For some reason Celia Johnson had approval of that role,' says Sir Alan, 'but because she was from a different generation and not very good with names she didn't recognise any of them and so they were all dismissed outright – including Richard. It's extraordinary really because Celia is one of the sharpest people I ever met and could do the *Times* crossword in a couple of minutes.'

Several weeks later, Peter Bridge called Alan with the good news that Celia Johnson had at last found her Greg. There was, however, one small problem.

'Celia had recently done a radio play with somebody she thought would be perfect for the part of Greg and had called Peter Bridge to tell him. "Brilliant, what's his name?" I asked. "That's the bugger," replied Peter. "I'm afraid she can't remember!" "Well, what was the radio play called?" I asked him. "She can't remember that either!"'

In the end Alan Ayckbourn assumed the role of detective and while Celia and Peter were wracking their brains he called up a friend in the radio department at the BBC.

'First, I asked him what the last thing Celia Johnson had done on radio. I think it was an Ibsen, or something? Once we'd ascertained that, I asked him if there were any young unknown actors in the cast list. "There's only one youngish actor in the cast," he said. "But that's Richard Briers. He's hardly unknown."'

When Ayckbourn reported his findings to Peter Bridge and Celia Johnson and mentioned Richard's name, a look of recognition suddenly swept over their leading lady's face. 'That's the fellow,' she said, enlightened. 'Richard Briers! He's the unknown actor!'

Within a day, Richard had read the script and had agreed to play Greg and, although Celia Johnson hadn't remembered his name, despite directing him in *Special Providence*, she had at least marked him out as a good actor. If it hadn't been for her (and Detective Inspector Ayckbourn, of course), he would never have been cast.

Richard later told Alan Ayckbourn that every moment he spent on stage with Celia Johnson was like a masterclass. 'It was her precision that fascinated Dickie,' says Sir Alan. 'She was beautifully disciplined, and her timing was just incredible. For an actor who was making his mark partly through the gift of timing, it was invaluable.'

With Michael Hordern things were slightly different and, as good an actor as he undoubtedly was, precision didn't rate highly on his list of talents.

'Michael Hordern was the dearest of men,' claims Sir Alan, 'but rather woolly and he had no idea what he was doing from minute to minute. Like Celia, he wasn't good at names and even after I'd known him for six months or so he still referred to me as "author". "Ah, dear author," he'd say in that wonderful voice of his while waving his script. "Could I have a woooord with yooooou?" Dickie and I couldn't believe that Michael and Celia worked so well together, but they obviously did.'

The only other person left to mention at this juncture is the play's director, Nigel Patrick, who had directed Richard in *Present Laughter*. Patrick had been brought in by Peter Bridge, right at the very beginning, and although Sir Alan respected him as a director he was slightly put off by Patrick's rather erratic mood swings.

'As an actor, if the audience ever coughed while Nigel was on stage he would stop, turn around and cough back at them, as if to say, "There, how do you like it!" Dickie told me this right at the start and it was his theory that when actors get to a certain age they become aggressive towards their audiences because they don't feel as loved any more. There'll be somebody younger in the cast who gets all the attention and they don't like it. Richard finished off by saying, "Old Nigel? He's a bloody nightmare, love!"'

By the time January 1967 had arrived, Richard was itching to start rehearsals. With the cast being assembled months earlier, it had been an agonisingly long wait but the more he read *Relatively Speaking* the more convinced Richard became that he was about to become part of something special. His wish had been to explore comedy, and it was about to come true.

'His enthusiasm was totally infectious,' claims Sir Alan. 'And for me that made a difference as I was as nervous as hell. I remember arriving on the first day of rehearsals and the only person there was Dickie. He was sitting in the stalls and the moment he saw me he got to his feet, ran over and shook me by the hand. I think he could tell I was nervous and he went out of his way to make me feel welcome. It's not often you get one of the junior leads putting the author at ease!'

But, despite Richard's warm salutation, after a few days he started regarding the young playwright rather suspiciously.

'Richard had started staring at me quite a bit. Not in a weird way. He'd just look up from his script occasionally, stare at me for a few seconds and smile quizzically. It would start the moment I walked in and would carry on periodically for most of the day.'

After a week or so Richard finally announced the reason for his bizarre behaviour, and it was all to do with the character he was playing, and a bag. Alan Ayckbourn concludes the story with a smile.

'I used to carry a folding briefcase around with me that basically had my entire life in it. In the play, when Greg arrives at Sheila and Philip's house, he's carrying something similar and one morning when Richard saw me carrying this thing he looked at his script, looked up and said, "Oh my God, it's him! You're Greg!" '

Richard had got it into his head that Alan Ayckbourn had based the character of Greg on himself and when he finally accused the stunned playwright he was told in no uncertain terms that he had got the wrong end of the stick.

' "I'm not that bloody stupid, Richard," I said to him. "Greg's an idiot! At least give me some credit." '

' "OK, sorry, love!" '

Once Richard was satisfied that he wasn't actually playing Alan Ayckbourn they were able to crack on apace and the try-out tour opened at the Theatre Royal Newcastle on 21 February 1967. It's an evening Alan Ayckbourn remembers well.

'I'd just passed my driving test and had driven up from Leeds in my new Mini. After the show I had a quick word with Dickie and he asked me if I'd like a drink. "I'd better get back to Leeds," I said. "I'm driving." Dickie was flabbergasted. "You can't go back to Leeds at quarter past eleven," he said. "I've got a couch in my hotel room. Why not stay on for a few drinks, then you can kip there?" '

The newly mobile playwright didn't take much persuading and, after sinking a few in the bar, they retired to Richard's room.

'It was more like a dorm really,' remembers Sir Alan. 'We'd had a couple of drinks and chatted for some hours. We talked to each other in a way that an actor and author perhaps wouldn't normally and got to know each other well. Dickie was a very interesting man and very bright. He was also incredibly perceptive.'

Now firm friends, Richard effectively became Alan Ayckbourn's eyes and ears on the tour of *Relatively Speaking* and, by the time they had reached the end of their short run at the Bradford Alhambra a few weeks later, his perceptiveness had allowed him to spot a potentially major issue. Something for which Alan and the producer would be extremely grateful.

'The director Nigel Patrick had a kind of hierarchy as to how he treated people,' says Sir Alan. 'Michael and Celia were treated with respect, of course, and because he and Richard had worked together before he was OK with him too. Jennifer Hilary and I, on the other hand, who were both in our twenties, were treated with mild indifference at best and because I wasn't around too often once the play was on the road (I still refused to leave the BBC!) poor Jennifer had had to bear the brunt of Paddy's anger and irritation.'

Nigel Patrick had given Jennifer Hilary a crisis of confidence, which had become so bad that by the time they had played the Alhambra for a few days she was threatening not to go on.

'By this time, I'd given Richard a nickname,' says Sir Alan. 'I called him *Anadin* Briers, which refers to the old strapline, "nothing acts faster", and he called me up one day and said, "Alan, it's Anadin. We have a problem!"'

According to 'Anadin', Nigel Patrick had become irritated by something Jennifer Hilary had done during the first scene and, because she hadn't understood his exact instructions as to how to rectify this immediately, he had started telling her that she wasn't capable of doing it. 'Nope. Sorry, love,' he'd said flippantly. 'It's no good, you just can't do it.' The story still riles Sir Alan.

'These days you'd quite rightly be had up for behaviour like that, but back in the 1960s you were just left to get on with it. That was no bloody use to us and so something had to be done.'

Shortly after Alan had finished talking to Richard, Peter Bridge was on the line. 'We need you to come and see Jennifer,' he said to Alan. 'The poor girl's in hysterics.' After asking Peter Bridge what he was supposed to do about it, the producer made himself clear. 'You're the author of a play that, thanks to Nigel bloody Patrick, has an actress who believes she's no longer good enough to perform in it. Therefore, you're the only one who's really qualified to persuade her otherwise.'

'Peter had a point,' admits Sir Alan, 'so, the following day, I drove down to Brighton, which is where the play was moving to, and I took Jennifer out for some tea. I'm glad I did because I'd never seen anybody so low on confidence before and after an hour or so I managed to turn her around. She was very, very good in it, by the way, so there was no need for any flannel.'

Later on during the tour, Alan Ayckbourn received another telephone call from Richard, this time bearing some good news. ' "I've just made the tonne, love," he said to me. "What do you mean, the tonne?" I asked, to which he replied cheerfully, "For the first time in my life I'm earning over a hundred pounds a week. It's a long way from the two pounds ten shillings I earned as a clerk!" '

About five years later, shortly after Richard had accepted the role of Sidney Hopcroft in Ayckbourn's *Absurd Person Singular*, he made another telephone call regarding his earnings, except this time he was less triumphant.

'Despite his love of money,' says Alan Ayckbourn, 'Dickie had a socialist instinct running through him that would make him question how much money he was earning. The producer Michael Codron told me this and it was all to do with how much he was earning compared to everyone else. "I'm getting a lot more than some of the other actors, love," he said to Michael. "Are you sure this is right?" Michael had a heck of a job persuading him apparently and Dickie told me later that it was quite a difficult pill to swallow.'

Alan Ayckbourn's *Relatively Speaking* opened at the Duke of York's Theatre on 29 March 1967 and, although the first night performance seemed to go extremely well, the author was being cautious.

'The reviews for my last West End show, *Mr Whatnot*, had been universally appalling. I'd done the traditional thing, you see, of sitting down with all the first editions and had had to endure all kinds of abuse, from Bernard Levin to Herbert Kretzmer. One of them had called it a disgrace to theatre!' So, when *Relatively Speaking* opened I said to my then wife that regardless of how well I thought it had gone, I wouldn't be reading a single review. "Oh, come on," she said. "Let's get one."'

Unfortunately for Alan, the first paper to arrive on the shelves early the following morning was the now defunct tabloid newspaper, the *Daily Sketch*, whose theatre critic, Fergus Cashin, was as well known for punching editors and getting pissed with Oliver Reed as he was for writing fair and thoughtful critiques of West End plays. Subsequently, his was the only review that was anything less than ecstatic about the new play and seemed to suggest that although the other 639 people had enjoyed themselves, Mr Cashin hadn't laughed once and it was to be avoided at all costs.

'I went to bed thinking that was the general consensus and when Peter Bridge rang me up the following morning I almost didn't take his call.'

Alan needn't have worried as what his producer had rung to tell him was that Fergus Cashin was a lone voice. Irving Wardle's review in *The Times* was far more representative of what Fleet Street thought and he called the play, 'A single-minded contribution to the theatre of pleasure. Rarely,' he continued, 'has dramatic irony been so thoroughly exploited in a single play, and like all good comic writers, Mr Ayckbourn is intensely thrifty; again and again one sees stray comic details being nurtured and blossoming into jokes. The preparation is masterly.'

Ayckbourn wasn't the only one to receive praise from the members of the press, although, such was their relief at seeing a good comedy in the West End – 'the rarest of commodities', according to Wardle – that the lion's share of the plaudits went his way. Even so, the four cast members all received exemplary notices, and in particular Celia Johnson.

Two days later, Alan Ayckbourn's telephone rang again. 'It's Dickie,' said the voice at the other end. 'You'll never guess who was in last night.' 'No, who?' replied Ayckbourn. 'The Master,' said Dickie. 'That's who!'

According to Richard, Noël Coward had enjoyed the show immensely, although on enquiring as to the identity of the playwright, his enjoyment had been curtailed.

'Ah, Dickie,' said Coward. 'What an awfully good show. Thoroughly enjoyable. But tell me, who is the author? I understand he's quite young?'

'That's right,' replied Richard. 'He's in his late twenties.'

On hearing this, the Master took a step backwards, put a hand over his eyes and said, 'Oh, dear God!'

The following day Alan Ayckbourn received a telegram from Coward, although at first he thought it was from an imposter. It read: 'Thank you so much for a beautifully constructed play. With all admiration, Noël Coward.'

'The telegram had an excess charge to pay on it and so I thought it was from Dickie,' says Sir Alan. 'I called him up and asked him what he was doing sending me telegrams from Noël Coward and he seemed perplexed. "Nothing to do with me, old love," he said. Because I thought it was a hoax I'd thrown the damn thing away but fortunately I managed to retrieve it.'

Relatively Speaking ran for approximately a year in the West End, notching up more than 350 performances. As one would expect with such a huge success, there was much talk of the show transferring to Broadway; although, thanks partly to the *New Yorker*'s theatre critic, Kenneth Tynan, who shared similar views with Fergus Cashin, but had slightly more clout, it wouldn't be produced on Broadway until 1984.

Even so, the play remained the toast of London's West End for much of its run. Despite Alan Ayckbourn still refusing to give up his day job as a producer of radio drama for the BBC up in Leeds (he finally threw in the towel in 1970), he and Richard kept in touch and whenever he had cause to come to London, the two would meet up.

'I remember Richard and I taking a taxi together not long after *Relatively Speaking* had opened in London,' remembers Sir Alan, 'and it's the only time I ever saw him lose his temper. The taxi driver recognised Richard and said to him, "I saw the show the other night and I thought it was very good." "Thank you

very much," replied Richard. "That's very nice of you to say."
"But can you tell me, Mr Briers," continued the taxi driver,
"why you're always the same?" Suddenly Richard became very
prickly. "How do you mean?" he asked. "Well, you know,"
said the driver. "You're always playing the same character,
aren't you?" I thought, *Hello! You're walking on dangerous ground
here, mate. It may be your cab, but you're about to get an earful*. He
didn't stop though. "How do you mean exactly?" asked
Richard, who, by this time was leaning forward in his seat.
"Well, I've seen you in that *Marriage Lines* thing, and I've seen
you in this play you're doing. What's it called, *Relatively
Speaking*? And you're exactly the same person." As opposed to
trying to familiarise the driver with the nuances of acting, Dickie
said, "Why don't you just drive the bloody cab!" The poor taxi
driver was ever so slightly surprised. "Blimey, Guvnor!" he
pleaded. "I was only saying!" '

Just a few days later Alan was reminded, in the nicest way
possible, what Richard Briers's customary disposition was while
conversing with members of the public. It happened shortly after
a camera crew from the BBC had arrived at the Duke of York's
to film some live excerpts of *Relatively Speaking* during a special
performance. This time, as opposed to almost causing an affray,
he helped avert a disaster. Sir Alan remembers it all too well.

'I'm pretty sure they were the same crew they used for football matches because they simply followed everybody across the
stage. They were swinging about all over the place. "And here's
Celia Johnson coming in from the right wing to meet a header
from Briers!" It was madness. Anyway, the director wanted to
start with Nigel Patrick on stage delivering a precis of Scene 1,
which I'd written for him, but for some reason he got very,

very nervous and, in the end, I had to rehearse him around the back of the theatre. He was sitting there on a dustbin and he just couldn't remember a line of it. "What's wrong, Nigel?" I asked. "Nothing!" he barked. "I'm fine." After about twenty minutes it finally started to register so we went back in.'

Although the lines had started going in, Nigel Patrick's willingness to deliver them in front of an audience was on its way out, and after much negotiating it was finally decided that he could record it in one of the dressing rooms.

'By this time,' says Sir Alan, 'we were running about half an hour late and the audience, not surprisingly, were becoming restless. The stage manager had already made an apology over the tannoy but that was fifteen minutes ago. In the end he went to ask Michael or Celia if they'd say something but as he did so a head suddenly appeared through the curtains. It was Richard! "Hello, have you been waiting long?" he asked. "We have! It's outrageous, don't you think? I mean, after all, we are professionals, damn it!" Richard had obviously realised what was going on after hearing the announcement over the tannoy and had taken it upon himself to try and placate the audience. To this day I've never seen a warm-up like it and despite the increasing delay he had them eating out of the palm of his hand. I'm pretty sure Richard Briers could do almost anything on a stage. He was quite amazing.'

CHAPTER FOURTEEN

Running Amok in Toytown

While he had been appearing in *Relatively Speaking*, Richard had also been gearing up to becoming a father again, and on 19 August 1967 Annie gave birth to another daughter, Lucy, who was also born at Queen Charlotte's Hospital.

One of Lucy's earliest memories is going to see Richard in Michael Frayn's first published play, *The Two of Us*, which premiered on 30 July 1970 at the Garrick Theatre and consisted of four one-act plays for two actors; the other being Lynn Redgrave. This was the first time either she or Kate had ever seen their father perform live, and for Kate in particular it was a thrilling experience.

'Because it was a grown-up play we were only allowed to watch the first half, although we did have a box, which was exciting. For the first time, the two halves of Dad's life finally came together; the half I knew from home, and the half I knew existed but hadn't seen yet, and I was totally wowed by it. I'd obviously seen him on television a few times but somehow that didn't seem real. Watching him become a different person was absolutely amazing.'

Lucy's memory of seeing *The Two of Us* is slightly sketchier, but it still had a profound effect on her. 'I think we went a few months after it opened so I would have been about three. The show was a farce, and I have this image of my father running on stage wearing a red curly wig and pushing this big table on wheels. First, I remember thinking, *I know you!* Then, I just burst out laughing. It was hilarious, especially to a three-year-old.'

Despite him being a family man and a doting father, Richard's day-to-day priority had to be his work, which meant Kate and Lucy had to dance to a certain tune.

'It wasn't done in an oppressive way,' says Lucy. 'It was never, "Oh my God, Dad's home, we've all got to be quiet." There were just certain rules we had to abide by. For instance, first thing in the morning we had to keep things down a bit as Dad wouldn't have got in until gone midnight. Also, if either of us ever had a cold we weren't allowed to go anywhere near him.'

This may sound drastic to some people, but the ramifications of an actor not being able to perform in a West End show could be damaging, and not just financially. 'The thought of letting people down filled Dad with horror,' says Kate. 'It was his worst nightmare and simply wasn't an option to him. So, if a bug did ever enter the Briers household, whoever was carrying it would have to go straight into quarantine. It was the only way.'

The word Lucy uses the most when describing her upbringing is 'security'; something that seems to epitomise Richard's domestic life in adulthood and was obviously a much-needed contrast to what he was doing professionally.

'We had a very safe and secure upbringing,' says Lucy, 'which is something Dad worked hard for. I think Kate and I always appreciated that, which is why we didn't mind seeing him less than we might have liked. We knew he was doing it for us and we were grateful.'

Although Kate and Lucy might have spent less time with their father than children in more conventional households, when Richard did manage to take time off he would focus totally on his girls.

'Whenever Dad was off duty he would just relax and have fun with us,' remembers Kate. 'He didn't have to do anything special. Just having his attention was enough and what I remember most is that he could be incredibly mischievous. It always got him into trouble.'

'Dad didn't do discipline very well,' says Lucy, 'and so if Kate or I were ever naughty he'd quickly move out of the way and leave it to Mum to do the telling off. Then, while Mum was busy reading us the riot act, he'd slowly creep up behind her and start pulling faces. That would make us laugh, which would in turn get us into even more trouble. And him. I guess it was terrible parenting! But great fun for Kate and me.'

Home wasn't the only place Richard Briers used to misbehave. In fact, if the testimonies of his friends and colleagues are anything to go by, one would be hard pushed to find somewhere he didn't misbehave. Lucy has experienced similar feedback and at first she was shocked: 'Since Dad died, I've heard dozens of stories from friends of his saying how naughty he was on stage and how much he enjoyed making people corpse. I was so surprised when I found out because I always thought he was the ultimate professional.'

To be fair to Richard, there was, on certain occasions, an underlying reason for this behaviour.

'Back in the 1960s and 1970s you might have been in a play

for anything up to a year,' says Lucy, 'and so as opposed to just putting people off it was actually a very clever way of keeping things fresh and preserving an energy on stage. I've done a run of about eighteen months as an actor and after a while you start going slightly mad. If you're expecting something a bit different from another actor every so often, which it sounds like people did with Dad, then it keeps you on your toes.'

Richard's second favourite environment for running amok and doing things he perhaps shouldn't was in a sound studio. While narrating twenty-five episodes of Enid Blyton's *Noddy* for ITV, which he did in the mid-1970s, he finished off by providing the ever-popular character with a slightly more risqué persona.

'He once sat there for an entire week narrating those *Noddy* episodes,' says Lucy, 'which are obviously written for children and are very twee. By the end he'd really had enough and so, just for the hell of it, decided to record an adult version.'

Richard improvised the dialogue for 'Blue Noddy' and, according to Kate, it was rather risque.

'It was so rude! Dad tried repeating it one evening when I was in my teens and after he'd had a couple of drinks. I couldn't believe my ears. It was all about Noddy and Big Ears running amok in Toytown. Nobody was safe! Poor old Enid Blyton would have been spinning in her grave. I wish I could find the recording of that. Or do I?'

Richard's career in children's television had begun at the start of 1969 when he was asked to narrate a story for the immensely popular children's television series, *Jackanory*. Starting in 1965, *Jackanory* had managed to attract as its storytellers some of the biggest names in British entertainment, including Margaret

Rutherford, Wendy Hiller and Joyce Grenfell, and when Richard was asked he jumped at the chance.

'I think being a father had something to do with it,' says Annie. 'Obviously it was a job, but because of the girls I think he felt he was qualified somehow, and because he loved children it seemed to make sense.'

Had somebody suggested to Richard then that he might one day become as synonymous with the genre of children's television as he was with theatre or even sitcom, then he might well have had something to say on the matter. But because of the size of the audiences involved, and the fact that parents often watched these shows with their children, he would quickly realise that, as a jobbing actor, which is how he always referred to himself, it would do his currency no harm whatsoever.

In 1970 Richard fulfilled two ambitions that a few years earlier wouldn't even have seemed possible. The first involved his mentor, Harold French, and one of the greatest farceurs of all time, Ben Travers. Forty-seven years previously, Travers had, with the help of a troupe of actors including Tom Walls, Ralph Lynn, Mary Brough and Robertson Hare, staged a series of farces that had taken London by storm, with the majority being turned into films that in turn became incredibly popular. Known as the 'Aldwych Farces', on account of them being staged at the Aldwych Theatre, they had fired Richard's imagination as a young man as they represented a genuine heyday for English theatre and in a period that Richard would have given his eye-teeth to have been around.

'Again, Dad's anachronistic side got the better of him,' says Kate, 'and when Harold French suggested that they remake the seven most popular Aldwych Farces with Ben Travers himself being involved in adapting the original scripts, Dad was thrilled.'

The two main stars of the Aldwych Farces, which are revived to this day by professional and amateur companies alike, were the actor-manager Tom Walls, who also trained racehorses while making the Aldwych Farces and in 1932 won the Epsom Derby with a horse called April the Fifth, and the monocle-wearing comic actor, Ralph Lynn, of whom Ben Travers once said, 'I have never seen or heard of any actor in any field with such an instinctive and unerring gift of timing.' Lynn specialised in playing the 'silly ass' characters in Travers's farces, who invariably – and incredibly, it has to be said – always gets the girl, while Walls was more suited to portraying authoritarian types, who generally had a fondness for drink, a battle-axe for a wife and a twinkle in one of their invariably bloodshot eyes. Not surprisingly, for the new series of television adaptations, Richard was to tackle the roles Ralph Lynn had made famous, with Arthur Lowe replacing Tom Walls.

'Richard was a big admirer of Arthur Lowe,' explains Annie. 'For a start, he'd been acting alongside John Gielgud at the National Theatre for a while and Richard had seen them both in *The Tempest*. Although he was a big admirer of John Gielgud and could do a marvellous impersonation of him, it was Arthur who he'd raved about afterwards and so with Harold directing the farces and Ben Travers being involved, this was just the icing on the cake.'

Anyone who is familiar with the original Aldwych Farces would naturally be chomping at the bit to watch these remakes, especially given the talent involved (the likes of Frank

Thornton and Megs Jenkins also appeared in most of them). Alas, they too are missing, believed lost, which is an incredible shame.

The second ambition that Richard managed to fulfil at the start of the new decade was meeting, and subsequently appearing alongside, the man who made him laugh more than anyone else on earth – Tommy Cooper.

'Dad was a born giggler,' says Kate, 'and he absolutely adored Tommy Cooper. Whenever one of his shows was on television and Dad wasn't working he'd sit down with a glass of wine and just laugh his head off. I think it was the physical side that he loved the most: the double takes and the looks to camera. Dad was a big fan of double takes!'

Believe it or not, one of Richard's all-time favourite double-takers was a family dog named Fred, who they had from 1981 until 1996. Fred's comic flair had been noticed by Richard soon after he arrived and, from then on, he would watch him like a hawk.

'Dad thought Fred was incredibly funny,' says Lucy. 'Because dogs react purely to any given object or situation their timing is immaculate and to Dad that was the key to engaging with your audience. When Dad played Malvolio, he stole Fred's hilarious "smile" which Fred used to do whenever he saw Dad.'

Such was Fred's influence on Richard that he even ended up incorporating some of his mannerisms in one of his most famous characterisations: Martin Bryce from *Ever Decreasing Circles*. Peter Egan, who starred alongside Richard in the series, remembers asking him about his influences for the character of Martin and couldn't believe his ears when he told him.

'During our rehearsals I noticed how cleverly Richard paced

his performance. He did terrific double takes and had a funny way of panting at times. I mentioned these things over lunch one day and told him how impressed I was. "It's all down to Fred," he said, by way of explanation. "Who's Fred?" I asked. "Fred's my dog," he replied. At first, I thought he was joking, but he said he wasn't. Like me, Dickie was a great animal lover and claimed that dogs were great comedians. He said: "If you want to learn how to do a double take, watch Fred, he's brilliant!"'

But in 1973, a good eight years before Fred arrived at Richard's house, he was to be influenced by a very different kind of dog. A green animated one, in fact, whose antics were based on those of a Welsh Border collie owned by a young writer and artist named Grange Calveley, and who, together with a purple animated cat, would help weld Richard's name to the burgeoning genre of children's television, where it would remain for the rest of his life.

CHAPTER FIFTEEN

Roobarb and Custard

It's fair to say that Richard's output in between appearing with Tommy Cooper in 1970, and being approached about the aforementioned animated animals in 1973, was eclectic to say the least; both in terms of category and reception. One of the more unusual jobs Richard accepted was to appear in a ten-minute cinema advert for the menswear giant, Austin Reed, in which he played a sartorially challenged character named Timothy, who, having tried and failed at achieving the right look, ends up standing outside the retailer's flagship store on Regent Street wearing nothing but his underpants and a Groucho Marx-style moustache and glasses.

Prior to this chapter in his career, Richard hadn't had to endure the ignominy of appearing in a flop, but the moment he agreed to star in Peter Yeldham's 1971 situation comedy, *Birds on the Wing*, the writing was on the wall. The synopsis, in which Charles Jackson (Richard) leads a small team of con merchants who, instead of looking for new targets, end up trying to con each other, sounds like a comedic precursor to the television programme *Hustle*, tells you all you need to know and the only saving grace from Richard's point of view was the size of the audiences.

'They were so bloody small that nobody really noticed,' he

once said. 'So, it was forgotten about very quickly. Thank God!'

According to Kate, her father's stock-in-trade response when encountering professional failure was the same one he used for adversity in general. 'Failure wasn't something he ever mentioned really,' she says. 'Although it definitely affected him, there's no doubt about it. As opposed to ever talking about it, though, he'd simply get on with the next job, and I'm pretty sure that was a generational thing. You just carried on.'

Richard's next two ventures, which both took place in theatres in 1972, were probably seen by more people than *Birds on the Wing* and they certainly received better notices. The first, which was *Butley* by Simon Gray, was directed by Harold Pinter and involved Richard taking over from his old friend Alan Bates in a role that he had originally made famous in July 1971. The play follows the fortunes of a gay university lecturer, Ben Butley, who shares his office and his apartment with a former pupil, Joey, who is now also a lecturer. On the day when the play takes place, Butley faces both the end of his marriage and the end of his friendship with Joey, with painful discoveries being made against a backdrop of trivial university politics and unease about student dissent. It would later be made into a film, with Bates reprising his portrayal, but, in the meantime, Richard was happy to fill in as the job presented an opportunity to put himself in a role that was obviously against type and, as an actor, would put him in contrast with a man who was considered to be one of the greatest stage actors of his generation.

'Richard was incredibly proud of his performance in *Butley*,' says Annie, 'and rightly so. His notices were among the best he ever received in theatre and, after *Birds on the Wing*, which was probably still weighing on his mind, it was exactly what he needed – a return to form.'

The Fergus Cashins of this world were otherwise engaged for Richard's maiden performance in *Butley* but those who were present had nothing but praise for his portrayal. R. B. Marriott of the *Stage* commented that,

> Richard Briers puts aside his glib, bright light comedy style, and changes his clear-cut, polished appearance, to play the title role in *Butley* at the Criterion, in succession to the creator of the part, Alan Bates. His study of the academic who is a badly self-mauled homosexual, a destroyer of the peace of mind of others, a man of intellect who has run to seed mentally and physically, is the best work I have seen him do. He creates a fascinating and entirely convincing characterisation which has real insight and depth of feeling. He strikes the barbed wit from his lines into fine flourishes.

But the most insightful appraisal of Richard's performance as Butley, and, bearing in mind what he was trying to achieve, by far the most complimentary, came from Charles Lewsen of *The Times*. Instead of assessing the performance on its own merits, he highlighted the differences between Richard's interpretation and that of Bates, which, in turn, underlined Richard's prowess as an actor as it seemed that he had effectively created the role from scratch. Given the number of plaudits and awards Alan Bates had received for his original creation, this was an incredible gamble on Richard's part and, had it backfired, it could well have changed his career. Lewsen wrote,

While the romantic actor [Bates] claimed a laugh every 20 seconds, the light comedian plays the first act, at least, through restraint of temperament. He wounds not by soaring but by pouncing from below. Where Mr Bates seemed to dance on the grave of his own innocence this Butley seems essentially still a child. Where Mr Bates implied a physical attraction towards Joey, this Butley has buried his homosexual impulse. Where the previous Butley used literary allusion purely as a weapon, this one suggests that he has been a decent teacher.

Lucy believes that this performance gave her father a new lease of life and helped to re-establish him as a stage actor. 'Dad had certainly done more theatre than television by this point in his career but since the mid-1960s there hadn't been much variety. The fact that he took on a role where he would be compared to Alan Bates was genius in a way; not only because it highlighted his ability, but because it started to re-establish his reputation in straight theatre, which was something he hadn't touched for over ten years.'

As if to prove that point, while Richard was appearing in *Butley* he was approached by Toby Robertson from the Cambridge-based Prospect Theatre Company about the possibility of playing Richard III on a national tour alongside Derek Jacobi, who would be playing Buckingham. It would be his first foray into Shakespeare for seventeen years since greatly curtailing the running time of *Hamlet* and, on the back of his performance in *Butley* and having just filmed a lucrative movie role, he felt well equipped for the challenge.

In an interview for BBC South to promote the company's visit to Bournemouth, which was well into the run, Richard commented that, far from losing his comic roots by tackling, as he put it, 'more legitimate theatre', one of the reasons he had decided to play Richard III was because he wanted to create his own, slightly comic interpretation.

'After receiving about twenty-three reviews,' he said, 'one is actually quite bruised, but one of the reasons I've come out of it quite well is because my interpretation is as a black comedy. Not as a stark historical drama. There is comedy in it, and while this man is trying to get this crown, he's funny and he's horrifying. It's sort of Grand Guignol melodrama really. When he gets to the crown at the end of the first half he goes potty as he gets frightened of assassination and he gets the full Adolf Hitler complex. Therefore, the first half is much more dramatic than the second.'

One critic described Richard's performance as being 'sardonic, verging on the demented', which pleased him no end. 'That's exactly how I saw him,' said Richard, 'so I'd obviously done the character, or at least my interpretation of the character, very proud indeed.'

The general public's reaction to Richard playing Shakespeare's most malevolent monarch was enthusiastic and they were always pleased to see him. Penelope Wilton remembers Richard explaining this to her during the making of *Ever Decreasing Circles*. 'Richard told me that one day, when he came on for the "Now is the winter of our discontent" speech, somebody in the audience shouted, "Hello, Dick!" He said to me, "Funnily enough, Pen, I felt my arm lifting ever so slightly and I waved to him." I thought that was marvellous. He did used to get a little bit annoyed about people shouting, "Hello, Dick". "Nobody does that to Paul Scofield," he used to say.'

Although she was only five years old at the time, Lucy remembers this period with a great deal of affection as, before Richard set off on tour, he invited a member of the company to stay with them. 'Derek Jacobi was between houses, I think,' says Lucy, 'and so we put him up for a few weeks. The problem was that I rather fell in love with him and so for the time he was with us I wouldn't leave him alone. Not surprisingly, Dad and Derek found this hilarious and whenever I came into the room Dad would say, "Your shadow's here again, Derek." I remember standing next to him in the garden once while he and Dad were having a chat and I was literally leaning into him. Poor Derek! He was very, very patient.'

Kate remembers Derek's stay for a different reason, but with an equal amount of embarrassment.

'*Godspell* was the biggest thing in the West End at the time and we used to spend hours and hours listening to the LP and dancing to it. You know how kids can take this sort of thing very seriously? Well, I remember my friends and I dancing to it in our living room one evening while Dad and Derek were chatting and having a drink. They were having to talk quite loudly because of the rumpus and, in the end, I'd had enough. "Could you be quiet please, Derek?" I snapped. "We're trying to listen to *Godspell*." I was only nine years old so he just pretended to be shocked, said sorry and put his hand over his mouth. I still cringe slightly when I think about that.'

The well-remunerated movie role that had enabled Richard to undertake the tour of *Richard III*, for which he was paid about fifty pounds a week, exemplifies the heterogeneous nature of his career in the early 1970s and proves beyond any reasonable doubt that his desire to be taken seriously as an actor was nothing compared to his desire to try new things, work with people he liked and earn a good living. In the long run, this is what probably prevented Richard Briers from receiving a knighthood, but he wouldn't have had it any other way.

The unfortunately named *Rentadick*, which follows a company of incompetent detectives – Rentadick, Inc. – as they attempt to track down the thieves of an experimental nerve gas that paralyses from the waist down, was written by Graham Chapman and John Cleese. It had Richard starring alongside his *Fathom* co-star, Ronnie Fraser, as well as Richard Beckinsale, James Booth, Spike Milligan, Donald Sinden and even, in an uncredited role, Penelope Keith.

The female lead in *Rentadick* was the Norwegian actor and sex siren, Julie Ege, who, according to Richard, was even more fun to work with than Raquel Welch, just as beautiful and had an excellent, if somewhat risqué, sense of humour.

'She was an absolute darling,' he said in the late 1970s. 'Nobody made me laugh harder on set. Not even Ronnie Fraser. Julie's an amazing woman. She's got a filthy mind though!'

A few months after they had filmed *Rentadick*, Richard was 'surprised' by Eamonn Andrews for an episode of *This Is Your Life* and Julie Ege was the 'surprise' guest at the end. Her sense of humour, however, almost got the better of her as, just for a laugh, she thought it would be fun to call Richard up the day before and give the game away, proving perhaps that she hadn't quite grasped the concept of the show. Fortunately for Eamonn, Julie made her intentions known to a friend who advised her against the course of action and a disaster was averted.

'I think that show was quite difficult for Dad,' explains Kate, 'as it featured a lot of people from school and from his first job, which he wasn't keen on revisiting. Having people like Julie and Harold French on the show brought him back into the present day and made the whole thing bearable. Just!'

In July 1973, while Richard was appearing in Alan Ayckbourn's second West End hit, *Absurd Person Singular*, alongside Sheila Hancock, he was sifting through the post one morning at home when he came across a script that had been sent to him by his agent. He had been warned about the script the day before and, apart from informing him that it was for a new children's television programme, his agent had told him that he hadn't known what to make of it. *Roobarb and Custard*'s creator, Grange Calveley, takes up the story:

'In 1973 the BBC contacted the agent Richard was with at the time and explained that they were looking for a "voice" to narrate a new children's animated TV series. The agent evidently told Richard that the characters were a bit weird – a green dog and a pink cat – and added that the programme probably wouldn't rate and would only last on air for about six weeks – but it was money.'

Born in Cheshire in 1943, Grange had attending art college before finding work with various advertising agencies; firstly, at a small agency situated in a magnificent house on Aldford Street in Mayfair and, secondly, at an equally grand address in St James's Square. 'I cooked up sales messages and slogans for jams and marmalades, package holidays and engine oils,' explains Grange. 'I wrote copy and I sketched out ads and TV storyboards. It was like *Play School* for grown-ups! Back then we drew with Magic Markers, which were basically felt-tips sticking out of small bottles of ink. "Squeakers", we called them, and to present ideas to clients we'd draw on to bonded paper layout pads. I always left my backgrounds white and clear of clutter in order to concentrate on the "product" and so, when it came to creating *Roobarb and Custard*, I kept that style.'

Roobarb had been based on the Welsh Border collie that Grange and his wife Hanny had come across after moving into a new house.

'After buying the house we didn't really have any money left to buy a dog,' says Grange, 'so Hanny telephoned the local vet to ask if they knew of a homeless dog who was perhaps looking for a family. Sure enough, there was a dog, a Welsh Border collie, and according to the vet he was a bit of a handful. "He's full of beans," the vet had shouted down the telephone above the noisy yapping, barking, woofing and carrying-on from a gang of dogs in the background. "However, I feel I must tell you," the vet continued, "that there is another young couple who are also looking for a dog. I am waiting to hear from them before the end of the afternoon to let me know if they want him or not."'

The vet had promised Hanny and Grange that if the other couple didn't want the dog they were welcome to come and meet him, but followed it up by saying that if they decided not to take the four-month-old dog, then she would have to put him down before leaving that evening. 'Those were the rules apparently,' says Grange. 'Or were they? Was she simply trying her best to find a poor unwanted dog a home?'

Fortunately for Grange and Hanny, the couple who had first refusal on the dog lived in a flat and so decided not to take him.

'Hanny and I almost tripped over each other as we tumbled out of the house, piled into the car and sped off towards the old Victorian stables that were now the veterinary surgery. We were on a mission, a mission of mercy. We were his last chance. We would save him!'

After screeching to a halt in the vet's yard, Hanny and Grange leapt out of the car and into the surgery's reception area. 'There was nobody in the waiting room, but we could hear the noisy gang of excited dogs and a gate clanging shut somewhere out at the back. All of a sudden, a door opened, and the vet was dragged into reception by a bundle of black and white Welsh Border collie, wriggling and tumbling at the end of a sturdy lead. "I thought it might be you two arriving in the yard," said the vet with a smile as she tried to undo the lead.'

According to Grange, once he was let loose the Welsh Border collie danced, barked, ran, licked and fidgeted non-stop. 'He was magnificent. We had to have him; and have him we did, along with a free dog lead, free dog meat, free dog biscuits, a free bowl and free inoculations. What had we done? He was mad!'

Grange was so taken with his new friend that he soon began writing short stories about his loony antics as well as drawing him either clanging his jaws at a fly or sitting up in a flowering cherry tree that he had very quickly claimed as his own. More characters were introduced to the stories, such as birds who were given sunglasses and teeth, with one of the last being a large, overfed cat from next door that would spend hours lying on the fence.

'All of a sudden, the stories really got steam up,' says Grange. 'I began to introduce more characters; guest characters like

Rover the duck, which was Hanny's idea of what a duck's name should be, Hugh, who was an owl, and then along came Moggy Malone and Poodle Princess as well as many other characters that would come and go. By the way, the cat on the fence had now become Custard. No deep thinking or soul searching was required on my part – the beast's name just happened quite naturally!'

The outline behind Grange's stories involved Roobarb, who had boundless amounts of energy and enthusiasm, presenting a constant flow of far-fetched ideas to Custard and to the birds in the trees, which he would then undertake. 'He'd then become famous in his own mind,' says Grange, 'but would also be totally oblivious of the fact that the cat was a cynic, that the birds in the tree had no loyalties whatsoever and the world in general saw him as a fool – including Poodle Princess and Moggy Malone.'

After a good two years of trying to garner some interest in *Roobarb and Custard* – 'I took the idea around the streets of London – from book publisher to TV station and back again' – Grange was put in touch with Bob Godfrey, an animation director whose most famous work to date had been a nine-minute short called *The Kama Sutra Rides Again*, that Stanley Kubrick had selected to be screened with his 1971 film, *A Clockwork Orange*. 'Everyone working in films knew Kubrick only ever phoned you to give you a bollocking,' Godfrey later said, 'so when I realised he was calling to do me a favour I nearly dropped the phone!'

Grange explains how he linked up with Godfrey. 'Tony Cuthbert, an animation director who made television commercials, said to me that he liked my work very much but that his company was not geared to make a television series. My heart momentarily sank until he added that I should really speak with Bob Godfrey. "He's mad enough to want to do this," Tony said and telephoned Bob who agreed to meet with me.'

During that meeting, which took place in a café in Soho, Grange showed Bob the drawings that he had made with the Magic Markers.

'Bob's hearing had been damaged by something that I believe had happened during the war when he was with the Commandos, and as his enthusiasm grew for the drawings that I was showing him his booming voice became louder and louder. Eventually, he became so loud that nearly all the customers in the grimy-windowed café seemed to be just as enthralled about my idea as Bob was.'

As well as his ideas, Bob also liked Grange's loose style of drawing and suggested, for starters, that they make a thirty-second animated clip.

'Remember, there was no animation software in them days,' says Grange. 'That was still years away! Bob Godfrey also liked the idea of drawing on paper with Magic Markers because both were cheap. This would be a plus, he said, as the chances are we'd be dealing with the BBC.'

For the thirty-second clip, Bob introduced Grange to an Australian animator called Peter Green.

'Peter and I sat in his small Soho studio and I relayed some of the antics of my real life Roobarb. I explained that in our leafy garden we had a conker tree, several apple trees, a pear tree or two and two flowering cherry trees, one of which forked at about three feet from the ground. I also told him that Roobarb would run down from the house and leap up into the fork of the cherry tree from where he could keep an eye on the garden birds and next door's cat that lounged on the fence. Oh, and there was the shed, of course.'

A few weeks later, Grange returned to Peter's studio and, rather surprisingly, he found him bounding from one side of the room to the other.

'He was panting, and his tongue was hanging out of his mouth when he suddenly noticed me,' says Grange. 'Without saying a word, he picked up a tennis ball, ran across the room and gave it to me – as a dog would.'

Grange had arrived at Peter's studio while he was in the middle of creating the Roobarb 'line test', which is a process used to check drawn frames prior to them being used for final artwork, and when Grange was shown the sequence of drawings that Peter had created for the scene, he understood immediately why the animator had acted out Roobarb's movements for himself before making the drawings.

'He had found his subject's character by performing the scene himself – and then captured it on paper. Peter Green was a very good artist and a wonderfully clever animator. He always put his very heart into his work!'

Green's thirty seconds of line animation showing Roobarb running down the garden and leaping up into the fork of his tree eventually became the opening to *Roobarb and Custard* and shortly after it was presented to Monica Sims, who was then the head of BBC Children's Programmes, a series was duly commissioned.

'I remember the day so clearly,' says Grange. 'I was standing by the yellow door to the garden, watching Roobarb standing quite still and staring at a chrysanthemum in a Percy Thrower kind of way. As I stood watching Roobarb watching the chrysanthemum, at the very moment he turned his head to look my way, the telephone rang. I answered and was so astonished at what I heard that I asked the caller to repeat what she had just said to me. "In a meeting yesterday afternoon, Monica Sims decided that she would like to go ahead with a *Roobarb* series. There will be a letter in the post to confirm. Oh, and Monica would like to see the films all finished in time to go to air in November next year." It was all very exciting. It was time to panic though. Thirty stories had to be written, and we had a deadline – November 1974.'

Soon after the series had been commissioned, Grange and Bob hired several animators, with each being asked to follow Grange's loose drawing style. 'The trouble was,' says Grange, 'that each artist drew slightly differently, which means throughout the series there are several different Roobarb "styles".'

What also developed during the making of *Roobarb* was the highly original style of animation that is now synonymous with the series. Sometimes referred to as 'boiling' or 'wobbling', it was completely at odds with the increasingly seamless American animation that was flooding the market but suited the anarchic nature of the series perfectly.

'As did the music,' says Grange. 'It was a great help in gaining recognition in those early days and is probably as important to *Roobarb*'s success as the stories and animation or Richard's wonderful characterisations.'

Written by the jazz musician, Johnny Hawksworth, 'Roobarb's Theme', with its punky electric guitar, was as anarchic as the cartoon itself and is without doubt one of the most popular children's television themes ever written. In addition to providing *Roobarb* with a refrain that would make children yelp with excitement and mothers flinch, it also gave Richard his first and only foray into the top ten when, in 1992, the rave band Shaft remixed the theme into a single, complete with samples of Richard's voice.

'*Roobarb* was just mad!' says Grange. 'The stories and the main characters were bonkers, the music was manic, and the birds were always close to hysteria, like kids when an adult trips over. All we needed now was a voice.'

When it came to finding a voice for *Roobarb*, which was the first ever fully animated series to be made in the United Kingdom, it was the BBC who first mooted Richard's name.

'Neither Bob nor I had met Richard before 1973,' says Grange. 'It was somebody at the Beeb that suggested we get together and when we did, Bob Godfrey said, "Ah, Richard! You were great in *All Gas and Gaiters*!" To which Richard replied patiently, "Erm, I think you'll find that was Derek Nimmo." Bob, who was slightly deaf, mumbled, "Oh, you don't think so? Well, I thought you were really good!"'

Once he had signed up for the series, Richard asked what style of narration they were looking for and Grange mentioned that his wife Hanny had suggested that it should be like 'reading bedtime stories to small children'. Thirty years later, when he started recording *Roobarb and Custard Too*, which was made in 2004, Richard looked Grange in the eye, scripts in hand, and said, 'And I suppose you'd like me to read this lot as though reading to grandchildren!'

So far as the question of character voices for *Roobarb* was concerned, Richard always trod carefully.

'At the very beginning of our *Roobarb* teamwork,' says

Grange, 'as though trying to avoid the subject of characters, Richard said to me, "I've got the dog, Grange. Now, what about that cat?" I told him that the cat on the fence belonged to a neighbour of mine who spoke like this, and, as I'm quite good at voices and accents, I presented this strangled, back-of-the-throat nasal impression of my neighbour. Instantly, Richard replied, "Aawwaaayeahh, rigghhhtyohhh. Wha'abaaat thathen?" and Custard's whining voice turned up, right there in front of my ears.'

' "Whatty' fink?" said Richard in a Custard kind of way.

' "Well," I said . . . panic set in – what had I done? "What about when the series goes to air? What about the voice? What about the . . ."

' "Oh, fuck!" cried Richard. "The neighbour! Well, I can't change it now. It's a gem! Tell him it's the bloke down the road." '

Roobarb went on air for the first time on 21 October 1974, just before the evening news, and was soon attracting over seven million viewers an episode.

'Not bad for a green dog and a pink cat,' says Grange. 'And not bad for an actor who, in his own words, once said, "I've done *Roobarb and Custard* and I've done *King Lear* . . . and I've done everything in between." For me to hear *Roobarb* and Shakespeare uttered in the same sentence by a national treasure was indeed a treat.'

At the time of *Roobarb*'s release, Richard was well known to the British public (but nowhere near as famous as he would be either during or after *The Good Life*) especially to children. 'The moment *Roobarb* hit the screens children began recognising me,' said Richard. 'But not by sight, of course; they recognised my voice. It hasn't stopped since 1974! "You're the man who does *Roobarb and Custard*," they say, to which I reply, "Yes, I am!" I love it!'

Throughout the 1980s and 1990s, Grange Calveley made several trips to London to try and gain interest and money for a second *Roobarb* series. During one of these visits he contacted Richard's then agent but was quoted a fee (without Richard's knowledge, it has to be said) that he figured was designed to make him go away.

'Richard and I were "close distant friends",' says Grange. 'He lived in London and I lived in Sydney, and of course I would never dream of approaching him personally on a business matter – that's what agents are for.'

Eventually, Grange did find a producer for what became *Roobarb and Custard Too*, which was televised in 2005, and sometime during 2004 they had lunch together at a restaurant on Shaftsbury Avenue. 'The producers of *Roobarb and Custard Too* had contacted Richard's latest agent and he had agreed to narrate the new series,' says Grange. 'Naturally, I was over the moon and the lunch was great fun. We sniggered over his old agent's foretelling in 1973 that it wouldn't last more than six weeks. "Six weeks, eh?" Richard cried while raising his glass. "Well, fuck that, love. Here we go again!"'

'Richard was a master of the art of swearing,' claims Grange (and just about everyone else who knew him). 'His obscenities were delivered as only he could; and were to be as relished and drooled over as freshly baked bread or newly mown grass. That said, I would not like to think I'd be first to herald that fact to Richard's world of loving fans.'

Grange's scripts for *Roobarb and Custard Too* were sent to Richard several weeks before the recording sessions and he obviously spent a lot of time going through them as the next time Grange saw them they were covered with Richard's personal notes, made in pencil, for things like inflection and delivery. 'I wish I'd have kept one,' says Grange. 'He must have spent days going through the scripts and that made the recording process a breeze. He was a consummate professional.'

As with *Roobarb* some thirty-one years previously, Richard again had trouble with just one of the characterisations in *Roobarb and Custard Too*; a character that he eventually delivered superbly.

'The character in question was Eric,' explains Grange, 'an Indian elephant from Yorkshire who had an Indian palace-shaped "exotic shed" on his back. "Mi Grandad were a prince and that were mi Grandad's shed," Eric had to say in a Yorkshire/Indian/English accent. "I were a pit elephant!"'

This obviously wasn't the first time Richard had been bamboozled by an accent and after they had completed the readings and the animation was complete, Richard wrote Grange a letter to say that he had received a disc from the production office with the new episodes. 'Have watched and enjoyed your genius during first fourteen episodes,' he wrote. 'Apart from Eric the Elephant's execrable northern accent (SHIT).'

'Richard was ridiculously modest,' says Grange, 'to the point where you wanted to grab him by the lapels and say, "What the hell are you talking about, man? You're the bloody genius, not me!"'

During recording Richard was in danger of running over time just once. 'It was my fault,' remembers Grange, 'so I edited quickly, with expensive studio time ticking away and crew tapping their fingers. Richard re-read the script and ended bang on time. At "wrap", he made an announcement from the open microphone to the Air Studios crew. He said, "In all my years of reading voiceovers and narrating animation, I can honestly say that Grange is the only writer who has put scripts under my nose that constantly read to time." I shrank into the carpet. To receive praise like that from somebody as talented and professional as Richard Briers was the ultimate compliment.'

In the years after *Roobarb and Custard Too* went to air, Grange and Richard kept in touch and even talked about working together a third time on something completely different.

' "Close distant friends" we were, and I would, over the years, send him new script ideas that he would always return with very helpful "crits", as he called his thoughts, about my work. In replying to me, he had obviously spent a lot of time with my ideas – crap or not. One letter begins, "Dear Mate – Thanks so much for script. You shouldn't really ask me for creative 'crits' because I'm an idiot." He then goes on with a flurry of well thought out and very helpful hints and tips. The letter ends, "Sorry not to be more helpful but plug on and do show me anything else." '

Three of Grange's favourite memories regarding Richard involve a telephone conversation they had after he and Hanny had moved to Australia, some culinary advice, à la Briers, and a recording session that took place in 1974 for the original *Roobarb*.

'The phone call happened shortly after we came to live in Sydney. It was the late seventies and we had just finished making *Noah and Nelly,* which was my second BBC TV series that Richard narrated together with Peter Hawkins. We'd decided to move to Australia because the work in Blighty had dried up. Everybody was on strike and there was no money for TV scripts. One gloomy afternoon, Hanny and I decided to call friends in

London. This was well before satellite phone services and if you wanted to call the UK you had to book a "call time" and wait up to two hours. I decided to call Richard that afternoon and after a long wait the operator finally called me back. "Put'n yaz though naaw," she said in a thick Aussie accent. Anyway, after about half an hour of us tittering merrily away, the operator cut in and said, "Yooz lot 'ave bin talkin' expensive rubbish fer 'alf an hour!" to which Richard replied, in a creamy Noël Coward kind of way, "I'll tell you what, why don't you fuck off back to your knitting, daaaarling?" At which the phone went dead!'

Richard's culinary advice is something Grange remembers with a great deal of affection.

'After my wife Hanny died, Richard knew that I was cooking for myself and, as one of the world's worst cooks, I would spend afternoons with a recipe book and expensive ingredients, making what was described as "delicious" on paper, before chucking the lot from kitchen door to the lawn where next door's cat (not called Custard!) would wolf the lot. "How's that fuckin' cat?" Richard would enquire gleefully. "Eating you out of house and home I suppose. Well, I've been thinking. Have you tried dousing everything with Worcestershire sauce?" Richard's ideas were unique; with words such as "douse", "smother" (pepper) and "swamp" (tomato sauce). "I'm told that curry powder can save the day, dear," he once said. "But be careful. We don't want to end up with the old Fireman's Arse'ole, do we, love? Montezuma's Revenge, eh? What!" It was all delivered in a voice resembling his cousin, Terry-Thomas, and teeming with cheer. Like a spring bubbling with chuckles!'

Grange's other favourite memory is of Richard at a reading for the original *Roobarb*.

'The poor kid on the sound desk (the ones with the millions of knobs on) was on his own for the first time and he didn't know how to create reverb – or echo, as it's also known. It was sod's law that the script Richard was reading required that, "Sir Roobarb, in his armour, would have to speak with an echo in his voice." To demonstrate just how affable Richard was, and how unlike some, shall we say, Hollywood types who would throw a tantrum if they didn't have the right coloured sweeties, he soothed the sound kid by looking over the sound desk and its million switches like somebody watching a tennis match, smiling and saying, "Oh fuck! Well, don't ask me, love." In the end we did record the lines, and Richard "spake" as Roobarb inside his armour – complete with a lovely echo! It was achieved by him standing in the studio with his head inside a tin waste-paper basket that had a microphone Sellotaped to its inside! It's still to be heard in "When a Knight Lost His Day" from the original series. What a gentleman he was.'

CHAPTER SIXTEEN

Enter the Parisitic Parsnip Grower

By the time the original *Roobarb* series first went to air in October 1974, it's fair to say Richard was in a good place, both professionally and personally. At the end of 1967, just a few months after Lucy was born, the family had moved into a new and much larger house in Chiswick. As well as the girls being happy in their respective schools, Annie, who had, in effect, sacrificed her career in order to look after them and Richard, was even managing to squeeze in the odd job here and there. 'Although Mum didn't go to drama school she'd done really well in rep and she had a promising career ahead of her. But she also wanted to be a mother,' says Lucy. 'If they wanted to have a family, which they did, one of them would have to stay at home. By the time Kate came along, Dad was endlessly busy and earning quite a bit of money, and so that was that.'

Even so, Annie still managed to carve out a pretty successful career as an actress, both before and after the girls came along. In addition to having a regular part in the TV drama series *Family Solicitor* in the early 1960s, she also made six appearances in *Doctor Who* alongside William Hartnell, four in the cop series *Z Cars*, and she even managed to make one or two stage appearances.

'If Mum had had to retire completely I think she'd have

found it really difficult,' explains Kate, 'especially being married to such a busy actor. Dad was never out of the West End and during the day he was either rehearsing television shows or recording voiceovers. Imagine doing the same thing for a living but having to wave them off every day and stay at home? She'd have gone bananas if she didn't get to do the same occasionally. Mum made an enormous sacrifice, for all of us, and nobody was more grateful than Dad.'

Because Richard was always so busy, holidays were hard to fit in and Annie had a job on her hands in persuading him to put things on hold and fly the nest for a week or two.

'Dad got better as he got older,' remembers Kate, 'but until the early 1970s we didn't really go away that much. We went to Austria skiing when I was quite young, but until Lucy arrived that was about it. I think Dad had this fear that if he went on holiday for a couple of weeks he'd somehow be forgotten about. It sounds irrational but obviously goes hand-in-hand with the precarious nature of showbusiness. Nothing scared Dad more than being out of work.'

One of the earliest holidays Lucy can recall is a two-week trip to Cornwall.

'One of the things I remember most about that holiday is how relaxed Dad was. I'm not saying that he was ever especially het up, but because he was always so busy he never seemed to have time to stop. The cottage we stayed in was tiny with a small kitchen, a living room and a bathroom downstairs, and upstairs there were two bedrooms. The stairs led up open-plan-style from the side of the living room and because it rained quite a lot Kate and I used to sit on them and read. Dad, who was quite a keen stamp collector, would get his albums out, light a cigarette and put Tony Hancock on the reel-to-reel. He was a Hancock fanatic and even though he'd heard them all a million times he'd sit there and howl with laughter. Only Laurel and Hardy and Tommy Cooper made him laugh that much.'

Kate's in agreement with Lucy as to how relaxed Richard was in Cornwall but feels there's a second adjective needed to complete the picture. Namely, sometimes inebriated.

'Dad being Dad, he got to know the locals in the village and he became especially friendly with the butcher and the owner of the local chip shop. Although they recognised him, which I think he was grateful for, they never treated him like a star and so he ended up in the pub with them every so often. I remember one evening he didn't get back until about three o'clock in the morning and it turned out he'd got lost. "I must have walked through a hundred fucking fields," he said to Mum. She just shook her head and told him to have a lie down!'

When Richard was first approached about appearing in *The Good Life* he had mixed feelings. 'I wasn't sure if a return to sitcom would be good for me,' he said in Richard Webber's excellent book, *A Celebration of The Good Life*. 'I had to ask myself whether I wanted to be a TV personality or a more serious sort of actor, performing at the Old Vic and places like that.'

It's fair to say that Richard's predicament probably happened at the programme's inception, as once he became familiar with the writers of the show and the team that was being assembled, he bought into the idea 100 per cent.

Although *The Good Life* hadn't been written specifically for Richard, à la *Marriage Lines*, it had been written with him in mind. The sitcom was a result of a conversation between two writers, John Esmonde and Bob Larbey, who had written the popular sitcoms *Please Sir!* and its follow-up, *The Fenn Street Gang*, and the new Head of Comedy at the BBC, Jimmy Gilbert. One of Gilbert's first ventures after joining the Beeb in the early 1970s had been to find a new vehicle for Richard, for no other reason than he was a fan. 'I wanted to find something good for him,' he said, 'because in my view, he was one of the best comedy actors we had.' During the meeting with Esmonde and Larbey, Richard's name came up in conversation and, after the two writers had said that they too were admirers of Richard's work, Jimmy Gilbert asked them if they could think up some ideas that might suit him.

'Bob Larbey was about the same age as me and we'd both recently celebrated our fortieth birthday,' said Richard. 'As far as I know, that's where the initial idea came from. A real midlife crisis.'

Richard was right, as Bob Larbey confirmed in 2000. 'We centred on whether it was a milestone age, when you're no longer young and have to admit that middle-age is starting to set in. It didn't worry me that I was forty or eighty, because I was happy and doing what I wanted. But it's a stage at which a lot of people start asking themselves what they've done in their life.'

Enthused by the idea, Esmonde and Larbey duly dreamed up a character who had reached the age of forty, was in a job he loathed and generally felt unfulfilled. The big question they faced was what he was going to do about it. 'There's got to be some basic truth in sitcom,' said Bob Larbey, 'and we felt the idea had that. A forty-year-old realising he was never going to be a raging success at business was an easy character to identify with.'

The first antidote the two writers dreamed up for their new character's crisis, of whom all they knew thus far was that he was forty and would be jacking in his job, was building a yacht and sailing around the world. Bearing in mind the budget constraints, that idea would never have got out of dock and so it was back to the drawing board.

There's a misconception these days that the idea of using self-sufficiency came from the fact that grow-your-own and vegetarianism were becoming popular at the time, but that's something of an exaggeration. Felicity Kendal certainly thinks so.

'There used to be a vegetarian restaurant in Soho called Cranks,' she remembers, 'and the reason it was called Cranks is because it was cranky to be a vegetarian. Even brown bread was seen as being a bit suspect and as for organic, it just didn't exist. At the time, people were embracing convenience, not self-sufficiency. That really started to happen after the show became popular.'

Although it wasn't exactly in vogue in the early 1970s, the concept of self-sufficiency had been written about extensively by the press for several decades and had also been the subject of a very popular book by a chap called John Seymour, entitled *The Fat of the Land*. This, more than anything, had helped keep self-sufficiency in the news throughout the preceding decades, which meant that when Esmonde and Larbey ditched their interesting but inevitably extravagant nautical idea, self-sufficiency became a natural successor.

'I can't honestly remember which one of us suggested it,' said John Esmonde, 'but the moment it came up in conversation we knew it had a lot of potential. The public might not have been practising self-sufficiency that much, but they were certainly talking about it. In that respect it was ideal, and it was also original.'

The Fat of the Land is autobiographical and follows the author and his wife as they move from the city to a five-acre small-holding in Norfolk. At first Esmonde and Larbey were tempted to follow a similar path, but very soon realised that they might be missing a trick.

'Having decided on self-sufficiency,' said Larbey, 'John and I thought that the obvious thing to do would have him buy an acre or two somewhere in the country. That would have provided a certain amount of comedy, but we eventually decided that it was a little bit too obvious.'

Esmonde and Larbey's alternative scenario was an absolute masterstroke and is as integral to the success of *The Good Life* as self-sufficiency or even the cast.

'We eventually decided that it would be a hell of a lot funnier if he did it at home in suburbia,' said Bob Larbey, 'primarily because we knew it would create tension.' John Esmonde agreed. 'Placing them in The Avenue, where a number of Margos and Jerrys lived up and down the road, not just next door, provided the abrasiveness. Amongst all those smart houses lived the Goods, with their front garden packed with leeks and their back garden full of pigs.'

The show's biographer, Richard Webber, made the important point that writers less experienced than Esmonde and Larbey might have created neighbours for the Goods who were against everything they stood for, thus focusing much of the action on altercations over the garden fence. As with the location, that would have been a bit too obvious, although the numerous exchanges that did occur between the Goods and the Leadbetters over their shared fence worked brilliantly; the point being that they were never overused, were against the run of play, and always resulted in an excellent piece of comedy, such as when Jerry, who is mowing the lawn, knocks over one of Margo's concrete toadstools while being goaded by Tom and Barbara.

Webber also makes the point that, with the show relying on four characters, weaknesses would be glaring and so each one had to be multi-dimensional. 'Depth of characterisation was essential,' he said. 'But if *The Good Life* was going to succeed it was imperative that the viewers liked the Goods and sympathised with their efforts, supporting them every step of the way in their fight for survival and independence.'

Bob Larbey felt that realism played a big part in achieving that. 'When we were defining the characters, it was obvious that Tom and Barbara had to have certain in-built characteristics. For a start, they needed courage to do what they were doing, as well as mental toughness. And Barbara had to be loyal and very much in love with Tom to go along with this kind of lunacy, because, at the end of the day, she was doing it for him, not herself.'

When it came to creating the Leadbetters, their characteristics – and their situation, of course – had to be at odds with the Goods'. Esmonde and Larbey plumped for, as John Esmonde described it, 'a Margo-driven household', with Jerry on hand to keep his wife happy. 'He had a faintly neurotic edge to him,' said Esmonde, 'because of his job and responsibilities, and although he didn't like the poverty and squalor his neighbours lived in, part of him envied what they achieved.' Esmonde went on to make the point that, while Jerry was a very capable individual who had made a success of his life, Margo suited him perfectly, especially as she was both socially adept and willing to entertain Jerry's business associates at the drop of a hat, regardless of number. 'She provided the strength he needed,' said Esmonde, 'even though she was pretentious.'

It was ultimately that pretentiousness (and snobbishness) from Jerry, but especially from Margo, that would almost lend the show a sub-theme that would often give self-sufficiency a run for its money. Once again, it was to be nuanced.

'We needed a reason why the neighbours would be disapproving,' said Esmonde, 'and what better reason than snobbery? But rather than giving them lines like, "I hate the smell of this mess," we felt, "This is Surbiton, and we *don't* want that kind of thing here," was much stronger.'

The characters of Barbara Good and Margo and Jerry Leadbetter enthused Richard when he read the first scripts, and, despite Margo's snobbishness and over-the-top pomposity, he quickly warmed to all of them. The same, however, could not be said for his own character, Tom, with whom Richard always had a kind of hate-hate relationship. 'Making the Goods and the Leadbetters old pals and Tom and Jerry [Tom & Jerry?!] colleagues, at least initially, was a stroke of genius on the writer's behalf,' he said. 'It gave the show a wonderful platform and led to conflicts of loyalty making the whole thing a lot more interesting. With Tom, who I actually thought was quite selfish and conceited, there wasn't really a great deal to latch onto, unlike Jerry, and especially Margo, who was a marvellous character, and so until we started making the show, and the characters began to mature, I just based him on myself.'

Over thirty years later in 2007, Richard declared all-out war on what had then become his most famous characterisation, by describing Tom Good to the *Daily Mail* as being 'a selfish parasite'. He said, 'I thought Tom was a very selfish person. Poor old Barbara never got any presents, any treats. He was so obsessed. It was always about him . . . his ideas, his plans. He had a parasitical side to his nature.'

Despite not taking to the show's main protagonist and namesake, Richard still lent the self-centred, parasitic parsnip grower one of his favourite songs. 'Because he was always quite cheerful, I made Tom into a whistler, which I am myself occasionally. I even taught my daughters to whistle. I wasn't asked to do this by the director, by the way. I just thought it fitted the character. The question was, what tune would Tom Good whistle? It had to be something memorable but also forgettable, if you know what I mean, and so I decided upon a couple of bars from "Over the Rainbow", which is one of my favourite songs. It's the part that goes, "Someday I wish upon a star, wake up where the clouds are far behind me." I'd whistle that myself occasionally, and, given what Tom and Barbara were undertaking, I think it was rather poignant.'

CHAPTER SEVENTEEN

'The power of the press knows no bounds.'

With the characters now ready to be brought to life, the production team assembled and the scripts coming in apace, it was time to put out a search for Barbara, Jerry and Margo. The first actor to be considered for the role of Barbara was Hannah Gordon, who would later appear alongside Richard in the much-hyped but ultimately short-lived 1982 sitcom, *Goodbye Mr Kent*, in which a recent divorcee (Gordon) is forced to take a lodger (a slovenly local journalist played by Richard) who ends up charming her and then sponging off her. Fortunately, given what finally came to pass, the softly spoken Scottish actor felt the role of Barbara Good was a little bit too similar to one she had just played, and so turned it down. The next actor to be asked to join what became British sitcom's version of the Fab Four was Richard's old friend and fellow RADA graduate, Peter Bowles, whom the producer and director John Howard Davies had approached about playing the role of Jerry.

'Strangely enough, the day I received the offer from John to appear in *The Good Life*, I also received an offer to appear in the new Alan Ayckbourn play, *Absent Friends*,' says Peter. 'I'd been waiting for a good theatrical role to come along for some time and so I took the Ayckbourn. When I first arrived at rehearsals, which started shortly before *The Good Life* started, the first person I saw was Richard, and he immediately asked me why I'd turned it down. "How on earth did you know about that?" I asked him. "Because I'm in it!" he replied.'

Having never done a sitcom before, Peter just assumed it wouldn't have been possible to do both at the same time, and so he had told John Howard Davies that he wouldn't be free.

'By the time I found out that they were rehearsing during the week and recording the show on a Sunday, Paul Eddington had already been cast in the role and so it was too late to do anything about it. Richard, who could be extremely mischievous sometimes, used to come into my dressing room while we were doing *Absent Friends* and inform me when his latest cheque for *The Good Life* had arrived. What an absolute swine!'

Peter goes on to make the point that if he had accepted the role of Jerry Leadbetter it might have had a detrimental effect on both his and Paul Eddington's career. 'First of all, I wouldn't have been offered *To the Manor Born*, as there's no way they'd have cast Penelope and I as husband and wife in two sitcoms back-to-back, and secondly, the lovely Paul Eddington, in addition to not playing Jerry – a part that he obviously made his own – wouldn't have been offered the part of Jim Hacker in *Yes Minister*, and that would be unthinkable!'

With several other ideas and approaches coming to naught, Richard, the production team and the two writers re-grouped and began to redirect their search for the remaining actors in a slightly different direction. 'I think the initial list was full of people who had lots of experience on television,' explained Richard, 'and for a variety of different reasons none of them worked out. Then, one evening, Annie and I went to see one of Alan Ayckbourn's plays on Shaftesbury Avenue, and suddenly everything started falling into place.'

Before the run of *Absent Friends*, Richard was already widely considered as being one of the definitive interpreters of Ayckbourn's work. 'He recognised what I wrote very quickly,' said Alan Ayckbourn shortly after Richard died. 'And his instincts were always right: when to speed up, when to slow down, when to leave that moment, and when to darken things. He was a true interpreter.'

Annie agrees with the playwright wholeheartedly, and, at the time when John Howard Davies, Richard and the sitcom's creators were first attempting to breathe life into the new show, she remembers her husband being almost synonymous with Ayckbourn's work, even though he only appeared in three of the writer's plays in the West End.

'Richard was, even then, known as being an Ayckbournian actor,' says Annie. 'In fact, I think he was the first one ever to be described as such. He took a great deal of satisfaction from that; partly because the plays were extremely popular, which meant he was associated with something successful, but also because he loved Alan's work. It was a perfect combination, really.'

It was Richard's affinity with Ayckbourn that led to the casting of Barbara and Margo. The play he and Annie went to see was the playwright's *The Norman Conquests*, a trilogy of plays that had opened at the Globe Theatre (now the Gielgud) in August 1974. Felicity Kendal, who played a rather put-upon character named Annie, for which she was later awarded the Best Newcomer Award by the Variety Club of Great Britain, remembers receiving a knock on her dressing-room door one evening shortly after the show had finished.

'It was the company manager asking me if I'd mind if Richard Briers popped around,' says Felicity. 'I'd never met him before, but he was a huge star even then. Anyway, he eventually popped round in the way only Dickie could, with everything moving very, very quickly! After saying some very nice things about the play and our performances he asked me if he could send me a script for a new sitcom he was making. "You'd be playing my wife, I'm afraid," he said, smiling. "It's a rather dotty little role, and it probably won't be a big series."'

For Richard to even suggest that Felicity, who hadn't had much experience on television, would be right for a leading role in a new series for the BBC alongside himself was manna from heaven for the young actor.

'I think I read the script, but I was already in. I'd been waiting years for something like this to happen and with Richard already on board things couldn't have been better.'

The following day Richard spoke to John Howard Davies and Jimmy Gilbert about his discovery and they immediately went to watch Felicity in the play and then meet her afterwards.

'But as well as seeing me,' says Felicity, 'they also saw my co-star Penelope Keith and when they came to see me afterwards I think John Howard Davies and Jimmy Gilbert thought they'd found their Margo.'

Funnily enough, around the same time that Davies and Gilbert had spotted Penelope Keith on stage in *The Norman Conquests*, Esmonde and Larbey had also noticed an actor on television who they were sure could bring Margo to life.

'The trouble was,' said Bob Larbey, 'that we'd only seen her in a Benson & Hedges commercial and so we had no idea what she was called. Eventually, after a lot of asking around, we managed to find out that her name was Penelope Keith and when we told John and Jimmy they were almost speechless. "But our Margo's called Penelope Keith," said John, "and there can't be two. Equity won't allow it."'

To ensure they were singing from the same song sheet, Jimmy Gilbert reached for a copy of the casting directory, *Spotlight*. 'I wanted to make sure we were talking about the same person,' said Gilbert. 'And fortunately, we were! It was an extraordinary coincidence.'

One of Penelope Keith's more bizarre roles pre-*The Good Life* had been as the German lesbian biker-nanny, Lotte von Gelbstein, in Marty Feldman's 1970 film, *Every Home Should Have One*, which, incidentally (although perhaps not surprisingly), had been directed by Jim Clark, the same man who gave us *Rentadick*. In 1974, just as *The Good Life* was coming into being, Penelope appeared in a twenty-six-episode television adaptation of Anthony Trollope's Palliser novels, in which she played a dominant Victorian matriarch called Mrs Hittaway. Unbeknownst to Penelope, the part of Mrs Hittaway would be a handy precursor for Margo. 'She was absolutely right,' said John Howard Davies while discussing how they cast the series. 'That middle-class, slightly authoritative woman with a touch of Barbara Woodhouse about her and a sexiness that was indefinable.'

By the time Peter Bowles had turned down the role of Jerry Leadbetter, both Felicity and Penelope had been hired to play Barbara and Margo and, when John Howard Davies asked them if they could think of anybody to play the part, Felicity suggested Paul Eddington.

'I'd recently worked with Paul on some television series and I absolutely adored him. I thought he'd be perfect in the role and so I suggested him to John.'

To complete the Alan Ayckbourn connection, Paul Eddington was then appearing in *Absurd Person Singular* at the Vaudeville Theatre on the Strand. The play had originally opened at the Criterion Theatre in July 1973 with Richard, Sheila Hancock and Michael Aldridge, and by the time it was re-cast in September 1974, Paul had taken over from Michael Aldridge, Angela Scoular from Sheila Hancock, and Peter Blythe, who would soon appear on television as Sam Ballard in *Rumpole of the Bailey*, from Richard.

'I think Paul Eddington was the least well-known member of the cast when *The Good Life* started,' said Ayckbourn in 2000, 'although he rapidly made a name for himself. He stayed with *Absurd Person Singular* until it closed in November 1975, seeing off another cast, and so by the time *The Good Life* started, and for a short period during the first series – sometime in June 1975, I think – all four cast members were appearing in one of my plays: Richard was touring in *Absent Friends*, prior to its run in the West End, Paul was about halfway through his tenure in *Absurd Person Singular*, and Penny and Felicity were about to finish their run in *The Norman Conquests*. All four actors were excellent performers. Some people tend to separate comedy from drama because they think each requires a different technique, but of course, the very best actors can play both. They're able to play comedy but retain the truth – the seriousness and integrity of the character. That's a great art, and one that Paul, Richard, Felicity and Penelope all mastered.'

John Howard Davies had been at school with Alan Ayckbourn and after the first episode was transmitted the playwright called Davies up. 'He accused me of casting plagiarism,' said John in 2003. 'And of course, he was quite right! I'd pinched his cast and I'd bunged them into a television series!'

Similarities were also immediately drawn between Ayckbourn's writing and Esmonde and Larbey's scripts, with Ayckbourn himself being one of the first people to pipe up.

'After it was televised I called Richard up and jokingly said, "What's going on here then, eh? This is all a bit familiar!" To be honest, had Richard not appeared in *The Good Life* I don't think anyone would have said anything. He was the reason.'

While Richard and the rest of the cast of *The Good Life* were working on their Ayckbourn or trying to familiarise themselves with Esmonde and Larbey's scripts, John Howard Davies and his production manager, Brian Jones, who acted as Davies's right-hand man throughout all four series of the show, were busy searching for a location. Both men were aware that finding the right location could be a chore at the best of times, so how they were going to find two adjacent houses in suburbia where one of the owners didn't mind having their garden churned up was anyone's guess. Clutching an *A–Z* of London, Brian Jones first set off west along the A40 in the direction of Oxford and within just a few miles he knew he was heading in the right direction.

'I was going against the traffic coming into London,' Jones told Richard Webber, 'so thinking about moving artists from Television Centre and the camera unit setting off from Ealing, everyone would be travelling west, avoiding the rush hour traffic travelling in the other direction. And in the evening, when we'd finished filming, we'd be London-bound whereas most of the London traffic would be heading out of the centre.'

After reaching Buckinghamshire and then working backwards, Brian finally arrived at Northwood, just around the corner from where Richard had done his National Service. 'All I was doing was looking at roads and houses,' said Jones, 'and one day I turned a

corner, drove down Kewferry Road, and thought, yes, this is it!'
After finding the two houses that would eventually become two of
the most recognised dwellings in the entire country, Brian Jones
took photos, showed them to John Howard Davies, and then set
about trying to persuade the owners to let them run riot – literally!

Richard Webber makes the point that finding homeowners
who are willing to let the BBC rip up their gardens, fill them with
livestock and have dozens of cast and crew milling about the place,
day in day out, ought to be nigh on impossible, but in this instance
Messrs Jones and Davies were in luck. In fact, Michael and Margaret
Mullins, who owned the Goods' house, were quite easily persuaded.
'We'd been living there for about two years,' Margaret Mullins said
in 2000, 'and hadn't done anything much to the garden. It really
needed digging up and starting again, so we were happy when the
BBC told us of their intentions. It was such an unexpected visit
that when they arrived I asked to see their identification!'

Brian Jones later admitted that his secret weapon when negoti-
ating with the residents of Kewferry Road was the leading actor.
'He was the carrot that I dangled in front of everyone,' said Jones.
'I'd tell them that it was a new series about self-sufficiency starring
Richard Briers, and everyone said, "Oh! Richard Briers."'

The most upheaval Margaret and Michael Mullins ever had to
endure during the making of The Good Life happened while Brian
and his cast and crew were filming the last episode of the first
series, which turned out to be one of the most beloved. Called
'Backs to the Wall', it's the one where a storm ravages the Goods'
garden, which forces them to harvest their crops immediately.
One of the reasons it's so memorable is that Jerry and Margo have
been enlisted to help bring everything in – one of Jerry's legs is in
plaster after breaking it while on holiday in Kenya, and Margo

turns up wearing rubber gloves, wellies and a bright yellow jump-suit complete with a matching hat. To give the effect that all hell had broken loose, the Mullins' garden had to be turned into a veritable mud-pit, but it did help to produce what is widely regarded as being one of the show's funniest scenes. It's the one where Margo – keen to prove she's equal to the challenge after being accused of being weak and feeble by Barbara – swings a large sack of potatoes over her shoulder, which knocks Barbara, then Jerry and finally Tom flat on their backsides and right in the mud. 'This scene needed one take,' said Brian Jones. 'You couldn't do it in two – or so we thought. We rehearsed and rehearsed and finally decided to record. The cameraman was ready, and every-body knew what was expected, so we started filming.'

Once the scene was completed John Howard Davies turned to the cameraman and, almost as a formality, asked him if everything had gone according to plan. 'I'd like to go again, please,' said the cameraman, which must have come as a bit of a shock. Especially as Felicity, Paul and Richard were still lying in the mud. 'I might have moved the camera and lost part of the action,' he added, at which point the cast had to be extracted from the bog before the scene was set up again. After filming it a second time, the camera-man piped up once more to say that the original take had turned out OK, so the second effort had been a complete waste of time.

One of the funniest stories regarding the owners of the two houses, Mr and Mrs Mullins and a chap called Albert Carr, who owned Jerry and Margo's house, involves them being accused of tax evasion by the HMRC due to rumours circulating in the press about how much money they were receiving from the BBC.

Mr Carr, who sold the house shortly after the first series had been filmed, thought he was in for a reprimand when Brian Jones first turned up at his door, having complained about a BBC presenter the night before. 'If I get annoyed at the BBC,' he told Richard Webber, 'I phone up and give them a telling off. I remember watching a political programme one evening and felt the interviewer was going on at his guest too much. I phoned the BBC and said that I hoped the presenter would be humbler when interviewing people in the future. I was asked for my name but declined. I told them that I wouldn't want to be on their programme because I liked having the last word, but they always had that!'

So when Brian Jones – from the BBC – paid Albert a visit, his mind immediately went back twenty-four hours. 'Oh yes, well, come in,' said Albert. 'I'm in a hurry but we can talk for a few moments.' When Albert discovered that the man from Auntie wanted to offer him money for using his house as a location for a brand-new sitcom, he had just one question to ask in return. 'How much?' he said with a grin. 'Not that it turned out to be a great deal.'

But it was the couple who bought the house from Albert, John and Betty Tindall, who attracted the attentions of the Inland Revenue. 'Newspaper reports said people were paying off their mortgages from the proceeds,' said Betty, 'but that was far from the truth. It might have taken a couple of friends out for a meal, but that was about it.'

As reports of the fees continued, the Tindalls were eventually brought in for questioning by the Inland Revenue. 'The taxman started showing an unusual interest in my income,' said John Tindall, 'presumably suspecting that all the newspaper reports must have been right, despite the fact that I'd sent them copies of all my correspondence with the BBC! The power of the press knows no bounds.'

CHAPTER EIGHTEEN

'Pure penicillin.'

Had *The Good Life* been judged entirely on its first episode it might not have made it to a second, and not simply in terms of its audience figures or the reaction from the press. 'In those days the sets for the show were put up overnight,' remembered John Howard Davies, 'and the designer, Paul Munting, had gone to a lot of trouble dressing the sets [with props] beautifully. Unfortunately, when we all arrived the following morning, the set dressings had been stolen.'

Perhaps not surprisingly, this piece of bad luck put a slight cloud over the new series and when the three hundred or so audience members arrived at Television Centre for the first recording in March 1975, the show's producer and director had convinced himself that it was jinxed. 'We'd started off fearing that nothing was going to go right with the series and I tried to hide my own fear and trepidation.'

The reaction from the studio audience, while not negative exactly, could only have been described as being tamely enthusiastic. But, instead of going home believing that he and his new show were destined for the scrapheap, which is what he had been expecting, John Howard Davies left the studio that evening hoping that it might just be salvageable. This pale glimmer of hope, which had been heightened by the fact that the press, who, as well as being intrigued by *The Good Life*'s 'sit', seemed to be confident that it would produce lots of 'com', only lasted until the morning after the first episode was transmitted.

'The first episode was pretty disastrous,' said Davies. 'The audience was about 5.5 million, where traditionally a good sitcom sometimes got 18 million viewers in those days.'

The producer's trepidation, while ultimately premature, was shared by the cast and crew alike and the six-week period over which that first series was transmitted proved to be a pretty harrowing time, especially for the lead actor.

'Watching a television series fail is like a slow death,' Richard once said. 'With a play, you can take it off, but with a television series, you've got to see it through to the bitter end. I'd had a failure or two by this time, one quite recently, in fact, and I must confess that when I started hearing on the grapevine about *The Good Life* I thought I might have made a terrible mistake.'

Two reviews from 5 April 1975, the morning after the first transmission, demonstrate just how polarised the British press were over the new series. The first is from the *Stage* and the other from the *Coventry Evening Telegraph*:

It was interesting to note that while three members of the cast of *The Good Life* (Episode One, BBC-1, Friday, April 4, 8.30) are projecting their recorded images on to the small screen, they are to be found in flesh in Alan Ayckbourn theatre plays: Felicity Kendal and Penelope Keith . . . are in *The Norman Conquests*, while Paul Eddington appears in *Absurd Person Singular*. From the first airing of BBC's new comedy series, it seems unlikely that John Esmonde's and Bob Larbey's scripts will pack viewers round the set, as Ayckbourn's have packed audiences into the theatre. Plough Your Own Furrow showed all the symptoms of first episode superfluity. Tom Good's determination to escape the bonds of what a radio programme contributor once described, in all seriousness, as the 'computer' belt, and attempt self-sufficiency in Surbiton, did not require so much exposition. Episode One should have started, not ended, with Tom rotavating his garden and awaiting the arrival of the goat. *The Good Life* shows no signs of bridging that gap in light entertainment. All good comedy must embrace at least an element of the universal. How far ploughing up the garden in Surbiton is going to intrigue viewers in council houses and high-rise dwellings remains to be seen. John Howard Davies's production has, so far, been too slow. Although Paul Munting's interior sets were attractive to look at, they could not enclose a situation ripe with humorous conviction. Barbara Good pacing reflectively behind French doors, for instance, risked none of the comic pitfalls or visual surprises which abound in Ayckbourn country. Good lines being scarce, the performing Goods coped well. Richard Briers as Tom conveyed a strong sense of the preposterous, while Felicity Kendal gave Barbara a demure countenance, engagingly split by infectious giggles. It would be unfair to dismiss an entire series at the outset. If subsequent episodes can sift the material more skilfully, prospects could well brighten. Perhaps hilarity may prevail when Tom and Barbara bring in the livestock. I certainly hope so. I could do with more laughs between news bulletins.

Take that utterly nice fellow Richard Briers and the mischievous-looking Felicity Kendal and there is a basis for a pleasant genteel middle-class suburban comedy. *The Good Life* has Briers reaching 40 and deciding that the world should have more to offer than a job designing plastic hippos to put in cereal packets. Mind you, it appears to be a well-paid job which gives him a home in which the kitchen sink is bound to be a gold-plated double-drainer. So, farewell to the fourth-floor office where he plays Mr. Chips to a bunch of younger men who don't invite him to play cricket. Farewell to the bosses on the floors above, where creeping makes up for a lack of ability. After he spends half the night working out the amount of gas that can be extracted from a given quantity of manure, and after his wife has deliberated by tramping in the garden in her dressing gown and gumboots, they decide to leave the rat-race and to become self-sufficient. The front lawn is turned in, three hundredweight of seed potatoes are waiting, and the goat is due to arrive. It's all slightly dotty, perfectly clean, deftly presented and it has enough digs at the commercialism of modern life and sufficient references to conservation to be topical, and there are enough of the dreams of escape to appeal to those of us who need fortifying. It also happens to be very funny, and that in itself, in a new series, is rare enough to be worth commending.

As luck would have it, the British public erred towards the opinion of the *Coventry Evening Telegraph* and by the second episode of *The Good Life* the audience had risen to 8.2 million, which is about where it stayed for the remaining five episodes. One of the reasons for the improvement was, in Richard's opinion, the increasing involvement of Margo Leadbetter as a character: something he was instrumental in promoting.

'Penny Keith was just a voiceover in episode one. She wasn't even seen. Then, as her part began to grow, we quickly realised that we were dealing with comedy dynamite and so as opposed to Jerry and Margo being just feature parts, which is what they originally were, I asked John Esmonde and Bob Larbey if they could build them up and turn us into a foursome. For God's sake, write them up, I said!'

John Esmonde was greatly impressed by Richard's gesture and spoke publicly about it several times. 'He was never afraid to give lines away for the good of the show,' said Esmonde in 2003. 'Not many actors would do that full stop, but with Richard it was automatic.'

Despite the rise in audience figures and the emergence of Jerry and Margo, that first series of *The Good Life*, while not a flop exactly, wasn't considered to be a success and once the weekend press and magazines had their say, it was the *Stage*, and not the *Coventry Evening Telegraph*, that held the prevailing opinion.

Even so, Jimmy Gilbert and John Howard Davies realised that the show needed time to bed in and, enthused by the potential amount of material it could produce, were willing to back it for at least another series. Bob Larbey was relieved when he heard the news, and he and John Esmonde immediately set to work on series two. 'The BBC in their *then* wisdom would persist with something they thought had some quality instead of just going, "Ooh, not very good figures. Just drop it."'

By the time the first episode of series two had finished at 8.10pm on 5 December 1975, the British public were more convinced than ever that *The Good Life* was essential viewing, and by the end of episode two the audience had climbed from a not bad 9.2 million viewers to a nicely respectable 10.2 million.

The actress Olivia Williams, who as well as hazardously introducing Richard to Bill Murray starred alongside him in the 2003 film, *Peter Pan*, in which he played Smee, remembers the lengths to which her father used to go to so as not to be disturbed during the show. 'My father used to take the phone off the hook when *The Good Life* came on, and I'm pretty sure millions of other people did exactly the same thing. There was so little output back then, and because there was no "watch again" option, you actually made an appointment to sit down and watch a television programme.'

Not only that, but you also talked about it the following day and it was that verbal interaction that finally began moving *The Good Life* into the upper echelons of British television. Well, that and a strike.

'Somewhere in the middle of the second series there was a strike at ITV,' remembered John Howard Davies, 'which shoved *The Good Life* to the number one spot instantaneously and it remained there.'

The timing of the strike couldn't have been better, as the episode that those migrating from the other side were about to see (they had been expecting to watch an episode of the sitcom *Yes, Honestly*, starring Liza Goddard and Donal Donnelly) is the one where Jerry is asked to accommodate a Dutch businessman at short notice by 'Sir', but has to refuse as Margo is appearing in *The Sound of Music* ('for that dreadful Miss Mountshaft'). As a consequence, Jerry is sacked from JJM Ltd, and so Tom hatches a plan to have him hired again. The fact that so many of the comedy migrants stayed with the series thereafter is hardly surprising, and that's no slight on Liza and Donal's efforts. Indeed, by the time series three had got into its stride in the autumn of 1976, *The Good Life* was attracting around 17 million viewers every week, which was well over a third of the entire adult population. Felicity Kendal remembers the effect this had on her life all too well, not least the emergence, en masse, it seemed, of those members of the viewing public who were finding it difficult to separate fiction from reality.

'I think I realised it was a success when I couldn't buy any vegetables without somebody asking me why I wasn't growing them myself. They genuinely seemed quite confused by this and so I either had to buy them very early, before anyone else was about, or try and reason with them and explain that it was only a television show.'

Even Lucy started suffering the effects of this, and it left her as confused as the people who were asking the questions, not to mention a bit frustrated. 'Girls at school used to say to me, "Do you have goats and pigs at home?" and I used to say, rather angrily, "No! That's on television." I simply didn't get the fact that they didn't get it, if that makes sense.'

Kate, on the other hand, was getting more frustrated with all the extra attention her father was receiving. '*The Good Life* took things to a completely different level fame-wise. Before that Dad would get recognised quite a bit and approached for an autograph occasionally, but after it started getting 15 million viewers he would be recognised and approached for a chat or an autograph almost constantly. Dad was in his element, by the way. It was me, Mum and Lucy who used to get fed up!'

It has been said before, but what separated *The Good Life* from other shows and made it so appealing, apart from the excellent performances and the sublime scripts, was that all four characters ultimately thought the world of each other, and that sometimes delicate but ultimately steadfast adoration, effortlessly and hilariously defeated every trial, tribulation and situation that befell them – even Tom's blatant selfishness. In a time of strikes and rising unemployment, it was the right tonic at exactly the right time. Despite the show being, as Richard once put it, 'overtly middle-class at times', it still managed to retain an inclusive quality that, just like the characters' affection for one another, transcended everything. Not only is that a fitting epitaph for the show, but it's also a heck of an achievement.

On 26 December 1977, about six months after the last episode of the final series had been shown, a Christmas special of *The Good Life* was transmitted in which Margo foolishly sends her entire Christmas delivery back on Christmas Eve afternoon because the tree that she had ordered is a few inches too short. Expecting it to be redelivered on Christmas morning, she is naturally furious when she finds out that this isn't going to happen, and with no other options open to her Margo picks up the phone and sets about cancelling Christmas. The Goods, whose festive period is obviously the antithesis of the Leadbetters' both in terms of cost and in terms of content, gallantly come to the Leadbetters' rescue. After gently persuading Margo that Christmas on a budget of 15p is actually possible, everybody ends up having a fine old time getting drunk on peapod burgundy, pulling homemade crackers with jokes inside – 'The Ooh Aah bird is so called because it lays square eggs' – and playing party games.

'That closeness that we created on screen was replicated in real life,' says Felicity. 'It's not necessarily unusual in a television programme, but the level of love and respect that we had for each other on that show was special. The day after a recording one of us would host a dinner party for the others and their partners, and because we were perfectly compatible drinkers, things could get rather rowdy. Richard and Paul in particular were like Morecambe and Wise once they got started. Penny and I used to call them "The Boys".'

About a year after what was supposed to have been the final episode of *The Good Life* had gone to air – the Christmas special where Richard falls off the arm of the sofa – Esmonde and Larbey were asked to write a special one-off episode in aid of an appeal to send teams from the British Isles to the Commonwealth Games in Edmonton, Canada. What made the request special was that it was to be recorded in the presence of Her Majesty The Queen, thus making the episode a Royal Command Performance. 'I was deeply, deeply proud,' said John Esmonde. 'When we were told, Bob and I decided we wouldn't do any Corgi jokes as I hate them. We'd simply write another *Good Life*.'

The episode John Esmonde and Bob Larbey came up with was 'When I'm 65', the one where Tom and Jerry decide to have a race, but end up in a pub. 'It worked quite well,' said Larbey, 'and overall it was a very happy, albeit frightening, sort of evening.'

In 2012, a poll of two thousand people suggested that *The Good Life* was the most effective televisual tonic for heart disease. The survey was based on medical research that has found links between laughter and heart exercise. Researchers at the University of Maryland Medical Center announced that test subjects who watched funny films had increased blood flow through the heart. Blood vessels that expanded during comedies contracted when the volunteers watched stressful films.

Chris Dark, clinical director of the company involved, said that they were convinced of the benefits of laughter. 'More and more medical evidence is emerging for the health benefits of laughter,' he said. 'These are thought to include protecting against heart disease, boosting the immune system, relieving stress and even increased pain tolerance.

'If laughter is the best medicine, then I guess this survey shows *The Good Life* is pure penicillin.'

CHAPTER NINETEEN

'Turn it over, quick!'

By the end of the 1970s Richard was desperate to do some straight theatre again, and preferably not in a role that required him to wear wellington boots or carry a spade. He was incredibly grateful to *The Good Life* for the exposure it had given him but there was no escaping the fact that the public's, and the industry's, perception of him had changed.

'On entering the series Dad had a reputation as being a versatile actor who was good at comedy,' says Lucy, 'and I think he was more than happy with that. The point being that he had a *reputation*, as opposed to an actual brand.'

By the time Richard left *The Good Life* things had changed somewhat, and this hard-fought reputation, something that had been built over the years and on countless different performances, had morphed into a kind of gilded middle-class persona that was based entirely on one show.

'Suddenly, as opposed to being just an actor,' explains Kate, 'he'd become middle-England's representative for just about everything. He'd become Tom Good. Or at least a nicer version of.'

In truth, this didn't bother Richard as much as it could have done. He did have the odd grumble now and then, especially when he thought people had forgotten the fact he had sustained a good career prior to *The Good Life*. Yet the potential creative restrictions of having a persona built on amiability and comedy, as opposed to talent and versatility, were outweighed by the fact that he was now approaching 'National Treasure' status. With a face that was now as familiar as his voice, even to children – not forgetting a ubiquitous smile – he was recognised everywhere he went and, most importantly, he was busier than ever. Richard's enterprise had now carved its own snuggly suburban niche, it seemed, and, providing he could step out of it occasionally and do something different, he would carry on giving the public what they wanted. There was a chance the persona might weaken over time, but, as was proved during a conversation he had with Penelope Keith shortly after *The Good Life* had come to an end, he was under no illusions as to how much the link would dissipate, if at all.

'That's it, Penny,' he said. 'It doesn't matter what we do now, *The Good Life* is what we four will always be remembered for.'

Regardless of the context of Richard's fatalistic statement, this must have taken some getting used to. After all, prior to *The Good Life* neither Paul Eddington, Penelope Keith nor Felicity Kendal had played a starring role in a television series, so imagine having to carry around such a strong association with a first effort.

When it came to Richard and his Good-esque persona, there wasn't that much between them; save for the strong language, the convivial drinking, the smoking and the fact that, as well as being an occasional curmudgeon, Richard Briers wasn't a natural gardener. The smile, however, was completely genuine. But what really perpetuated the association, at least in the public's eyes, were the sartorial similarities; something that still makes Lucy laugh today.

'Dad was absolutely useless with clothes, to the point that if he ever needed to buy a pair of trousers for himself, he'd walk into Marks and Spencer, pick up the nearest pair, pay for them, take them home, and then have them altered so they'd fit him! The thought of actually trying them on first would have been absolutely unthinkable to Dad.'

In May 1975, after *The Good Life* had started, the journalist Nancy Mills wrote an article for the *Guardian* in which she juxtaposed two actors whom she thought represented both ends of the British sartorial spectrum: Richard and Jeremy Brett, then a fashionable heart-throb who had recently been convinced by the famed mannequin-maker, Adel Rootstein, who had already made window dummies of Donyale Luna, Twiggy and Lady Jacqueline Rufus Isaacs, to model for her. 'He represents modern man,' Mills said of Brett, while Richard met the journalist wearing, as she put it, 'a blue and white striped shirt vaguely tucked into plaid trousers. The pocket of his grey cardigan was stuffed with a pipe and what looked like about 12 Kleenexes. I couldn't see if his socks matched."

'I've kept pretty old-fashioned,' Richard explained to the journalist. 'I can't stand trousers flapping around the ankles. I had to wear them for a part once and that was awful. I like to be comfortable.' Richard then points out that he favours Hush Puppies (what else?) because they don't make any noise. 'I guess I'm very English,' he continues. 'What I mean is, I'm sloppy. I've always wanted to get up in the morning, zip myself in and go. I usually reach for the nearest thing. Clothes are to cover yourself in. I buy them only when I absolutely have to. Right now, I need a dark blue mac. I lost the last one. In fact, I lose three a year.' Richard then states that he replaces his macs at Burtons, but for his shirts, he's a Marks and Spencer man. 'I need ones that will cover a middle-age spread,' he says, before muttering to himself, 'I really must go on a diet.'

Mills goes on to describe Richard as being a friendly, homely kind of person. 'It didn't seem even slightly odd,' she writes, 'when he opened a jar at the table, and offered me some apple chutney. "Here," said Richard, "try some of this. It's home-made."' Before she moves on to Jeremy Brett, Nancy Mills asks if Richard might have taken to heart the self-sufficiency theme he's been promoting in his current TV series, *The Good Life*, which perhaps should have rung some alarm bells. After all, any actor can become typecast, but if the public start to believe that a character you play on television and the real you are in fact one and the same, there's going to be no escape, especially if the character is one of the most famous on British television.

But another two areas where the public and the private Richard Briers didn't really harmonise were background and education, with the public assuming, understandably, given his accent and the fact that he was obviously quite bright, that he was university educated and that he came from a well-to-do family.

'The public are always quite shocked when I tell them that my parents didn't have two pennies to rub together,' he once said. 'Or that I was rubbish at school. That really surprises them. It doesn't fit the voice, you see. They all think I went to Cambridge or somewhere and have lots of O-levels. O-levels? I didn't even get a Z-level!'

When it came to what kind of drama he liked, again, people who didn't know Richard personally would often assume that

Coward, Wilde and possibly Shakespeare would be top of his list. They also wouldn't have been too shocked had he turned up playing, for instance, Bottom in *A Midsummer Night's Dream* (*Richard III* was a distant memory by then).

But while Noël Coward, Oscar Wilde and William Shakespeare all featured high on Richard's list of favourite dramatists, it was the avant-garde Irish playwright and novelist, Samuel Beckett, who gave him the most amount of pleasure. Indeed, when Richard first appeared on *Desert Island Discs* in 1967 (he appeared again in 2000), the book he chose to take with him to the island was a volume featuring the plays and novels of Beckett.

His fascination with the Irish Nobel Prize winner, whose works often provided a very bleak outlook on human existence, has been the subject of several conversations between the author and Richard's family and has given rise to a rather interesting theory; something that Beckett himself could easily have dreamed up.

'In my opinion it has something to do with the life he'd have led had he not become an actor,' says Annie. 'A "petty conman or a door-to-door salesman with a drink problem", was how he put it, which is so Samuel Beckett. It was a darkness that always followed him: a fear of his success disappearing and everything going to pot. I think that's why he also loved the plays of Harold Pinter. A sudden knock at the door either disrupting or ruining a successful life. That's where the fascination came from. It put him in touch with his parallel life.'

Sadly, Richard never got the opportunity to perform in one of Beckett's plays. In fact, the closest he came was in 2009 when he and his close friend, Adrian Scarborough, with whom he had appeared in Alan Bennett's award-winning adaptation of *The*

Wind in the Willows at the National Theatre nineteen years previously, were due to star in Beckett's existential masterpiece, *Endgame*. Shortly before the play was due to open at the Duchess Theatre, Scarborough had to leave the production unexpectedly, and Richard, who was in pretty poor health at the time, decided to pull out. It was supposed to have been Richard's last ever performance on the West End stage, and not going ahead was one of the few regrets he had during his career.

Had Richard enthused about the Irish dramatist, whose plays often offer a bleak, tragicomic outlook on human existence, as often as he had done publicly about Henry Irving, it might have made his relationship with the public more interesting. Prior to *The Good Life*, nobody would have batted an eyelid about his obsession with Beckett; partly because he was a well-respected theatrical everyman, but also because nobody would have given two hoots. By the end of the 1970s, he was closely associated with woolly jumpers, spades and those dreaded French windows, and certainly not with an experimental playwright. What Richard needed was a vehicle that would challenge him as an actor, satisfy his yearning to play straight theatre and fly under the radar of the telly-watching populace, who were effectively paying his wages. Enter a nineteenth-century Norwegian playwright called Henrik, a Tony Award-winning director, and a Liver Bird.

The closest Richard had come to playing a straight dramatic role since *The Good Life* had started was when he appeared, in voice only, as Fiver, in the 1978 animated classic film, *Watership Down*. Based on a novel of the same name by Richard Adams, it tells the story of a rabbit warren facing imminent destruction, which forces its inhabitants to flee the warren and search for a new home. The film, which includes scenes of bloodied bunnies fighting tooth and nail over their territory, is often mistaken by television schedulers these days as being made for children; partly because it's animated and features rabbits, but also, to a lesser extent, because Richard – Mr Children's Television – voices one of the lead characters. A character, incidentally, who has apocalyptic visions of the sun soaking the land with blood – not exactly Noddy.

On Easter Sunday 2017, Channel 5 showed the film at 2.25 p.m. when the vast majority of the country's infants were just coming down from a six-hour sugar rush after inhaling their parents' bodyweight in Easter eggs and chocolate bunnies. About twenty minutes into the film the words, 'Turn it over, quick!' could no doubt be heard echoing all over the land. Once the traumatised wee ones had been placated with no doubt more chocolate and a Disney DVD, the furious parents took to social media to voice their fury. What made the channel's faux pas funny, to those not affected, was that the broadcaster had done exactly the same thing the year before. Even so, it ended up defending its decision to broadcast a film depicting the slaughter of innocent bunnies on Easter Sunday by stating that, '*Watership Down* has become a seasonal tradition on Channel 5 so we've decided not to buck the trend in 2017.'

Fair enough.

Richard's big opportunity with regards to appearing in a straight play first came to his attention in the spring of 1980 when he received a telephone call from his agent. 'I actually took the call for him,' remembers Annie. '"Tell Richard

Michael Blakemore's been in touch," he said to me. "He wants to know if he might be interested in playing Håkon in *The Wild Duck*." Richard was over the moon when I told him. "What, Ibsen?" he replied. ' "That's perfect. Tell him yes!" '

One of the reasons Michael Blakemore wanted to cast Richard in *The Wild Duck* was the same reason that the actor wanted to do straight theatre: he wanted to try something different. But there was also another reason.

'I'd always felt that Richard was a very underrated actor,' explains Michael, 'and was much better than people gave him credit for. He was recognised as being a successful actor, as opposed to a great one, and I felt that was wrong. What I found interesting about Richard's comedy is that it was often based on observable reality, rather like Nigel Hawthorne in *Yes Minister*. The part I was offering him obviously wasn't a comedy role, but it did, I felt, have a lot of comic potential, and I wanted to try and unlock some of that without losing the character. Håkon's such a feeble man – nice, but fallible – and I thought Richard would be terrific in it. I'd never met him, but I just had this feeling he'd be perfect.'

As one of the world's most renowned and prolific theatre directors, Michael Blakemore had worked with literally thousands of actors over the years, but soon after starting rehearsals with Richard, Michael came to the decision that this one was unique. 'To this day, I have never known an actor work as hard as Dickie Briers. He knew his lines right from the off and also helped to create a very warm environment. But he also had a kind of nervousness about him, as if he was in a hurry to get it right. I had so much respect for him and I remember it being a very happy rehearsal period.'

The actor Nerys Hughes was in a similar boat to Richard in that she was primarily known for playing comedy (especially in *The Liver Birds*) but had a long association with drama and wanted to do more. She also remembers the rehearsals being quite jolly and was very much looking forward to the prospect of, potentially, changing people's opinions about Henrik Ibsen.

'Ibsen is sometimes thought of as being quite heavy or a bit wordy,' explains Nerys, 'and Michael Blakemore is one of those brilliant directors who knows that to get the best out of a tragedy, which is what *The Wild Duck* is, you have to get to the comedy. It was the juxtaposition of those two things that made the production so wonderful. I especially remember a scene just before Hedvig, who is the daughter of Håkon and his wife Gina, which is the part I played, shoots herself. Richard, as Håkon, was saying yet again that he was going to leave, and Gina's so used to it now that, as he's walking around the room ranting I'm very calmly opening his drawers and packing his suitcase. It was such a brilliant idea of Michael's because as the audience are laughing away at Richard being irate and terribly pompous and at me nonchalantly packing his clothes, they suddenly hear this shot out of nowhere and then they realise that Hedvig has shot herself. It caught the audience out every single night because one moment it was very funny, and the next it was horrifyingly sad. If it hadn't gone from high comedy to tragedy so quickly and unexpectedly, it wouldn't have had the same effect.'

Richard and Nerys's experience in the genres of comedy and drama was clearly an essential component in making Michael Blakemore's production a success, so casting the two was a moment of genius on his behalf. But, despite them being such experienced performers, Nerys did get a helping hand from reality.

'When the play opened, I hadn't long since had a child,' continues Nerys, 'and so every night when Hedvig shot herself I'd cry real tears. That, I think, added to the contrast we'd created.'

Something else that contributed to Blakemore's deliberate juxtaposition of comedy and tragedy was Richard's face.

'Richard's face in repose had a terrible sadness about it,' remembers Nerys. 'I wasn't used to seeing him like that because he was usually smiling, but whenever I did, even for a few seconds, I'd always feel slightly sad. The sad face of a clown, some might say, but that's wrong. Richard wasn't a clown or a comedy actor. He was an actor. An actor who had this wonderful ability to move people. You can see it in some of those later productions he did with Kenneth Branagh. It was an important part of what he had inside him; this ability to move people, but he also had this amazing gift of subtleness. I saw Richard in some outrageous farces and comedies over the years, but I never saw him overact. People often say he was quite a nervous performer, but I think that was down to a lack of confidence, which is slightly different.'

Alan Ayckbourn remembers going to see Richard in *The Wild Duck*, although he admits that even with a first-rate cast and director, he wasn't at all looking forward to it.

'I'd seen quite a bit of Ibsen over the years and to tell you the truth I'd always found it quite depressing. Then, when I went to see Richard in *The Wild Duck*, I was falling about all over the place. It was refreshing, but I have to admit I was confused.'

After the show Alan took Richard for dinner and immediately challenged his friend about the apparent transformation.

'Richard said to me, "Ibsen? Terribly funny. I mean, you

remember the scene where I leave home to go to a dinner while the rest of my family are starving hungry? Naturally, the family ask me to bring something back, expecting a doggy bag, and what did I bring? The bloody menu! Look what we had, I cry! Mark my words, Alan. Only a farceur could write a sick joke like that." '

After seeing *The Wild Duck*, Alan came to a conclusion about Richard's acting that was partly informed by having seen Richard's former co-star, Celia Johnson, in another Ibsen play about thirteen years previously.

'While Celia was appearing as Sheila in *Relatively Speaking* she was also starring as Mrs Alving in a production of Ibsen's *Ghosts* for the BBC. "They're actually very similar in a way," Celia said to me one day, but at the time I couldn't really see what she meant. Luckily, I managed to catch *Ghosts* when it was transmitted and as opposed to noticing any actual similarities between the two plays, what I did notice were the variances in Celia's execution of comedy and drama. Ultimately, it was all about timing. That was the biggest change of all, which led me to the conclusion that Celia Johnson was a straight actor with an uncanny comic instinct. After watching Dickie in *The Wild Duck*, I came to exactly the same conclusion. That's what Dickie was: a straight actor with an uncanny comic instinct. He'd previously told me that every moment he spent on stage with Celia Johnson had been a masterclass, and that precision of hers, which is what fascinated him so much, is ultimately what bonded them.'

Sir Alan remembers another scene from *The Wild Duck* that got an awful lot of laughs, except this time it was purely down to the director.

'There's a scene in the play where Hedvig [played by Michelle Wade] falls over,' explains Alan, 'and Richard told me that Michael Blakemore, who is a great director, came up with the idea of her splintering her glasses. Dickie and Nerys thought this was marvellous and so a second pair were made that had all the lenses smashed. So, when the actor falls over, instead of getting straight to her feet she quickly changes her glasses. Then, she gets to her feet. I remember it got a very big laugh but at the same time it made her death all the more tragic. Dickie said it was the funniest scene he'd ever had to play and found it very difficult not to corpse.'

Although the reviews for *The Wild Duck* were generally quite positive, there was a certain amount of condescension towards Richard's recent success on television, thus demonstrating that even the critics had bought into this new persona of his, despite many of them once praising his efforts as a stage actor and bemoaning the fact that he was highly underrated. Nobody was as annoyed by these comments as Michael Blakemore.

'I honestly couldn't stand that,' he says. 'And I was absolutely furious at the time. Furious! I'd been longing to cast Richard Briers in something for years and he'd exceeded all my expectations tenfold. The critics who were condescending towards his performance were simply being cruel. It was very sad.'

Despite one or two punitive critics, the general consensus was that Richard Briers's return to straight theatre, albeit with the odd smidgen of comedy thrown in to accentuate the tragic elements, had been a roaring success and the invigorated actor celebrated the fact by popping into a recording studio and fulfilling a life-long dream. In truth, he had been fulfilling this dream, on and off, since 1973, but after several months of playing Ibsen it was exactly what he needed.

'One thing Dad never stopped doing was reading the works of P. G. Wodehouse,' says Kate. 'It had been a constant joy in his life ever since he was a child and so when he was asked to play Bertie Wooster in a radio adaptation for the BBC, he couldn't believe his luck.'

It was the renowned radio director and producer, David Hatch, who first approached Richard about playing Bertie Wooster, and notwithstanding the fact that he was offering him a role that he had dreamed about playing for decades, he was full of admiration: 'David Hatch was a first-class director and producer, but he was also a wonderful human being. I think he was producing *Just a Minute* when we first met, which I was a big fan of, and because he was a fellow Wodehouse fanatic we seemed to have a lot in common.'

What made this experience especially enjoyable for Richard was the fact that David Hatch had hired his old friend and co-star, Michael Hordern, to play Jeeves. This was inspired casting by Hatch and the listening public were thrilled by the results.

'David Hatch had gathered a First Eleven cast together,' Richard said. 'So, as well as Michael Hordern, who was simply sublime as Jeeves, we had the likes of John Le Mesurier and Jonathan Cecil with us. We couldn't miss, really.'

Presented under the umbrella title *What Ho, Jeeves!*, fifty-four episodes were recorded between 1973 and 1980, encompassing the stories from *The Inimitable Jeeves*, *Right Ho, Jeeves*, *The Code of the Woosters*, *Thank You, Jeeves*, *The Mating Season*, *Joy in the Morning*, *Jeeves and the Feudal Spirit* and *Stiff Upper Lip, Jeeves*, plus 'The Ordeal of Young Tuppy'.

One of the biggest admirers of this long-running series was

the actor and author, Stephen Fry, who, as well as becoming a friend of Richard's in the late 1980s, had the pleasure of bringing one of his favourite characters to life when he appeared as Jeeves alongside his friend and then collaborator, Hugh Laurie, in the immensely successful ITV series, *Jeeves and Wooster*.

'I had grown up loving P. G. Wodehouse, adoring him,' said Stephen for a BBC tribute to Richard in 2013. 'And I'd been reading the books since the age of ten. Back then it had never occurred to me that I might get the chance to hear Wodehouse brought to life. Michael Hordern was a magnificent Jeeves. His voice, to quote Wodehouse, was "like gravy pouring out of a jug". The quality Richard brought to Bertie Wooster was like-ability, I think. A sunniness of nature. An optimism. He was always being abused by his friends, yet he always adhered to the code of the Woosters. The series was magnificently done, and it was one of the BBC's great achievements of the 1970s and early 1980s. To have managed to bring off something that lives in every reader's mind so exactly and with such perfect clarity, without ruining it – I little knew that I was going to go on and attempt to do the same thing on television, of course – was a fine achievement.'

The main difference between Richard's portrayal of Bertie Wooster and Hugh Laurie's is that Richard's has a bit more nous and tends to be a tad more assertive. He's also a bit quicker to temper than Laurie's and does indignant wonderfully. Both are obviously 'fatheads', to coin Aunt Dahlia's description, but, as Stephen Fry pointed out during his Radio 4 tribute to Richard, Bertie Wooster wasn't a complete lost cause. 'He knew a lot of poetry,' said Fry. 'He didn't necessarily know who the poet was, and he wasn't precisely sure of the context, but he knew it a lot better than, say, Bingo Little or Gussie Fink-Nottle.'

In 1997 Richard was invited to become the first Honorary President of the newly formed P. G. Wodehouse Society, something that gave him a huge amount of pleasure and pride. In a message to the society's members after he had accepted the position, he wrote, 'I don't normally undertake commitments outside acting, but when I was asked to become president of the newly-formed P. G. Wodehouse Society, I felt I couldn't refuse. And I'm glad I didn't.'

Richard's final outing as an interpreter of a man who the revered American magazine editor William Shawn once claimed wrote, 'the purest sentences in the English language', took place in 1995 when he was offered the role of Galahad Threepwood, a kind of late middle-aged worldly-wise Bertie Wooster, in a feature-length adaptation of Wodehouse's popular novel from his Blandings Castle series, *Heavy Weather*. He starred alongside a stellar cast including Peter O'Toole, Roy Hudd, Judy Parfitt, Ronald Fraser and Samuel West. Not only is Sam the son of two of Richard's dearest friends, Prunella Scales and Timothy West, but he is also Richard's godson and is quick to acknowledge the vitally important part his godfather played on the occasion of his birth.

'While my mother was busy giving birth to me at Queen Charlotte's Hospital in June 1966, my father was with Richard. He and Annie lived practically opposite Queen Charlotte's at the time and so instead of waiting to be called in for the birth, my father popped across the road to sample some of Richard's whisky. When he was finally wanted in the delivery room nobody knew where the heck my father was. They tried everywhere. Eventually, somebody suggested Richard's and they managed to get hold of him just in time. My father ran into the delivery room and was told to put a mask on immediately, which might have helped to mask the smell of whisky. A few minutes later, I was born.'

Over forty years later, in 2007, Richard went to see his godson in a production of Harold Pinter's play *Betrayal* at the Donmar Warehouse and Sam remembers being knocked for six by his powers of recall.

'It was very sweet of him to come and see me at the Donmar. Entirely by chance my godmother was there, and I arranged to meet them both in the bar afterwards to say hello. Richard, who hadn't seen my godmother for over forty years, went straight over to her and said, "Hello, we met at the christening." I could not believe my ears!'

Although they both had leading roles in *Heavy Weather*, Sam and Richard only had a solitary scene together, but it was memorable.

'I had to come down some stairs very crossly having just been fired by Lord Emsworth and I had to say something like, "While I was out of the way, *being fired*, Pilbeam sneaked up to my room and stole the manuscript." Afterwards Richard said, "It is nice to be working with you, *being fired*," and then he laughed. Richard Briers laughed at something I'd said! I thought, wow, he thinks I'm funny. That's really good!'

Later on, during another break in filming, Richard started talking to Sam about comedy. 'And, of course, when Richard Briers starts talking about comedy you listen. He likened comedy to an orange. He said that when you present a joke to an audience you can't just go, "Ta daaa!" You must include them and bring them towards you. "Just imagine your hand is cupped around a small orange," he said. "When you hold it out for people to see everyone has a look and then goes, 'Oh, it's an orange!' The point being that the audience have had to do a little bit of work which means that when they conclude that it's an orange, they feel clever for having done so." I remembered that, and I took it with me.'

Unfortunately, *Heavy Weather* was the first and last time Richard got to play in a Wodehouse on screen, which, given the fact he was such a consummate interpreter of his work, is a crying shame. That said, he did get to share a scene with Peter O'Toole for the first time and the result is hysterical, like two old actors having a boozy afternoon at the Garrick Club, of which, incidentally, both Richard and Peter were members. Since leaving RADA their paths hadn't crossed much professionally, and the club was where they cultivated what became quite a lively friendship. The film director, Roger Michell, remembers seeing Briers and O'Toole in action at the Garrick Club one day, and it was exactly what one would expect. 'There was a commotion,' said Michell. 'Then, all of a sudden, O'Toole was there, climbing up the marble staircase arm in arm with compatriot Richard Briers. They were hanging on to each other and laughing. Although I'm not sure who was holding on to whom.'

CHAPTER TWENTY

Briers in the Woods

By 1983, Richard had added yet another genre to his ever-broadening repertoire – pantomime. In fact, since appearing, and shaking, in front of Her Majesty the Queen and the Duke of Edinburgh in the final episode of *The Good Life* in 1978, he had appeared in two: *Babes in the Wood* at Norwich Theatre Royal, in which he played Dame Nanny Goodlife (who else?), and the same pantomime again at the Ashcroft Theatre in Croydon, in which he starred alongside Beryl Reid.

Richard enjoyed doing pantomime, to an extent. As a man who thrived on being part of a theatrical company and liked being recognised by the public, especially children, he was in the right place. After all, that's precisely why the producers had offered him roles in the first place, because people recognised him. The emoluments too, were not to be sneezed at, and despite having to spend the Christmas of 1978 holed up in a hotel over a hundred miles from his beloved Chiswick, he and the family made the most of it.

'It was actually quite fun,' says Lucy. 'Some of Dad's dresses were enormous and it was the first time I'd seen him in drag. He looked hilarious. It snowed a lot and I remember that the crew made a sledge for me and Kate, which was really kind of them. During the pantomime, Dad had to sing the song, "Spread a Little Happiness". He had the beginnings of a good voice but no confidence. It was oddly perfect for the role.'

Although Annie's memory of Richard's maiden outing as a pantomime dame is rather sketchy, there is one part of the proceedings she will never forget. 'I was standing at the back of the stalls during a performance one day, when Richard did something that made the entire audience rock forward and back as one. I can't remember what he said or did, I'm afraid, but I remember the reaction. It was absolutely astonishing. Hundreds of people rocking back and forth and laughing their heads off in unison. It was a marvellous sight and I was terribly proud of him.'

The only thing Richard didn't enjoy about pantomime was the style of acting. As a dramatic actor who specialised in light comedy, it was a far cry from what he enjoyed or what he was used to doing. Even so, Richard respected the genre immensely and seemed to thrive on the atmosphere and camaraderie that such intense productions tend to create.

'There's no hiding place in pantomime,' says Annie. 'Everybody needs to pull together as one, and that was ideal for Richard. Professionally, it was always where he was happiest.'

Dame Judi Dench, who appeared with Richard, firstly, in a television adaptation of George Bernard Shaw's *A Village Wooing*, in 1979, and then in several Shakespearean productions for Kenneth Branagh, echoes Annie's comments and says she can't think of anyone else she would rather have alongside her in a company.

'I think most people who worked with Dickie would tell you that he was the ideal company man. Very jokey – he was the master of comedy – and very easy going. He also cared for *everybody*. Actually cared for them. And it didn't matter what he was doing, he was always the same. During the making of *A Village Wooing*, which David Cunliffe directed, I had a lot of trouble remembering my lines. It's a two-hander, and for some reason I found it very, very difficult. Richard, though, was incredibly supportive. Nothing flustered him, you see. When you say that somebody was so full of integrity, it gets kind of flattened out these days, but Dickie really was. It was just a joy to be with him.'

Such was Richard's admiration for the genre of pantomime that when he was offered a second opportunity to wear outrageous dresses, trot out some innuendo and, when all's said and done, fill some coffers for his enterprise, he said yes immediately.

'It was commutable this time,' says Kate, 'which made a big difference. Dad was very much a home bird, so to be offered a run just fifteen miles from Chiswick was ideal. He definitely enjoyed doing pantomime, but he was never completely at home. As well as being exhausting, I think it was all a bit chaotic for him. He made a brilliant pantomime dame though. Had he enjoyed it more, it could have become a speciality.'

Incidentally, when Richard died in 2013, the *Eastern Daily Press*, which covers the Norwich area, paid an especially warm tribute to him. This was driven partly by the national narrative, which focused mainly on his contribution to television, but it also made reference to the myriad appearances Richard had made at the Theatre Royal, which ranged from the aforementioned *Babes in the Wood* to *The Tempest* and were made over a forty-year period. The fact that the newspaper acknowledged his regional contribution is heartening, but also serves as a pretty accurate barometer for the sheer breadth of Richard's work on the stage.

When it came to fast-moving theatre that's teetering on the verge of chaos, Richard's genre of choice was undoubtedly farce, but that genre still threw up a surprise in 1983 when he was offered a role in a new production that was against type, both personally and professionally.

The farce in question was Ray Cooney's *Run for Your Wife*, which, with a multitude of different line-ups, ran continuously in the West End from March 1983 until December 1991, making it the capital's longest-running comedy ever. The role, which was the lead character, was a cockney taxi driver called John Smith who, as well as being in his thirties, happens to be a bigamist. Richard, who was touching fifty at the time, couldn't do a cockney accent to save his life and was as devoted to his wife as it was possible to be. Even so, he accepted the role gratefully, and, not surprisingly, made a huge success of it. When the critics had their say, not one reference was made to the discrepancies regarding accent or age, and the excellent initial cast, which included Richard's old friend, Bernard Cribbins, gave the production a perfect start.

Bernard remembers clearly Richard's own take on the accent situation, but it was imparted to him at the worst possible time.

'On the opening night, literally seconds before we were due to go on, Richard turned to me and said, in that wonderfully cheerful voice of his, "Do you know, love, I must be the poshest fucking taxi driver in London!" I came so close to corpsing that night. I just couldn't get it out of my head!'

★   ★   ★

About the same time that Richard and Bernard Cribbins were due to leave the cast of *Run for Your Wife* and give way to James Bolam and Ian Ogilvy, he was contacted by Bob Larbey. He and John Esmonde had happened upon a scene that they thought would not only be the basis for a great situation comedy but would also provide a great role for Richard.

'John and Bob were walking through Clapham Common one day and they saw a football match on,' recalled Richard in 2006. 'Right in the middle was this little referee who was shouting and nagging and blowing his whistle. This is offside, that's offside. That's not right. What are you doing? He was a nightmare! When the match ended, everybody glared at him and then rushed off to have a drink, leaving this bloke saying, "Hey boys, where are you going?" All they wanted was to get him out of their sight. That was the influence behind Martin Bryce, and the genius was that they created a character with whom people could identify. Everybody could recognise a little bit of Martin Bryce in somebody they knew.'

But in order to make their new character watchable, as opposed to just annoying, the writers had to inject an extra ingredient; something they hadn't seen much of on Clapham Common. 'Bob Larbey called me up one day,' said Richard, 'and he said, you're the only actor we can think of who will give this appalling character some kind of charm! They knew I could be vulnerable and so that's what I did with Martin. I made him vulnerable.'

Kate remembers well Richard's reaction to this new character, and to the suggestion of him taking another dip into the waters of sitcom.

'He became quite enthused when he was asked to play Martin,' says Kate, 'and that was good to see, especially as *Goodbye Mr Kent*, which he'd made the year previously, had been such a flop. After that I think he started questioning whether he should ever do sitcom again, and you can understand why. Had it not worked out that would have been two flops in the space of two years, and it could have been disastrous. Agreeing to do *Ever Decreasing Circles* so soon afterwards was a big risk but, in a way, I think he thrived on that kind of pressure.'

Despite his concerns, Richard was confident that Esmonde and Larbey's new vehicle for him would capture the public's imagination; partly because, as he said, everybody knew somebody who was 'a little bit Martin Bryce'.

In a tribute to Richard's portrayal of Martin Bryce, which was published after he died, Andy Dawson from the *Daily Mirror* summed up the character perfectly: 'On the surface, he was the group leader, jollying everyone along with his never-ending programme of events, like the holiday camp entertainer from hell. But scratch that surface and there was a man who was desperately clinging on to sanity by attempting to control every situation that he found himself in. A right pain in the arse in other words!'

With Richard now safely (although probably slightly nervously) on board, the show's producer and director, Sydney Lotterby, whose CV already included shows such as *Porridge*, *Yes Minister*, *Open All Hours*, *Butterflies*, *The Liver Birds* and *Some Mothers Do 'Ave 'Em*, set about finding Martin's wife, Ann Bryce, and selected Penelope Wilton.

Unlike Felicity Kendal, Penelope Wilton had worked with Richard before on a television adaptation of, what else, but an Alan Ayckbourn: *The Norman Conquests*. Oddly enough, when

Richard had first spotted Felicity playing Annie in the stage version of *The Norman Conquests*, Penelope had been playing the part of Ruth, who is a similar sort of character. In the television adaptation, however, which was made in 1977, the part of Ruth was played by Fiona Walker, with Penelope playing Felicity's role. Yet again, a significant episode in Richard's career was all down to that man Ayckbourn.

Richard once said of Ann Bryce, 'Like many women, I think she realised she'd married a child, and she just coped with it, as many women do.'

Once Martin's wife had been cast, it was time to find his nemesis. The character of Paul Ryman, who moves in next door to Martin and Ann Bryce and slowly but surely proceeds to turn the unsuspecting Martin's world completely upside down, was the final leading role to be cast in the new sitcom, and it was by far the most difficult.

The actor who was eventually cast as the suave, Cambridge-educated salon owner with a rather complicated love life was a suggestion of Annie's: Peter Egan, who had already appeared alongside Richard on stage, in George Bernard Shaw's *Arms and the Man* at the Lyric Theatre in 1981. Peter explains that they had bonded during that run, partly courtesy of the IRA.

'We actually had two cancellations due to bomb scares during *Arms and the Man*,' remembers Peter. 'We were all standing out on Shaftesbury Avenue in full costume, me as a Hussar and Richard as a Serbian army officer. We got some very strange looks!'

One of these two cancellations happened mid-performance, while Richard and Peter were playing a scene together and, at first, they feared the exodus might have been because of their acting.

'About halfway through a very long scene featuring just the two of us, we both became aware that the auditorium was being emptied, not silently, but quite surreptitiously. Our eyeline at the time was on the same level as the royal circle and out of the corner of our eyes we could see row upon row standing up and then tiptoeing out. We knew what was going on, but after about eight rows had been cleared Richard stopped, turned to the audience that was left and said, "Come on! Surely it's not that bad?" Five minutes later we were being ushered out onto Shaftesbury Avenue to be stared at while a robot searched the auditorium for bombs!'

The reason Peter, whom, together with Paul Eddington, Richard later claimed was his favourite-ever male co-star, had been so keen to work with Richard in the first place was simple. 'It's because he made me laugh,' says Peter. 'I'd seen Richard in sitcoms and all the Ayckbourn plays during the 1960s and 1970s, and he always seemed to have a sharp vulnerability about him. Almost bitter and resentful, in a way, and I found that very human. Equally, he could also be very acerbic when he wanted to be, except that instead of that penetrating other people, it tended to rebound back on him. It was more a rhetorical judgement of the world or even himself, than a bitter judgement of other people.'

One of the first things Richard said to Peter after they first began working together was that he had given himself a nickname. 'Richard used to refer to himself as "Mr Anorak",' explains Peter. '"You, Peter, you're a tall glamorous actor," he used to say to me. "And look at me. I'm just Mr Anorak." "But you're a brilliant actor, Richard," I'd say. "Yes, but I'll always be an anorak."'

While rehearsing *Arms and the Man*, Richard would sit in on every scene, regardless of whether he was involved. What's more, he would also show his appreciation whenever things went according to plan.

'I used to love the fact that he sat in on the other scenes,' says Peter. 'To have somebody of his stature watching you rehearse is obviously an honour, but to make them laugh is really something. If Richard saw that you were working towards trying to make something funny, he always fed into that and encouraged you. That's very rare with somebody who is known for comedy, because comedy is the hardest of all the disciplines and is the one people protect most fiercely. Drama is universal, but comedy is deeply personal. He was flattering, generous and liked other people to get laughs. That was just a great gift and me doing *Arms and the Man* with him was a great introduction.'

When Peter was offered the role of Paul Ryman in *Ever Decreasing Circles* he accepted it immediately, although he had no idea what it was about.

'I'd been in New York for three months and one day I got a call from my agent. I'd been talking to him for some time about me doing a comedy and he called and said that I'd been offered one. "Well, send over the scripts and I'll have a look," I said. "There isn't time," he replied. "They start filming in two weeks."'

Peter was due to leave New York in a few days' time, which meant the scripts would have been arriving just as he was setting off back to England. 'There was obviously no internet back then and I couldn't get access to a fax. I'd never usually accept something sight unseen, but I was interested. "Who's in it?" I asked my agent. "Richard Briers and Penelope Wilton," he replied. The moment he'd finished saying Penelope Wilton, I said, "Yes, I'll do it." If those two were involved I knew it must be good, and I was right. I was also dying to work with Dickie again, so by the time I arrived back in England it was all systems go.'

Peter soon found out that they had endured an awful lot of trouble casting the part of Paul, mainly because the character, in its early stages at least, didn't quite ring true. 'On the page, Paul was a poncey, superior kind of character, and I didn't feel that would work. Somebody that snobbish would never move into a place like The Close, with Martin, Ann, Howard and Hilda. It was far too provincial and suburban.'

What brought the character of Paul down to earth a little and made his presence more believable was laughter, and it was all thanks to his co-star. 'Richard made me laugh so much that I decided to invest my appreciation of his humour into Paul,' says Peter. 'On paper he's quite a humorous individual, so for the sake of the character, which needed softening, and of the director, who, had the character stayed the same, would have had to cope with me corpsing all the time, Paul became a giggler with a smile and a sunny disposition. I think I humanised him.'

The final and most elusive component of Esmonde and Larbey's new sitcom was the title. 'Titles are always terribly difficult,' said Sydney Lotterby. 'And I think we tried something like thirty-nine in all. "E=mc^2" was one. I can't tell you the trouble we had.'

Other titles that were considered for the show (none of which are especially inspiring) include 'May I Have a Seconder?', 'He Does Try', 'Yours in Haste', 'The Close Friend', 'The Pillar of Society', 'Close Connections', 'Martin's Way', 'One Man's Close' and 'For the Love of Martin'. In the end, and after much deliberation, the writers settled on the cryptic *Ever Decreasing Circles*, an astute reference to Martin's tendency to disappear into his own obsessive compulsive little world.

Like *The Good Life*, *Ever Decreasing Circles* was a slow starter and attracted an average audience of about five million during the first series. Today, that would mean a top-three position in the overall television ratings alongside the likes of *Coronation Street*, *Emmerdale* and *EastEnders*, but on 29 January 1984, when the first episode went to air, it was disappointing. Even so, the powers-that-be once again saw enough potential in their fledgling sitcom to give it another go, but instead of broadcasting the second series on its own, which was the norm, they decided to repeat the first series in its entirety directly beforehand. This turned out to be a masterstroke on the scheduler's behalf as the first series got seven million viewers this time around, and the second series over nine million.

Unlike *The Good Life*, which took more than an episode to set its stall out and a series or two to bed in, *Ever Decreasing Circles* does the first part in its opening three scenes, culminating in what must be one of the most brilliant lines ever written or delivered in the opening of a sitcom, and one that, just as importantly, tells the viewer all they need to know about the main character.

After dropping off the junior football team that Martin manages, which, unbeknownst to him, is quite obviously made up of children who would rather not be there and is undoubtedly the worst team in the league – 'Thirteen – one was the final score, although the score flattered them' – Martin makes his way to the kitchen, but only after marching on the doormat while giving his wife Ann a blow-by-blow account of his latest defeat, before turning his attentions to the telephone receiver, which must always be placed so the lead is on the left.

As soon as Martin enters the kitchen, Ann attempts to introduce him to Paul, their new next-door neighbour. Martin, however, is in full-on 'doing mode' and without even drawing breath or acknowledging his wife or their new neighbour, he proceeds to carry on about his business while vocalising every thought and opinion that comes into his turbulent and often tortured head.

'Word of advice for your wife, Paul,' says Martin, before he's even set eyes on his new neighbour, let alone shaken his hand. 'Put her on compound rubber and the moment she starts to vibrate, you won't have any trouble.'

The fact that Martin assumes that Paul is, A) married, and B), knows he's referring to the washing machine, is obviously part of the joke, but, like the doormat and the telephone receiver, it's also symptomatic of the character, which again enables us to get a grip on things and buy into the situation. Martin Bryce assumes that everyone thinks along his lines, and when he realises that they don't, he becomes incredibly frustrated. Finally, the gag gives birth to one of the most ingenious and most enjoyable nuances of Martin Bryce's character – humanising inanimate objects. Together with Howard Hughes, these objects are his only real friends; partly because they are often integral to what he's doing, but mainly because they don't answer back.

The usual subjects are either application forms for one of his multitude of societies or grub screws; both of which he addresses like a dog owner would an obedient and well-loved Labrador.

'You sit over there,' he says tenderly while carefully moving a pile of forms. 'You'll be much happier.'

The grub screw, which he accuses of doing a runner, is treated like a five-year-old boy who is late for his tea. 'Come along, young man,' he says after finally tracking down the errant screw. 'Back to where you belong.' Even irony becomes humanised in the Bryce household. 'Let's put Mr Sarcasm back in his box, shall we, Ann?'

It was obviously the writers' intention to cram as much of Martin's character as possible into the opening few scenes, and they do it to perfection. Penelope Wilton and Peter Egan, too, are only given lines that are very typical of their characters, and so, with at least twenty minutes remaining of the opening episode, all that's left to do before Martin gives himself a nervous breakdown is introduce the sitcom's two supporting characters, the often correspondingly attired fusspots, Howard and Hilda.

Ever since that first episode of *Ever Decreasing Circles* was shown over thirty-four years ago, comparisons have been made between it, *The Good Life* and the characters therein, and Richard was quizzed about this on a regular basis.

When asked about the difference between Tom and Martin he made the point that, despite Tom Good being well educated and evidently quite worldly-wise, you never tended to consider what his background might have been or what he did prior to becoming a draughtsman. 'It just never really entered your head,' said Richard. 'With Martin, on the other hand, it's the opposite, and while he's rushing around organising other people's lives or driving all the way to Brighton to buy a crochet hook for an old woman he insists on visiting but who doesn't really want one, all sorts of things pop into your head. First of all, you have to ask yourself how it all happened. How he became so complicated. A man who, underneath it all, happens to be charitable, kind, and really quite sensitive. Where on earth did it all come from?'

Martin Bryce is a conundrum that would have sent a room full of psychiatrists into a spin; something that Esmonde and Larbey latched onto when they wrote an episode for the second series entitled 'Psychiatrist', which is dedicated to solving that very same conundrum. Martin doesn't realise what's going on until shortly before the episode ends, by which time he has tried to persuade the therapist, who, like many of his potential tormentors, is a mate of Paul's, that it is Ann who is in need of therapy. The list she reels off when asked by the psychiatrist what most annoys her husband is wonderfully eclectic and is delivered with comic aplomb by Penelope Wilton: 'Enemies, friends, molehills, clocks, trousers, skirting boards, committee meetings, no committee meetings, the council, NATO, Magnus Magnusson, tin openers. I'm only just scratching the surface,' she says. And she means it. By the end of the episode the psychiatrist, Ann, Paul and even the ever-loyal Howard and Hilda are convinced that Martin is going mad, whereas Martin, of course, is convinced that everyone else is.

But it wasn't just Martin's childhood that used to take the viewer out of the here and now and make them think retrospectively about the character. His marriage did the same. That's something else that didn't happen much in *The Good Life*. 'Tom and Barbara were so well-matched that you never really questioned where or why they got married,' remarked Richard. 'Well, perhaps you did while Tom was being selfish or conceited, which was often, but you could always understand the initial attraction. Also, the fact that they were so obviously in love with each other prevented you from questioning their union any further.'

Martin and Ann, on the other hand, are about as well-suited as Ozzy Osbourne and Dame Vera Lynn, and this might make one believe that there must have been something specific – an event, perhaps – that had melded them together. After all, why else would somebody as beautiful and as intelligent as Ann end up marrying somebody like Martin? This is proven to be the case when, several times throughout the series, cryptic references are made to a night they shared in the unromantic-sounding town of Kidderminster, which usually results in the lights being switched off a few minutes earlier than usual. 'Shall I take my pyjama top off, Ann?' Martin asks in one episode. 'Yes, why not?' she replies.

Esmonde and Larbey, who had always tended to work in the present moment, are going off track slightly here, but, as with their other ingenious comedic nuances, it never dominates proceedings and is something viewers merely consider while they are watching the show. Although they would end up talking about it afterwards. 'How on earth did Martin and Ann ever get together? He's an absolute nightmare! Imagine what he was like as a child.'

Penelope Wilton, who, like Peter Egan, remained close to Richard for the rest of his life, used to receive dozens of letters every week asking her why she tolerated, 'that horrid little man'.

But the real crux of *Ever Decreasing Circles*, apart from Martin imposing his will on his neighbours while trying to suppress the complete mental collapse that continually froths away under the surface of his psyche, is his ongoing relationship with Paul. Paul drives Martin absolutely round the bend and, as well as featuring prominently in all twenty-seven episodes, this is the main subject of at least ten. The dilemma is best represented in an episode entitled 'The Cricket Match', from the start of the second series.

Martin, who has been captain of the local cricket team since time began, finds out that Paul used to play for Cambridge and so is forced to consider him for the team. At first, Martin refuses to budge, claiming that he already has eleven men at his disposal, but when one of them breaks a finger while practising with who else but Paul, he's forced to give way. As Martin feared, Paul goes on to win the match almost singlehandedly by scoring the majority of the runs and taking most of the wickets. Martin is demoralised, but it doesn't stop there. After the match his opposing captain accuses Martin of unfair play for allowing a Cambridge Blue on to his team. 'Anybody who's that keen on winning and picks somebody of that class, is nothing but a cheat,' says the opposing 'Skip'.

Ironically, Peter Egan couldn't play cricket to save his life. 'I think I'd only played the game a couple of times and I was dreadful.'

When Peter Egan came clean about his shortcomings at the crease it left the director with a dilemma. 'We were all left scratching our heads,' said Richard. 'Then somebody, I forget who, suggested that they film Peter bowling and playing a few shots. Then, slow everything down and play some dramatic music over it. By slowing it down you can't tell how bad he is, you see. I have to say it looked wonderful. They actually managed to make my mate Peter Egan look like a cricket hero – which he certainly wasn't!'

For Martin Bryce, however, having Paul in his team was his worst nightmare. 'It was like cutting him through with a knife,' said John Esmonde. 'He, the captain. He, the man who arranged all the teas. He, the man who varnished the stumps. It was the end of his world!'

At the end of the match, in an effort to placate her demoralised husband, Ann suggests he goes next door to the bar. 'Get in there, get on the piano, and we'll have a sing-song,' she says encouragingly. 'We've had some terrific evenings with you on that piano.' 'Yes, I suppose I could do that,' says Martin, seeing some light at the end of the tunnel. 'Yes, you could,' agrees Ann. 'Come on!' As she leads Martin off towards the bar you hear the sound of a piano being played. A sing-song then ensues, but even before a single word is sung you know exactly who's tinkling the ivories. 'Yes, it is him,' says Ann, after peering around the door.

What makes the relationship between Martin and Paul so very interesting is that despite his athleticism, his good looks, his popularity and his success, Paul doesn't have Ann. Martin does. Esmonde and Larbey tease us occasionally, intimating that one day it could happen, but we know it never will. The two writers had tried writing the endgame of this storyline in one of the early scripts, but it was shelved by the director. Ann may become distracted by her neighbour occasionally, just as Martin becomes distracted by committees and by pieces of plywood, but when all's said and done both are devoted and would never stray. Perhaps this gives rise to some of Paul's mischievous behaviour?

After all, if he can't win the war, he can at least win a couple of battles. Ultimately, though, Martin Bryce is the real victor. The fact that he never realises it is Esmonde and Larbey's final frustration in this, their most analysed and talked-about situation comedy.

The writer and comedian Ricky Gervais is a huge fan of *Ever Decreasing Circles* and over the years has tried doggedly to get the show repeated again on its original channel. In 2013, shortly after Richard's death, he even put up one of his own creations as a bargaining tool. 'Dear BBC,' he tweeted. 'I'll let you repeat *The Office* for free if you repeat *Ever Decreasing Circles* this year.' It was a serious proposal, but hasn't been taken up.

One of the first people to recognise the influence *Ever Decreasing Circles* had on Ricky Gervais's work was Richard himself. 'Martin was like a mild David Brent,' he told the *Guardian*. 'We all knew an irritating little man who wanted to manage everything. It was a very recognisable type. But we were a cosy, escapist show. Gervais's stuff is hysterically funny but almost too close for comfort.'

'*Ever Decreasing Circles* is such a lost treasure,' says Ricky. 'One of the most underrated comedies of all time, in my opinion. It's such a gentle show, but also very sweet and very grown up. It was a big influence on me. Take Martin Bryce. OK, he was a bit of a buffoon. A bit of a nerd. The thing is, he had the best life imaginable. He had his perfect life. He was the kid in the playground who organises things and who everyone wants to play with. And then Paul moved in next door. That's pure drama. If the cat sits on the mat, that's boring. But if the cat sits on the dog's mat, we've got a bit of drama. We've got a situation.

'What I really like about the relationship between Ann and

he cast of *The Good Life* with the show's director John Howard Davies (top right), Lucy (bottom ft) and Kate (bottom right).

)ear BBC, I'll let you repeat *The Office* for free if you repeat *Ever Decreasing Circles*.' Unfortunately .icky Gervais's proposal fell on deaf ears. *(© BBC Photo Library)*

Richard as Nanny Goodlife with Kate and Lucy before a performance of *Babes in the Wood* at the Theatre Royal, Norwich, 1978.

'What, Ibsen? Tell him yes!' With Nerys Hughes in *The Wild Duck*. Although the director Michael Blakemore had never met Richard before he knew he'd be perfect for the role of Håkon.

Richard and Annie with a still intact Fred.

think you've got this for making people laugh.' Receiving his OBE in 1989.

(above) Meeting the Queen Mother alongside his friend and occasional co-star, Sir Michael Hordern.

(right) 'I remember when he asked me to play King Lear because I went rather pale.' Playing Lear was a huge risk for Richard.

With Kenneth Branagh, Michael Keaton and Ben Elton on the set of *Much Ado About Nothing*. One of the happiest (and sweariest) film sets Richard ever set foot on.

With Denzel Washington and Sean Leonard on the set of *Much Ado About Nothing*.

Blink and you'll miss him. With Kevin Whately and John Thaw in *Inspector Morse*. Richard based some of his character's mannerisms on a real-life serial killer.

(above) Rehearsing Eugène Ionesco's
The Chairs with Geraldine McEwan.
Richard's first and only appearance on
Broadway earned him a Tony Award
nomination, not to mention adulation
from Bill Murray.

(right) With Lucy outside the Golden
Theatre on Broadway clutching a copy
of his calling card, the *Daily Telegraph*.

ith the cast of *Monarch of the Glen*.

nnie and Richard in Simon Paisley Day's play, *Spike*. The theatre-going public just couldn't get to
ips with Richard playing, as he put it, 'a complete and utter bastard'.

Collecting his CBE in June 2003, accompanied by grandchildren Harry and Rachael.

His favourite role. Richard adored being a grandfather.

Richard and Annie in their garden. All roads led to Chiswick for Richard, especially as he got older

Paul is that Ann would never, ever go there. Martin had nothing to worry about and that's why it was funny. If she really had flirted with him, that wouldn't have been funny. That would have been horrible! Regardless of whether they were suitable or not, the strength of Martin and Ann's marriage was integral to the comedy as it allowed it to take place. That setup and the sweetness of them all was remarkable, *and* it was funny! Let's not forget that. It was *so* funny. Howard and Hilda, for a start. The reason they were Martin's two favourite people was because they indulged him. I remember in one episode there was Howard, Hilda, Martin, Ann and Paul, and out of the blue Martin says, "What's everyone's favourite jam?" As he goes around the table, Paul and Ann start rolling their eyes at each other, and when he's finished they think that's that. But it isn't. "So," he says, "what's everyone's second favourite jam?" On paper that's not funny but because of the situation, and the performances, it's just incredible.

'You always have a family in sitcom,' continues Ricky. 'And you always have an outside threat. Sometimes they're literal, sometimes they're subtle, and sometimes they're metaphorical. Take *Bilko*, for instance. The soldiers were thrown together so they were a family, and the outside threat was the Colonel. In *The Office*, which was my thing, the family were the people David Brent had working for him, and the threat was the fact that he didn't have control over the documentary team. In *Ever Decreasing Circles*, the family was the residents of the close, with Martin as their self-appointed leader, and the outside threat was Paul. The thing is, Paul never did what Martin always feared he was going to do, which was try and take over. He still ruined it for him by trying to be helpful, but Martin didn't want that either. He didn't want Paul saving the day, just as he didn't want Paul running the committees. He'd rather lose at cricket than have Paul get the winning runs. But Paul – again, played beautifully by Peter Egan – wasn't a nasty person. He was a bit mischievous, but he wasn't nasty. There was nothing obvious or predictable about that show. It was a work of genius.'

In 2006, Ricky found an opportunity to work with Richard on his hit TV show, *Extras*, and he lived up to every expectation. 'What's special about Richard and the way he played his characters is humanity. He was obviously a great actor. Everybody knows that. He may have been particularly famous for playing comic roles, but at the end of the day an actor's an actor, and there's lots of those. What's rare is that whatever Richard did he brought humanity to it and you can't write that. OK, some of it's probably luck. He had a nice face, and he moved well, and he was excitable, and he had a nice voice. But he always brought a humanity to his roles because he was made of it. He was made of kindness. You trusted Richard Briers even though you didn't know him. I think people would be devastated if they found out that Richard wasn't a nice person in real life. Luckily, he was, which I think we all knew, but that just reinforced his power as an actor. Whenever Richard Briers came on the screen you only ever had good feelings. It's a kind of alchemy, really. Something you can't put your finger on. A few people have got it, but very few. He also transcended age, so he was either your dad, your grandad, your brother or, if you were ancient and on the verge of death, your son. When I first met him on the episode of *Extras* he was becoming frail. He had to sit down between takes – luckily there weren't many because he nailed it – and every time he stood up again he had a smile on his face and he gave it his all. He was so professional. The reason I asked him to do *Extras* was because I wanted him to play against type – against everything I've just mentioned. The joke being that the main players, who disturb a eulogy Richard's delivering at the BAFTA Awards, become so infuriating that they actually make Richard Briers lose his temper, which is impossible, isn't it? Or, should I say, wasn't it? I can't imagine Richard Briers getting up grumpy, being unkind to anyone or being unnecessarily fussy or having an ego. His face was literally made of warmth. I loved him.'

CHAPTER TWENTY-ONE

Renaissance Man

One of the biggest dilemmas Richard faced during the early to mid 1980s was the prospect of his daughter Lucy becoming an actor. Kate, who is four years older than Lucy, had already worked in stage management (she trained at LAMDA followed by nearly six years in rep and the West End) but, much to Richard's relief, she had decided it wasn't for her. 'I really enjoyed my time working in stage management, but eventually decided it wasn't for me,' says Kate, who is now a primary-school teacher. 'For a start, as soon as people hear the surname, they immediately think, "You're only here because you have a famous parent." Sometimes that's obviously the case, although it never was with me. The only way you can get over that is by being better than everyone else. It can be really tough.'

When it came to Lucy wanting to become an actor, Richard had a real fight on his hands. Although he didn't do himself any favours.

'Dad *really* didn't want me to be an actor,' says Lucy, 'yet when I was in my teens he would take me into work with him often. I would sit in the wings watching him on stage. It's impossible not to be influenced by that environment and so what he thought he was doing I have absolutely no idea!'

The reason Richard was so against his two daughters entering the profession was twofold: first, the precarious nature of the business enflamed his fear of them being poor, a predicament he was determined his daughters shouldn't suffer; and second, it was even harder for women, especially as actors, to succeed in the industry as it was men; not only harder in terms of the amount of parts that were on offer but also because you were often expected to look a certain way.

'I think Dad certainly had different aspirations for Kate and me, but he never really vocalised them. The idea of me becoming an actor or Kate becoming a stage manager must have been incredibly frustrating for him, but instead of trying to put me off he decided instead to put me through my paces.'

What Lucy means by that is that if she was going to become an actor, Richard was going to be nothing but honest about how he thought she was faring and, although he would support her by watching her performances, he would not be dishing out praise unconditionally. She was going to have to earn it, just as he had, and he would be her biggest critic.

'People are often shocked by this but when I was in my teens Dad used to come and watch me in school plays or in plays by the National Youth Theatre and afterwards when I came out he'd just look at me, shake his head and say, "No. You're not good enough. Sorry, but you're not good enough to do this professionally." Some people react by saying, "Isn't that cruel?" but no it's not, and I understood why he was doing it; he was testing my convictions which only ever made them stronger.'

Lucy believes that Richard was simply trying to test how much she wanted to become a professional actor, primarily because he feared that she had been seduced by the fact that he was famous. 'I think he knew that if it genuinely was what I wanted to do then I'd turn around and say, "I don't care what you think, I'm going to do this," and that's exactly what happened. It was a classic case of tough love, I suppose. My God, he was frank though. I'd walk into the bar after giving it my all for two hours and there would be my father just shaking his head and looking disappointed. That's either going to make you or break you, but every time he did it I just said to myself, fuck you Dad, I'm doing this.'

The straw that finally broke the camel's back with regards to Lucy winning Richard's approval happened when she won a place at the Bristol Old Vic Theatre School, which is one of the most prestigious in the country.

'From that moment on he was totally brilliant,' remembers Lucy. 'His attitude changed. It was the beginning of another layer to our relationship. Not only father to daughter but actor to actor. The first example was when he came to see me playing Helena in *A Midsummer Night's Dream* for the National Youth Theatre. When I went to meet him in the bar, I thought, *Well, if he doesn't like this I don't know what I'm going to bloody well do*. In fact, had he said no this time I think I might have barred him from attending any of my performances! Fortunately, when I made it into the bar he was standing there with a bottle of my favourite beer in his hand and he just handed it to me, smiled and said, "That was fucking brilliant, love!" I can't tell you how relieved I was, but also incredibly proud.'

Despite Richard eventually accepting his daughter's decision, there was an occasion later on when his long-held belief that financial security should be the ultimate ambition for an actor usurped his newfound approval, and resulted in, initially, quite a big argument and some swearing at each other, followed by a cracked door frame.

'After I graduated from Bristol Old Vic I did rep for a while at Worcester and Salisbury,' explains Lucy. 'Then, I started doing sitcoms for the BBC. I was a regular in a Carla Lane sitcom called *Screaming*, alongside Penny Wilton, Gwen Taylor and Jill Baker, and then I started getting guest parts in things like *Red Dwarf* and *The Brittas Empire*. It sounds strange, but I felt like I was being groomed in a way – Richard Briers's daughter specialising in sitcoms? What else! – and so after a while I made the conscious decision to move away from television and concentrate on stage work.'

Lucy's first move in turning away from the one-eyed goggle-box was to turn down a well-paid role in yet another situation comedy in favour of a poorly paid role in a play in Birmingham.

'When I told Dad he absolutely hit the roof,' says Lucy, 'and we ended up having the mother of all arguments. In his mind you only ever turned down television if you could afford to, which I obviously couldn't. But the fact was, I was simply becoming a less funny, less successful female version of him and the prospect of carrying on that role filled me with dread. I just had to break away. I'm afraid I became so angry that I got up, stormed out of the house and slammed the front door so hard that I broke the frame! Dad, not surprisingly, sent me an invoice for the repair, which I duly paid.'

Lucy's dilemma with regards to being compared to her father wasn't something Richard had ever had to endure, and it's probably fair to say that his judgement on the matter was clouded slightly by his long-held obsession with solvency. Indeed, his experiences with Terry-Thomas had all been quite positive in that respect, and free from comparisons or emotional ties.

'After time, Dad began to understand my decision,' says Lucy, 'and, as importantly, I think he respected it. Subsequently, he and Mum came to see everything I was in, regardless of where it was, and would often traipse the length and breadth of the United Kingdom.'

The story of Lucy's attempts to find her way as an actor, and of Richard finally coming to terms with her endeavours, reached its conclusion at the Sheffield Crucible Theatre in 2004. Lucy was appearing there in a play called *Cloud 9* by Caryl Churchill, and, as per usual, her mother and father had made the journey to see her.

'They'd asked to come to a matinee performance, as by that point Dad didn't like travelling after dark. "I'm too old for that, love!" he used to say. After the show we went out for something to eat and just after the meal he quietly said to me, "I'm going to pass the baton on now, love. It's over to you." It was symbolic, of course, but bearing in mind who he was and what he'd achieved, it was an incredible gesture. It's one of the greatest gifts my dad ever gave me.'

In July 1986, shortly after he had completed filming series three of *Ever Decreasing Circles*, Richard travelled to Chichester where he was due to play Lord Foppington as part of that year's Chichester Festival in Sir John Vanbrugh's Restoration comedy, *The Relapse*. The previous year, he had started appearing in another sitcom, his first for ITV, entitled *All in Good Faith*. Written by John Kane, the man behind *Terry and June*, it tells the story of a middle-aged vicar who decides to swap his cosy affluent Oxfordshire parish for an urban parish in the Midlands, resulting in a slight culture shock for him and his nicely spoken, ever-so-caring family. You can probably guess the rest. The public reaction to the sitcom, which in the end managed to spawn eighteen episodes, was almost a metaphor for the direction in which his career was going.

Buoyed by the success of *Ever Decreasing Circles*, Richard had said yes to *All in Good Faith* thinking he was on a roll, but although the telephone was still ringing, everything he was being offered, on television at least, was much of a muchness. '*Ever Decreasing Circles* was a one-off,' says Kate, 'whereas *All in Good Faith* was quite typical of those 1980s Saturday-night sitcoms that were very twee, very middle class and safe. No disrespect to *All in Good Faith*, but Dad was better than that.' Indeed he was, and Richard knew that something had to change. It wasn't a desperate situation, not by any means, but the longer he went without being challenged as an actor, the less enthused he became about a profession to which he had been addicted for well over three decades, and that wasn't right. Something or somebody had to remind Richard Briers exactly why he had wanted to become an actor in the first place, just as Brian Murphy had done all those years before. The problem he faced was that, despite being a risk taker, those he had taken so far had always come to him. The telephone would ring, a script would arrive and he would either say yes or no. He didn't have the time to go looking for a new challenge. Unfortunately, it would have to find him.

Appearing at the Chichester Festival in a Restoration comedy was a change from the norm as opposed to a change of direction. Nevertheless, Richard was looking forward to being part of a large company again; a company that included his old friend

Ronnie Stevens, who played Tommy Cooper in *Ever Decreasing Circles*, Jan Ravens, Harold Innocent and John Sessions.

About four years earlier Lucy had been to see Julian Mitchell's play, *Another Country*, at the Queen's Theatre; a show she would eventually see no fewer than seven times. During its run, which lasted over two years, *Another Country* featured all manner of soon-to-be-big names, including Rupert Everett, Daniel Day-Lewis, Miles Richardson and Colin Firth. But the actor who had made the biggest impression on Lucy during her many trips to the Queen's was a twenty-two-year-old named Kenneth Branagh, who ended up winning the Best Newcomer Award for his performance in *Another Country* at the 1982 Society of West End Theatre Awards.

'After seeing Ken in *Another Country*,' says Lucy, 'in which he was absolutely amazing, I started going to see him in everything he did, including a one-man show at the Way Upstream Theatre. The day I saw it there were six people in the audience and afterwards he took us all out for a drink!'

After getting wind of his daughter's admiration for the Belfast-born actor, Richard decided to take her to see Kenneth Branagh in the RSC's production of *Henry V*. 'Dad had never met Ken, but he was so impressed by his performance that after the show he said, "Let's go around and say hello." God, I was so nervous! Ken actually recognised me from the one-man show; he has an incredible memory for names and faces. He was thrilled to meet Dad.'

With lots of mutual admiration flying around the dressing room regarding that evening's performance and shows like *The Good Life*, Richard and Ken chatted away merrily for about twenty minutes and seemed to get on like a house on fire. 'That would have been in 1984,' says Lucy, 'and although they struck up a friendship they didn't see each other again for about two years.'

John Sessions, who was playing Foppington's younger brother, Tom, in *The Relapse*, had been at RADA with Kenneth Branagh and during the run he called his old friend and asked if he would like a ticket. 'My good mate Mr Branagh came down to see me mince around in my Restoration garb,' said Sessions, 'and ended up being amazed by Dickie. He thought, this man really hasn't had his potential stretched at all.'

This time it was Kenneth Branagh's turn to visit Richard in his dressing room, and once the 'Branagh and Briers Mutual Appreciation Society' had reconvened, the young actor-director started talking about a project that he and his friend David Parfitt were working on.

'David Parfitt and Ken were about to form the Renaissance Theatre Company,' says Lucy, 'and their first production, which was due to take place just after Chichester at the tiny Lyric Studio in Hammersmith, was going to be *Romeo and Juliet* starring Ken and Samantha Bond.'

The story goes that Kenneth Branagh offered Richard a role with the Renaissance Theatre in the dressing room at Chichester, but that's not the case. 'All he did there was invite Dad to come and see *Romeo and Juliet*,' explains Lucy. 'And Dad obviously accepted.'

The only person who could say for sure whether he already had any plans for Richard in the dressing room at Chichester is Branagh himself, but by the time Richard arrived at the Lyric Studio a month later to see Renaissance's maiden outing, the aspiring actor, producer and director had more than just an idea as to what he wanted Richard to do: he had a role. Branagh says, 'I knew Richard had toured with Prospect Theatre as Richard III, and drew the conclusion that he had classical aspirations in performance. But mostly I just thought that he would have that combination of gravitas and humour that would be great to see in Malvolio. He was surprised to be asked. Frankly, I was surprised to have had the gumption to ask him. His reaction? Perplexed, and rather worried, but I sensed he was also excited.' Despite this, Richard's answer was immediate.

'After the show,' says Lucy, 'which was absolutely wonderful, Mum, Dad and me were waiting in the bar to say hi to Ken. When Ken arrived he immediately took Dad to one side and offered him the role of Malvolio in *Twelfth Night*. Dad said yes without even taking a breath.'

Renaissance's production of *Twelfth Night* wasn't due to take place until the end of 1987, so Richard, Kenneth and the new company he had helped to form had plenty of time to get to know each other. This was the fruit of Richard's labours: being able to take a low-paid stage role without having to worry about money – which he did. Frequently. Nobody recognised this more than Kenneth Branagh.

'A challenge Dickie felt he had when I first met him was that people saw him as one particular thing – a sitcom actor. Although he loved doing it, he definitely had ambitions to do other things. I was twenty-six years old when I asked him to come and be in our production, and I had five years of a career to show him that it was worth getting involved. But he did it. This was a significant risk for Dickie and he certainly didn't need to do it. There was no money. It was un-glamorous, unprofitable, and risky in terms of his reputation. But as I said, you could tell he was hungry to do something that challenged him as an actor. Something where he could laugh, cry, shout or be angry or funny. He took the opportunity with both hands.'

The film composer, Patrick Doyle, who is a long-time collaborator of Kenneth Branagh's, co-wrote the music for *Twelfth Night* with none other than Paul McCartney, who Branagh had approached personally about collaborating with Doyle. Patrick remembers being amazed at how well Richard adapted to playing the Bard in a small theatre. 'I had the great joy of working every night on stage as part of the band for *Twelfth Night*,' says Patrick. 'Towards the end of the play, Malvolio had to appear from this hole he'd been hiding in at the side of the stage, and one night, about a second before he came on, Richard just looked at me and rolled his eyes, as if to say, "Here we are again, eh love? Not long now. We'll soon be home." The audience couldn't see him at the time, but they could certainly see me. I was in absolute hysterics! He had that effect on me, unfortunately. He creased me up.'

Patrick believes that the reason Richard fitted in so well at Renaissance was his lack of ego. 'Richard Briers didn't have a starry bone in his body,' claims Patrick. 'Not one. And for all his modesty and his self-deprecation, he knew exactly what he was capable of as an actor. His performance in *Twelfth Night* was just extraordinary.'

One of the things that made this transition possible was the relationship Richard had struck up with his new director. 'We got on well,' remembers Ken. 'He had an almost permanent twinkle as if he was on the edge of a laugh at all times. He made you take things less solemnly, though he was perfectly serious in his approach. I loved his description of himself as "an emotional comedian". He was quick-witted but also clownishly funny with his body and voice. He could time a laugh conversationally, but also access deep silliness which was very infectious. He could also be waspish and sharp when tired, and it was altogether a compelling mixture. He was always kind.'

Like Michael Blakemore with *The Wild Duck*, Kenneth Branagh really went to town on juxtaposing the comedic elements of *Twelfth Night* with the tragic, and to equally great effect. Lucy believes this was down to three members of the company: the director, the set designer and the leading actor. 'Ken and his designer created a very stark set for this production,' remembers Lucy, 'which gave the whole thing an incredibly dark feel. The comedy was still hilarious, but at the end of the play when the mood turns and Malvolio suddenly explodes, that bleakness really helped to highlight the tragedy. The effect it had on the audience was extraordinary. You were left with a sense of deep sadness.'

Richard Briers made many stage appearances during his career – at least a hundred – but the one for which he is best remembered is undoubtedly this one. Indeed, in conversation about Richard, many of his friends and colleagues refer to 'his Malvolio' somewhere along the way. Richard's reviews were like nothing he had ever received before, with many of the critics describing his performance as 'a revelation'. One of those critics was Gerard Werson from the *Stage*, who, after the revelation bit, claimed that Richard's Malvolio was, 'making us see through his consummate timing and ardent seriousness to the deadly centre of this sublime comedy. This is a beautifully played and directed performance that never shades into caricature.' Although complimentary, it was his new boss, Kenneth Branagh, who made the most accurate and succinct summation. He said, 'His humanity and his comic brilliance came together as Malvolio and it was an illuminating performance of a great role, in a great play, by a great actor. He found great pathos without cheap manipulation. He was hysterical in the great comic set pieces because he was so real. And his constant reiteration and emphasis on the question "why?" in Malvolio's last great speech railing at his mistreatment was heartfelt, tragic and profound. It was a pleasure to see Richard experiencing that particular kind of success; it was a great compliment to his nationwide fame as a much loved household name.'

After lulling Richard into a false sense of security by asking him to play the relatively small part of Bardolph in his 1989 star-laden and multi-award-winning film adaptation of Shakespeare's *Henry V*, Branagh approached Richard about playing what is widely considered to be the most demanding role for a senior actor, namely, King Lear.

'I remember when he asked me because I went rather pale,' said Richard. '"Now come on, Ken," I said. "I know I was terrific as Malvolio, but now you're talking about the big ones!" Fortunately, Ken was wonderful. He's a very hands-on director, who'll get you in a room, talk to you, and get the best out of you. To get me, a middle-class boy from the suburbs, to open up this enormous emotional power you need to play Lear seemed impossible at first, but he did it. We did it. It was the complete opposite to sitcom.'

Kenneth Branagh remembers Richard's initial reaction to playing Lear well. 'Richard had to take a few deep breaths before agreeing to the world tour of *King Lear*, but he had a really strong capacity for creative risk, and was at a point in his life where a new adventure for he and Annie was something intriguing. The biggest challenge was leaving Fred, the dog, behind.' Once Richard had said yes, he and Branagh began discussing how he might approach the role. 'We talked a lot about other performances of King Lear. He was especially fond of Donald Wolfit and, of course, in every role he imagined how his great hero Henry Irving might have approached it.'

For a man who enjoyed taking risks, the issue for Richard was never going to be whether he was good enough to play King Lear. It was going to be whether he could *afford* to play King Lear. Even the fact that he would be playing him all over the world – 102 performances in thirty countries, no less, and over six long months – paled into insignificance compared to the prospect of playing him with a diminishing bank account, especially as he wouldn't be able to supplement it by doing voice-overs. Not on tour. The only way it was going to happen was if he was offered a well-paid job beforehand, so he wouldn't have to worry. Strangely enough, it was the very genre that had driven him into classical theatre in the first place that ultimately allowed him to carry on with it. That, and a popular brand of coffee.

'Although *Ever Decreasing Circles* had finished a year previously, it was being repeated all the time,' explained Richard. 'And, just when I was beginning to give up hope about Lear, Penny Wilton and I were offered the coffee bean commercial. You know, the one where you shake your hand and flash your beans? That paid for the entire year – income tax, corporation tax, VAT, the lot.'

As opposed to people being shocked at the prospect of

Richard 'cuddly' Briers playing King Lear, most were simply interested. Curious, even. 'I think everybody knew that Dad was more than just a sitcom actor,' explains Kate. 'They just needed reminding occasionally. In fact, they weren't the only ones. *He* needed reminding occasionally.'

Kenneth Branagh was in no doubt that Richard had what it took to play King Lear. 'His range was derived from being a truthful actor, and having the ability to imagine and embody great emotion. Because of television characters that focused on him in suburbia, he was sometimes seen as someone whose world view was quite enclosed. Not so with Richard. He was passionate and imaginative, and it always provided a delightful surprise when he became the so-called mouse that roared,' says Ken.

But as far removed as *King Lear* was from things like situation comedy, coffee adverts and guest appearances on *Morecambe and Wise*, it was still considered to be mainstream. What's more, it had been written by a fellow national treasure, albeit a dead one. What the public often found difficult tolerating, however, was Richard Briers playing nefarious or unlovable characters, especially on television.

This had come to light in 1977 when, before *The Good Life* had finished, John Howard Davies, who was by then Head of Comedy at the BBC, commissioned John Esmonde and Bob Larbey to write a new show especially for Richard. The result was *The Other One*, a sitcom about the unlikely friendship between two boring bachelors, Ralph Tanner and Brian Bryant. Also starring Michael Gambon, it ran for seven episodes initially and, despite it being a firm favourite of almost everyone involved, the public loathed it.

'Michael played the most boring man in the world,' said Richard, 'and I played this bumptious little man with an awful moustache. It was beautifully written by Esmonde and Larbey and it became one of our favourites, but I'm afraid it was the most dreadful flop.'

Michael Gambon was yet another Alan Ayckbourn regular who had very little experience on television. That, however, had no bearing whatsoever on the show's failure. It was all down to Richard, apparently, and how the public perceived him.

'I'm afraid Richard wasn't very lovable in *The Other One*,' said Bob Larbey. 'That was the problem. I remember the first time we did it in the studio. I could actually feel the audience recoil when Richard came on with this moustache and a kind of smarmy look about him. You could see them looking at each other saying, "Ooh, that's not our Richard."'

John Howard Davies was so taken with *The Other One* that he ended up commissioning a second series, despite the show's dismal reception first time around. 'You could do that in those days,' said John Esmonde. 'It wasn't expensive to make so John Howard Davies asked us to write six more. It didn't make a blind bit of difference though. The public still hated it.'

Two years later, Richard had another go at playing a nasty, unsympathetic character, this time on radio. The actor, Siân Phillips, who had appeared with Richard in *Saint Joan* at Coventry Rep back in the 1950s, was his co-star on this occasion and it's fair to say that, prior to watching him record the role, she had one or two misgivings.

'The play was called *A Chaste Maid in Cheapside*,' says Siân. 'It's an early Jacobean play by Thomas Middleton and this production also started Peter Jeffrey, Sarah Badel, Norman Rodway and Hugh Paddick. To say it was an enlightening experience would be an understatement, and all because of Richard's performance. He was at the height of his powers as a sitcom actor with *The Good Life* still fresh in everyone's minds, and regardless of what he'd done on the stage, comedy is what the public associated him with. I remember thinking while I read the play, which is an extremely dark comedy, *I wonder who they'll get to play the male lead?* He was a particularly evil and quite serious character and when I found out it was going to be Richard I must admit I was slightly taken aback. *The lovely Richard Briers*, I thought. *Surely they've made a mistake?'*

In those days, it took about a week to record a radio play at the BBC and at the end of the first day's recording Siân was in a complete state of shock. 'He was absolutely magnificent in the role and I remember being totally stunned by his performance. I think we all were. Whoever cast Richard obviously knew something I didn't, but they got it absolutely right. He was terrifyingly menacing – more so, I suppose, because of his reputation of being so nice. What a contrast! Many years later, when he was cast as King Lear, I wasn't the least bit shocked. I knew exactly what he was capable of.'

Two other noteworthy performances by Briers the baddie are Sir Clixby Bream, a deeply unpleasant academic he played in an episode of *Inspector Morse* in 1997 alongside his close friend, John Thaw, and Vernon King, an aggressive, self-satisfied bully who has reduced his wife to a state of servile submission. The latter was in a play entitled *Spike*, which ran in Southampton for four weeks in 2001 and also starred Lucy and Annie. It was a black comedy by Simon Paisley Day who'd written the script with Lucy specifically in mind for the role of the daughter. Both Sir Clixby Bream and Vernon King represented the dregs of humanity, yet each provoked a very different reaction.

The appearance in *Inspector Morse* was the only time Richard played a genuinely evil character in front of a prime-time audience. He did play a murderous vicar in an episode of *Midsomer Murders* once, but he was eccentric as opposed to evil. Just like the programme itself, really. '*Midsomer Murders* was terribly over the top,' said Richard. 'But loads of fun. I had to decapitate somebody and then jump off the top of a church!'

Sir Clixby Bream, on the other hand (despite the Wodehousian name), was a disturbingly demonic individual. As well as having his hair dyed black for the role, Richard based part of him on a real-life serial killer. 'I forget who it was,' says Annie, 'but while Richard was preparing for the role in *Inspector Morse* he remembered reading about a serial killer once who never blinked. God knows why he remembered it, but he decided to apply that to his character, who was also very calm and sinister looking. It worked brilliantly. He was very scary.'

For some strange reason the millions of people watching this episode seemed to accept Richard in this role, and, instead of berating him for shattering their illusions, they simply congratulated him. Kate remembers the reaction clearly. 'The day after the episode was televised, Lucy and I received dozens of texts from people saying how much they'd enjoyed it. And how evil he was. I think it was considered an acceptable novelty.'

Like Shakespeare, *Inspector Morse* was obviously part of our cultural fabric, and its star, John Thaw, was, like Richard, a bona fide national treasure. This is undoubtedly what prevented the un-blinking Richard, or the show's producers, from being castigated for his portrayal of such a malevolent individual. The theory is validated by the reaction he received while playing Vernon King in *Spike*. 'Dad was never even considered to play the part of Vernon,' says Lucy. 'He'd read the script while we were casting the role and out of the blue he rang up and said he'd like to do it. I couldn't believe my ears. It was great for the play, of course, but I did wonder how the public would react.'

Having Richard involved ended up becoming a double-edged sword for the producers of *Spike*. It certainly put bums on seats, which was encouraging, and it generated a lot of column inches. The headlines, however, failed to allude to either the quality of the play or the strength of the supporting performances, which, when mentioned in the text, were generally positive. What the headlines concentrated on was the fact that Richard Briers was playing a complete and utter bastard, and while the critics were, at best, confused by his appearance, the theatregoing public were horrified.

'The reaction was, in the main, very positive,' remembers Lucy. 'We had a few letters of complaint and some people walking out but we also had letters saying how exciting it was to see Dad playing such a different role. Especially as during the play Dad had to hit me. In my mind it was a Marmite production. People either came three times or occasionally walked out. It was an amazing experience to work on this play as a family.'

CHAPTER TWENTY-TWO

'My God, he's on fire tonight!'

About halfway through rehearsals for the world tour of *King Lear*, which was due to open in Los Angeles at the start of 1990, Richard broke his ankle. As you might expect he insisted on carrying on despite the injury and having a pot on his foot and ankle.

But it was the example Richard set to the rest of the company that really caught Branagh's eye. 'He was a leader without pretension. He was on time always (which meant early). Always ready with his lines and prep. Always physically up on his feet ready to go for it. No hanging about. Plenty of smiles. Held nothing back. Didn't walk around the part, or see himself in slowly. He always threw himself at it. Full energy, full voice, full commitment from day one. That was a great example to all,' remembers Ken. 'Richard was serious in rehearsal. Worried. Humour was always against himself, and we loved to share a little showbiz camp to release tension. He was also a great scholar of acting and actors, so the greats of the past were often invoked. We wondered how they would have tackled a moment in the same play.'

A few days before that, while he was still wearing two shoes, he had caused quite a stir around the hotel swimming pool. The composer Patrick Doyle remembers it well, although he does have a bit of a problem getting the words out. 'I can't even think about this without becoming hysterical,' he says – slowly. 'Dickie was such a fish out of water in Los Angeles. A real Englishman abroad. One day, while we were all lying by the pool, he suddenly appeared wearing some awful shorts, some awful socks and a pair of black Oxford shoes! "How are we all doing then?" he said cheerfully. "Fuck me, it's hot!" When I finally stopped laughing and asked him about his attire, he said, "It doesn't matter, love. No one knows who the fuck I am!" He was more English than English and I loved him for that. We were laughing for days.'

Despite the cast and crew being able to sit by the pool occasionally, January in Los Angeles could still be incredibly cold at times, and when the company had first arrived in the city, some of them realised that they should have packed their coats. 'We were freezing our arses off,' remembers Patrick. 'Richard, who was the last person to leave London, got wind of this and do you know what he did? He bought a great big suitcase, collected up all the coats from God knows where, and took them with him. Nobody asked him to.'

For somebody who had never been further than Spain before and who would rather drive and take the ferry than endure a forty-minute flight from London to Paris, setting off on a ten-hour flight to Los Angeles, with dozens of flights to follow, must have been daunting for Richard, especially coupled with the fact that he would be required to play *King Lear* every other night.

'Going abroad as a family had to be negotiated as something we'd do every other year,' says Kate. 'But even then, we'd normally end up getting a ferry and then drive to wherever we were going. The reason Dad conquered his fears and went on that world tour was because of Ken (and because Mum went with him!). He not only inspired Dad, he empowered him. I always remember Dad saying that for the hanging scene in *Henry V* there had to be a closeup of his face before they put the noose around his head. For some reason Ken wasn't happy with it and, after about the third take, he went over and said, "Dickie, stop acting!" Dad had been trying to do an "Oh my God, I'm about to die" kind of expression, and it was too much. Ken gave Dad the courage to give a more natural performance and it ended up being very moving.'

When Richard and Kenneth Branagh started working together some people mistakenly believed that Richard was doing it as a favour – a grand old actor helping out an up-and-coming actor. But that's not the case. 'No, no. It was a partnership,' insists Lucy. 'Ken was learning, but so was Dad. He enjoyed learning about his craft. For instance, Dad was a big fan of Shakespeare, but he wasn't a Shakespearean scholar. To be approached by somebody, regardless of their age, who quite literally lived and breathed Shakespeare was incredibly exciting for Dad. Nobody had ever had the imagination to cast him in roles like that before. The RSC never approached him. Not once. He'd had so much stage experience and had they contacted him he'd have said yes immediately. They didn't, though, because at that time they didn't have Ken's imagination.'

Although incredibly proud, Lucy found watching her father play King Lear almost as challenging as it must have been playing the role. 'I found watching Dad play King Lear a really traumatic experience,' she admits. 'But what I admired most about the production, as well as the direction, was the fact that he played the character as a bit of a bastard, which meant the journey was a true journey. Some actors play Lear as quite a benevolent King, but he's not. He's a horribly divisive character who plays his kids off against each other. Dad had the courage to do this, and the fall and the madness he conveyed were just heart breaking. He was fantastic.'

The theatre critic Michael Billington came to a similar conclusion, although he admits that it took him two bites of the cherry. 'I confess that when I first saw Richard's Lear, at the jet-lagged end of a tiring week in Chicago, I shamefully fell asleep. Seeing the performance later in Edinburgh, I was impressed by his ability to encompass the hero's rage and madness.'

The courage Lucy speaks of definitely came at a cost for Richard, and accentuated a problem that he had always had, even as a bit-part player. 'I think Dad had always suffered from stage fright,' says Lucy. 'He'd talk about it sometimes, but always in a jokey way. In fact, as opposed to it being a problem, I think it was something he eventually managed to feed off. I think it challenged him though.'

But it wasn't just the prospect of appearing on a stage that gave Richard the willies. Television studios were just as bad. 'He used to get so, so nervous before we recorded *The Good Life*,' remembers Felicity Kendal. 'But the moment he went on, he was fine. It was anticipation, I think, plus lots and lots of nervous energy.'

Appearing in *King Lear* took Richard's stage fright to a completely new dimension, where, as opposed to having just a 'quick shake', which is how he often referred to it, his entire body would start trembling uncontrollably just prior to going on stage. 'He made his first entrance via these enormous double doors,' remembers Lucy, 'that were situated at the back of the stage, and I remember him saying to me after the tour that he never got over the fear of standing there waiting for those doors to open – and the mountain he then had to climb. I think Ken went to see him just before his first entrance on the opening night, and he couldn't believe what he was seeing. Dad was literally quaking with fear.'

'It would be hard not to be nervous attempting King Lear,' says Branagh, 'particularly if you break your ankle, as he did, during rehearsal. It meant the opening performances were inevitably tense, but he showed immense bravery to combat pain and apprehension and deliver a very powerful king.'

Having Annie on the tour was obviously a great comfort to Richard, especially given the size of the role and the length of the tour. But there was still somebody back in Chiswick who, as well as being very dear to Richard, rarely left his thoughts. And who, in his absence, would be having a life-changing operation. Emma Thompson, who played the Fool, remembers Richard opening up to her about this dilemma, and she did everything she could to help him. 'Richard really missed his dog, Fred, and one day he told me that he was having to have his balls cut off. That's Fred, by the way, not Richard. After he'd told me I found two little circles of foam rubber, painted them red, and then hung them up in the hovel with a note attached to them saying, "Thanks a fucking bunch!" and a paw print. So, that night, when Richard came into the hovel from the storm, there waiting for him was a note from his bollockless dog. There were one or two giggles, I remember. Things like this used to happen all the time. They were a necessity!'

Out of the hundred or so performances of *King Lear* (the company also performed *A Midsummer Night's Dream* on the tour, in which Richard played Bottom, a role he didn't enjoy), Richard claimed he only got it right twice. 'But that's Shakespeare,' says Lucy. 'I've only done four Shakespeare plays, but the moment you think, *Great, I've got it*, Shakespeare goes, *I don't think you have, actually*, and spits you out to ensure you try harder next time!'

As one might expect with a long and punishing world tour, the performances were sometimes a bit hit and miss, especially with *King Lear*. This resulted in one or two unfavourable reviews along the way, but all in all the reception was enthusiastic for Renaissance's maiden voyage, with both the productions and the actors receiving a great deal of well-deserved praise. One benefit of Richard performing abroad (to the audiences, at least) was that he was unknown to the vast majority of critics and theatregoers. This meant he was being judged and appreciated with a clean sheet for a change, with neither a spade nor a woolly jumper in sight. Not that he was particularly bothered. The only other time Richard had this kind of anonymity thrust upon him as a stage actor was when he appeared on Broadway in *The Chairs*, for which he was nominated for a Tony Award. It wasn't something he ever craved, however, and he always admitted that he was far happier being a familiar face than an unfamiliar one, regardless of the baggage or cries of 'Hello, Dick!'

His lack of concern was fortunate, as a year or so later, after opening in *Uncle Vanya*, which, like *The Wild Duck*, interweaves comedy with despair, the theatre critic from the *Spectator* observed that Richard only had to grin for sections of the audience to fall about. 'Surely that must nag occasionally,' Kate once asked him. 'Yes,' he replied. 'But the alternative is far worse.'

One of the most favourable notices Richard received on the entire Renaissance world tour was from the *Chicago Tribune*, which said,

This production of *King Lear* has the benefit of a ripened, knowing and wisely apportioned portrayal of Lear by Richard Briers. Briers, who also portrays Bottom the weaver in 'Dream,' paces his Lear brilliantly. He enters first as a proud old monarch, swollen with pride, whose quick anger and petty vanity more than fulfil his daughter`s description of him as 'an idle old man.' As his pride and his power are brutally taken from him, he moves believably from an outraged king to a homeless madman and finally to a dying, distorted shadow of his former self, stripped of all his earthly goods and ready now for the sweet release of death. This is an acting obstacle course of mammoth challenges, and Briers navigates it with barely a stumble.

The first time Richard nailed King Lear became one of the most talked about events on the entire tour. At the time, however, it rendered everyone who saw it completely speechless.

'This story is the stuff of legend,' says Patrick Doyle. 'We were in Zagreb, and because Richard had broken his ankle during rehearsals he'd been playing Lear with a cast on right from the opening night. He'd incorporated it into his performance, and because he was playing an old man that worked well. What a trooper, though. Not only was he playing King

Lear for heaven's sake, one of the most physically demanding roles in theatre, but he was doing it with a disability. One night in Zagreb, shortly before the show was due to start, I was in the wings waiting to play keyboards as there was no recorded music. When Dickie made his entrance I immediately thought, *My God, he's on fire tonight.* He was immense! Without a word of a lie, as the actors came off, rather than go back to their dressing rooms, everyone stood next to me in the wings and watched him. Nobody said anything, we just watched. We knew that something extraordinary was happening. I'm not joking here, but Dickie was totally unrecognisable. Like a man possessed. During the interval everybody went back to their dressing rooms, but again, nobody said a word. Then, when the second half began, everybody who wasn't due on stage came and stood next to me in the wings again and watched. Nobody moved, nobody spoke. I think we thought he'd been possessed, some-how. After the show, every member of the cast and crew spon-taneously followed Dickie back to his dressing room; first and foremost to congratulate him, but also to ask what had happened. "I've no idea where that came from, love," he said. "No fuck-ing idea. It was just there!" In my opinion, what actually happened was that his technique and his instincts aligned just at the right moment. With a role as big as Lear, that's only going to happen once in a blue moon. Like seeing Halley's comet or winning the bloody lottery. I remember reading an interview with Laurence Olivier once and exactly the same thing had happened to him. He had no idea *what* had happened. All he knew was that something *had* happened. He also knew that it was impossible to reproduce, more's the pity.'

Kenneth Branagh agrees. 'His connection with the role

seemed to transcend all other performances and the audience and other actors felt what it was like to be in the presence of greatness. Richard was perfectly real, effortless and magnificent. He was never anything less than impressive in the part, but, on that evening in Zagreb, he was incandescent.'

Part way through that mammoth tour of *King Lear* and *A Midsummer Night's Dream*, Richard was contacted by his agent who asked him if he would be interested in playing Ratty in a production of *The Wind in the Willows*. Alan Bennett had adapted it for the stage and it was due to open at the National Theatre on 1 December 1990. Should he accept, his co-stars were going to be Griff Rhys Jones, who would be playing Toad, Michael Bryant, who would be playing Badger and David Bamber, who would be playing Mole.

Ever since its formation in 1963, when it was based at the Old Vic, Richard had been hoping for an opportunity to appear with the National Theatre Company, and, despite being exhausted on his return from what seemed like everywhere, he started rehearsing almost immediately. Griff Rhys Jones, who was thrilled when he found out Richard was playing Ratty, remembers being fascinated by his new colleague right from the word go.

'One of the first things I remember after meeting Richard, apart from thinking how incredibly charming he was, was a conversation we had about funny lines one day, not long after we'd started rehearsals. He told me that when he was at RADA he'd been taught that when delivering a line you should always finish with an upward inflection, as if throwing the line to the next person. They used to have classes in which they taught things like that, and I remember being very impressed by it. Richard also said that in his opinion the most important thing to remember when performing comedy was to sing your lines. "All the great comedians sing their lines," he said to me. When I thought about it I realised he was absolutely right. Walter Matthau is one of my own favourite actors and comedians and when I started reciting him in my head I realised that he sang his lines. Tony Hancock, who was one of Richard's favourites, also sang his lines, and I think he got that from Sid Field. I don't know how much of it's instinctive, but great comedy performers do manage to find a musical intonation in the lines they're delivering. Richard, too, had a wonderful sing-song feel to his voice. I found that absolutely fascinating and it's something I've passed on to young comedians.'

In order to do their animal subjects justice, he and his co-stars were each given some visual assistance. 'Before we started rehearsals we were all given videos of the animals we were playing by our movement director,' says Griff. 'You know the kind of thing; rats, toads and badgers in their natural habitat. Richard and Michael, who were fairly old school, were absolutely horrified by this. It was all a bit modern and a little bit too close to method acting for their liking, I think. They did as they were asked, though, and took their videos home with them, although I'm sure they never watched them. The following week when we returned the movement director went to Michael Bryant and asked him if he'd learned anything from the video. "Yes," he said earnestly. "I've watched this video very closely indeed and have come to the conclusion that badgers move exactly like Michael Bryant."'

In truth, Richard probably did watch the video, although

according to Alan Bennett, it didn't help his portrayal much. 'Richard was quite subdued to begin with in rehearsals. He was quite cheerful, but he was obviously having difficulty character-ising the part, which must have been frustrating. Then, the costume department gave him this huge tail which he proceeded to wear at every rehearsal, and that somehow released him. He then became much more expansive as Ratty.'

Annie confirms this, but also says that the tail became an integral part of every performance. 'I'm fairly sure Richard did watch that video,' says Annie, 'although I can't say for certain. I know that he and Michael Bryant had a jolly good laugh about it! I remember him being quite worried prior to getting the tail and I think he felt a little bit self-conscious. The tail made him feel like a rat, I suppose, and allowed him to behave like one. In the end it became more of a prop, and he ended up using it to great effect. Every night he did some-thing different.'

Despite glowing reviews and being sold out for months on end, *The Wind in the Willows* suffered from one or two technical issues early on in its run. The second time it happened, Richard was forced to do something he hadn't done for over thirty years.

'The one thing Richard didn't like about the show was the revolving stage,' remembers Griff. 'We used to call it the poppa-dum, and although it was integral to the production, Richard was scared to death of the damn thing. I don't think he liked moving stages! One day, about twenty minutes before curtain-up, the entire mechanism of this blasted thing packed up and we were left with no show. The same thing had happened about a week before and on that occasion the front-of-house manager had been sent on to the stage to deliver the bad news.

The Wind in the Willows was one of the hottest tickets in town at the time and these people had been waiting months to see it. Subsequently, that poor front-of-house manager had received a barrage of abuse on telling the eleven hundred people they should all go home and when it was suggested to him that he might like to make a repeat performance, he refused point blank. In the end it was decided that Richard and I should go out there and spoil everybody's evening, which was absolutely marvellous! As luck would have it, Richard had done something like this before years ago, and the way he handled it was just incredible. Some of these people would have travelled miles to see our play and so telling them all to go home without being lynched or even heckled was a minor miracle. After that, we decided to come up with an alternative version of the play. One that didn't require a revolving stage!'

When it was working, the poppadum became the location of some rather interesting conversations between Griff, Richard and Michael.

'Just prior to the final act of the show, all three of us had to be crammed in together just behind the set on the revolving stage,' remembers Griff, 'and usually we'd have a quick chat. One evening, while chatting about this, that and the other for a while, Richard and Michael suddenly started smacking their lips. "What on earth are you doing that for?" I asked them. "Wine, dear boy," replied Michael. "Wine!" "What do you mean, wine?" I asked. "In just a few minutes' time I'll be having my first glass of chardonnay and Michael will be having the first glass of whatever he's having," said Richard. "That is correct, dear boy," confirmed Michael. "Not long now, Richard, old chap." It was quite bizarre watching these two old actors standing there dressed as animals and smacking their lips. Neither of them ever touched a drop before the curtain came down but when it did they'd sit back and enjoy themselves. They both said that the great advantage of being in a play is that you don't start drinking until at least 10 p.m. "If you're not in a play," said Richard. "There's always that temptation to open a bottle at 6 p.m. After that, it's goodnight Vienna!"'

At some point during the production Griff was approached by a famous producer, who will have to remain nameless, about appearing in a new play after he had finished in *The Wind in the Willows*. 'I remember telling Richard about this and the moment I mentioned the producer's name he piped up and said, "Oh, him! I know him of old. I'll tell you what'll happen there, love. If you take the job, about a fortnight into the run he'll knock on your dressing-room door and suggest that because the production isn't making any money you should take a pay cut. I'm telling you now, love. That's what'll happen."

'Dickie was being deadly serious about this and so after accepting the role and then starting in this play I waited for the knock. Sure enough, about a week and a half into the run there was a knock at my dressing-room door one evening and in walked this producer. "I'm terribly sorry," he said, "but the returns are down and everybody's taking a pay cut." Because Richard had warned me about this, and because I'd been expecting it, I'm afraid I started to laugh. This went down rather badly, I'm afraid, as he assumed that I was laughing at the show's misfortune. It also didn't do my negotiating position much good either! Richard was in hysterics when I told him.'

One of Alan Bennett's favourite memories from this period is watching Richard run the gauntlet every day up some steps and past an exceedingly enthusiastic beggar. 'Richard could be quite crotchety occasionally, although I think he played up to it a lot, and because he was so loved it became a bit of a joke really. After rehearsals, Richard would have to take the steps that lead from the National Theatre to Waterloo Bridge and there was a beggar on the landing of these steps who always managed to extract some money out of him. After a few weeks Richard had had enough of this and in his best crotchety voice he said, "I'm not going to do it, Alan. I'm not going to give that man anything today." Sure enough, after rehearsals had finished Richard walked past the beggar without giving him anything, but as he passed he heard him say in a sad voice, "Awww, he's my favourite actor," so he went straight back and gave him a pound.'

CHAPTER TWENTY-THREE

'This, is anger!'

By the time Richard's tenure in *The Wind in the Willows* was coming to an end he was already in discussions with Kenneth Branagh about what they should do next. 'Ken phoned me up one day and suggested I play Uncle Vanya,' said Richard. 'It wasn't quite as daunting as Lear, of course, but the previous two London Vanyas had been played by Michael Gambon and Timothy West, who, as well as being pals of mine, were both considerable actors. They were going to be hard acts to follow.'

The first person to have suggested that Richard take on the role of Uncle Vanya was his friend Peter Egan, although that had been several years before during *Arms and the Man*. 'Richard and I would often have a few glasses of chardonnay after the show,' remembers Peter, 'and one evening I told Richard that he should have a go at playing Uncle Vanya. I thought he'd bring pathos to the role and also humour. Chekhov is often played so turgidly, in my opinion. It's all a bit one-dimensional.'

Strangely enough, shortly after talking Richard into playing Uncle Vanya, Kenneth Branagh contacted Peter Egan and asked him if he'd like to play the part of Astrov, the once youthful doctor who has aged prematurely due to overwork and excessive drinking.

Since finishing *Ever Decreasing Circles*, Richard and Peter Egan had become firm friends. As well as talking on the phone quite often, they would meet for curry nights on Chiswick High Road. 'We often had long evenings with curry and chardonnay,' remembers Peter. 'We'd worked together for six whole years without a single cross word and loved being in each other's company.'

Shortly before rehearsals began for *Uncle Vanya*, Kenneth Branagh was called to Hollywood to finish off a new film he was working on called *Dead Again*. This presented a big problem for Peter Egan, but Kenneth Branagh was having none of it.

'After telling us that he was going to have to go to Hollywood for most of the rehearsal period, Ken presented us with a list of possible replacements. The problem I had with this was that I'd agreed to do this play for two reasons; one, because I wanted to work with Dickie again, and two, because I wanted to work with Ken. With him now gone that took away half the attraction and so I told him that, regrettably, I was going to pull out while there was still time to recast me. Ken then informed me that the advance for the play was the biggest the company had ever had and the reason for that was the prospect of seeing Richard and I. Far be it from me to blow my and Dickie's trumpets, but *Ever Decreasing Circles* was still relatively fresh at the time and so I suppose it may have had something to do with it. "I'll tell you what," said Ken. "Why don't you direct it?" "What, you mean direct it and don't play Astrov?" "No," he said. "Do both!" "I couldn't direct and act at the same time," I pleaded. "Laurence Olivier did," said Ken. That was really helpful!'

Peter finally agreed to Ken's suggestion on the proviso that the leading actor was happy, so when Richard gave the new appointment his blessing it was all systems go. 'Richard said, "Yeah, that'll be wonderful. I'd love you to direct me." That was an amazing gesture by Richard. I was by no means a proven director and Uncle Vanya was a hugely difficult part from his point of view. For him to put his confidence in me like that must have taken an immense amount of courage, not to mention an unbelievable amount of loyalty. I was thrilled when he told me.'

With Branagh's occasional help, Peter Egan went on to direct the play and it became a great success, both critically and commercially. 'It really was a unique experience,' explains Peter. 'To watch Richard develop through a Chekhovian character like Uncle Vanya, and to bring his wonderful suburban humour and his mania to it was a privilege. He was one of the best Uncle Vanyas I've ever seen, and I promise you I've seen dozens them. Dozens! Although he's a supreme actor, I never believed in Michael Gambon as Vanya. He was far too powerful and too saturnine for my liking. There was no conflict there emotionally as he's such a bull of a man. Richard, on the other hand, gave Vanya humour and vulnerability, not unlike Michael Redgrave. His is probably my favourite portrayal of Uncle Vanya and is still considered to be the benchmark. Richard isn't far behind, though.'

'Richard had a real fondness for Uncle Vanya,' explains Branagh. 'He loved his dreamy poeticism, his doomed romantic tendency and his (finally) explosive temper. The character could be noble and then absurd in the twinkling of an eye, and I think he loved playing that, and the character's rage. Richard didn't try to make Vanya heroic. He was just very transparent and honest in the role and let Chekhov do the heavy lifting. He seemed as relaxed and happy in the part as any I'd seen him do.'

Perhaps Richard's least known collaboration with Kenneth

Branagh, which was made in 1991 at about the same time as *Uncle Vanya*, should have been one of his most celebrated as not only was it nominated for an Oscar for Best Live Action Short Film, but it also had a small but perfectly formed cast: Richard and Sir John Gielgud. The film in question, *Swan Song*, was based on an early one-act play by Anton Chekhov and tells the tale of an eighty-eight-year-old stage actor who becomes overwhelmed by despair as he stares out over an empty, rundown theatre. The actor then confesses to a sympathetic elderly prompter (Richard), who has secretly been sleeping at the theatre, that after a long-ago rejection in love, the theatre lost its magic for him. Gradually, the prompter cheers up the elderly actor who starts reciting soaring passages from *King Lear*, *Romeo and Juliet* and *Othello*. As is often the way with short films, which are too short to be granted a theatrical or DVD release and often too obscure to be given an airing on primetime TV, *Swan Song* is rarely seen, which is a shame as the chemistry between Richard and his idol is both joyful and interesting, and both performances are sublime. The only slight downside to the film is that it is the only time these two actors ever appeared together on screen. There really should have been more.

Of the eight films that Richard made for Kenneth Branagh (nine, if you include *Peter's Friends*, in which he never made the final cut), the most enjoyable to film was undoubtedly *Much Ado About Nothing*. Filmed in Tuscany in the summer of 1992, it had the biggest budget ever for a Shakespearean film at that time at over $11 million and featured a handful of Hollywood A-listers among a cast that can best be described as the best of British. Representing Tinseltown were Denzel Washington as Don Pedro, Michael Keaton as Dogberry, Keanu Reeves as Don John and Robert Sean Leonard as Count Claudio, and, representing the home team, were Kenneth Branagh as Benedick, Emma Thompson as Beatrice, Kate Beckinsale as Hero, Brian Blessed as Antonio and Richard as Leonato. The film went on to take over $36 million at the box office, making it one of the most financially successful Shakespearean adaptations of all time. It was also nominated for a host of prestigious awards, including a BAFTA and the coveted Palme d'Or at Cannes.

'They had so much fun doing that film,' says Lucy. 'I went out there just for a week, and I had the best time. You can see it in the film. It's just joyful.'

According to Patrick Doyle, the atmosphere both on and off the set during *Much Ado* was convivial to say the least, and this resulted in some unlikely friendships being formed. Brian Blessed, for instance, taught Keanu Reeves how to meditate during those three months in Tuscany, but when Keanu wasn't filming or asking large, bearded Yorkshiremen about *dharma*, he was being taught how to impersonate Victorian actors by Richard. 'My dad and Keanu Reeves bonded from day one and they adored each other,' explains Lucy. 'Dad ended up teaching him all of the Victorian actor poses – à la Henry Irving – for all the different emotions, such as anger, love and jealousy, etc. When I was out there we all went for a meal one night in a restaurant that overlooked the main square in the local town. Keanu left early because he had to be up at 5 a.m. and as he was walking back to his apartment he stopped in the square, called up to Dad and started doing all these poses. "Richard, watch this," he shouted. Then, after assuming the required stance, he called out, "This, is anger!" We all applauded so he changed the pose and shouted, "And this is love!" Dad was sitting there going, "Left arm higher, love, left arm higher. And bring the knee down a bit. That's it, Keanu, that's it! Well done. Bloody well done!" The whole thing was absolutely hysterical, but it was also very heart-warming. After all, there aren't many industries where you can bring two people together from such different backgrounds.'

Kenneth Branagh must have had this in mind while casting the film and, fortunately, the experiment worked.

'You know, it was just fascinating,' he later said. 'You put Michael Keaton and Richard Briers in a scene together – I find that both bizarre and rather moving. I remember Keaton saying to me afterwards, "This guy knows about timing. This guy is funny. This is a funny guy." And I said, "Darling, he's been funny in our country for about the last thirty years, you know, he's a kind of national institution."'

The only slight downside to the amalgamation, as far as Richard was concerned, was not being able to hear some of the American actors. 'Dad did say that because of the differences in the style of acting he found it very difficult making out what the American actors were saying,' says Kate. 'They were so filmic they were simply too quiet for him. In the end, and you can see this in the film, he just waited until their mouths had stopped moving and then delivered his next line.'

Despite the hearing issues there are some superb exchanges between Richard and Denzel Washington, none more so than when Leonato accuses Don Pedro of killing his daughter, Hero. Nobody was more impressed by this exchange than Kenneth Branagh, who saw a different side to Richard.

'When we got to the scene where Dickie had to berate Denzel Washington, he was incredibly moving. And he was pretty butch, for Dickie. I think he frightened himself that day.'

The language on set, at least while the cameras were rolling, would normally have been restricted to what's known as Early Modern English. The language off the set, however, was slightly more Anglo-Saxon. This was primarily down to a series of swearing competitions that took place between Richard, Brian Blessed, Kenneth Branagh and Patrick Doyle. In breaks between filming, the four men would huddle around a table and take it in turns to see who could come up with the most ingeniously profane statement. In street-dance parlance it would be referred to as a 'battle', and, although he claims to be quite adept at using fruity language, Patrick Doyle admits that the competition was fierce.

'The first time I heard Dickie swear I was on my knees laughing because it's not something you expect, is it? Richard Briers saying the f-word?! The thing is, he rarely got into trouble for it because it was very rarely gratuitous. He turned it into an artform, if anything. I'd usually come third or fourth in these swear-offs, depending on the day. Briers and Blessed were just masters.'

But the ability to curse at will was a skill that needed to be honed, and Emma Thompson remembers seeing Richard and Brian getting some practice in more than once. 'They were absolutely disgraceful. I remember seeing them clinging on to each other like a couple of old hooligans, swearing and blinding. They were just heaven.'

But not everybody who worked on *Much Ado About Nothing* appreciated the ribald language flying around, and, not long into the shoot, one person decided to make their feelings known. 'I can't say who it was for obvious reasons,' says Patrick, 'but there was one person working on the film who was very religious, and the look on their face when they heard what was going on was a picture. "Until today," they said to me, "I had heard the C-word only twice in my entire life. Today, I have heard it three hundred and twenty times." I said, "I'm sorry about that, but the place is full of 'em!" That didn't go down well.'

Patrick has a theory as to why Richard might have developed such a prolific potty mouth in the first place. 'People involved in the arts and especially children's television are often big swearers. Because, at the end of the day, you can't be nice all the time, can you? You need to let off steam occasionally and act against type. It's quite a cathartic experience. Richard didn't swear all the time, by the way. He could switch it on or off, just like that. He was at his best when telling an anecdote, which he would embellish beautifully with swear words. You never felt offended listening to him. If anything you felt blessed.'

Patrick Doyle's memories from this period are recalled with a not insignificant amount of laughter. 'Because I was quite ruthless with everyone, Richard started referring to me as Hitler's musical director. It all started when Ken asked me to write a song for Hero's funeral. We were filming it the following day, so that afternoon I wrote the song and then called a rehearsal on the tennis court at the villa we were filming in. Dickie, who had this kind of curmudgeon persona that he loved playing up to, came trudging along and immediately started moaning. "It must be about a hundred fucking degrees out here! What if we all melt? What will you do then? You'll be buggered, that's what! By the way, where's Adolf? Is he coming?" Despite the wigging, Dickie was always first there and never caused me any trouble. In fact, he'd do anything you asked him, as long as he could swear and have a good moan.'

CHAPTER TWENTY-FOUR

'Come along, matey, come on in.'

On 26 November 1992, just a few months after returning from Tuscany, Richard's mother passed away. His father Joe had died in the late 1970s and, although Richard had often bemoaned the fact that his father could never hold a job down, his death had hit him hard. 'Dad may have had a different work ethic to Joe,' says Kate. 'And he may also have had a different outlook. There were definitely some similarities though – a sunny disposition, being one – and they always got on well together. Joe was also extremely proud of Dad, and I think he got a lot of satisfaction from that.'

With Morna, there existed a more complex relationship. As a promising concert pianist whose career had been cut short by the war, not to mention a frustrated actress, she had followed her son's career with forensic interest and had, at one time, endeavoured to fulfil some of her own dreams and ambitions via his continued success. This had been achieved by Morna becoming, in effect, a professional actor's mother, and she had even given talks on the subject at the local Women's Institute. Not on what it was like to be Richard Briers, but what it was like to be Richard Briers's mother. Although understandable, Richard sometimes felt like he was talking to a fan rather than a parent but what ultimately prevailed was a realisation that her actions were born simply of a sense of extreme pride.

A few years after Joe's death, Morna had lost a leg to type-1 diabetes and ever since then she had been confined to a wheelchair. To save her going into a home, Richard's sister Jane had volunteered to look after her full-time, with Richard then suggesting that, 'I'll provide the money, if you provide the care.' With the two of them working in tandem, Morna's final years had been happy, and there is no denying that she loved her children very much and was obviously tremendously proud of them both, as they were of her.

It isn't terribly well known, but between 1981 and 1997 Richard wrote a total of six books, and on subjects ranging from the pleasures of the table to places of worship. His first book, called *Natter Natter*, was a compendium of anecdotes about life in general, each with an accompanying cartoon drawn by the *Punch* and *Private Eye* cartoonist, Larry (Terence Parkes). This venture, which had been suggested by a publisher, ticked three important boxes for Richard. First, it was something he hadn't done before, and, regardless of his popularity, it was going to be a risk – tick. Next, it paid well, which fed the enterprise – tick. And third, he got to work with one of his favourite cartoonists – tick. Unfortunately, very little is known of that particular relationship, but another of Richard's favourites, the ever-popular Giles (Ronald 'Cal' Giles), corresponded with Richard for many years and would always include cartoons at the end of each letter. Richard's number one favourite was Matt at the *Telegraph* and Matt used to send Richard a signed copy of *The Best of Matt* every year. The rest of Richard's bibliography is slightly less mainstream, but every book published under his name did well and it was obviously something he enjoyed doing. The other five are *Grow Your Own Nosh* (1987), a gardening book written with Peter Heseltine that was obviously inspired by *The Good Life*, the aforementioned *Coward & Company* (1987), which was undoubtedly Richard's favourite, a horticultural version of *Natter Natter* entitled *A Little Light Weeding* (1993), *A Taste of the Good Life*, which was an anthology compiled by Richard and Annie featuring musings about food and alcohol, and last but perhaps least, *English Country Churches*, which was published by Robson Books in 1991.

While Richard was compiling *A Little Light Weeding* at the start of 1993, his friend Kenneth Branagh, with whom he had been working now for over five years, was on his way to New York to see a rather famous American actor who he was hoping would take the leading role in his next movie. This, and several subsequent meetings, would eventually give rise to what became one of the most bizarre pairings that has ever been committed to celluloid, and something that eventually became one of the main talking points of Richard's career.

In a retrospective that went to air shortly after his death, Richard's friend John Sessions introduced the episode brilliantly when he said, 'Dickie was Bardolph in *Henry V*, he was Leonato in *Much Ado*, and then, of course, came the great meeting of the twentieth century, that between Richard Briers and Robert De Niro.'

Branagh's adaptation of Mary Shelley's *Frankenstein*, which was eventually released at the end of 1994, had been a long time in the making. While courting Mr De Niro – or Mr Denero, as John Cleese called him – Branagh had promised him the final say on casting. Once on board, Kenneth Branagh then visited Robert De Niro in his apartment in New York and, in the actor's private cinema, began showing him showreels of the people he wanted to cast.

'OK, Robert,' said Branagh. 'This is the actor I want to cast as the old blind man. He's called Richard Briers.'

'Richard Briers, Richard Briers,' mumbled De Niro. 'OK, let's see if he's any good.'

After the showreel De Niro thought for a moment, and then spoke. 'Mmm, Richard Briers,' he said thoughtfully. 'Good actor.'

The most famous scene the two actors had together lasted just a couple of minutes yet took hours to film. This was mainly down to the difference in acting techniques, which were in stark contrast. Richard was asked to recall the occasion many times over the years and was always happy to oblige.

'There is a small but very famous scene in *Frankenstein*,' said Richard, 'where the blind man has to ask the monster, who's lurking outside, to come in and sit by the fire. Before we started filming Ken said to me, "Now look, Dickie, when you say, 'Come in, don't be frightened,' you might have to say a bit more than that." At first, I panicked because I thought he wanted me to adlib, and I'm not very good at adlibbing.'

What Kenneth Branagh meant was that Robert De Niro would only come in if he felt Richard genuinely *wanted* him to come in, thus pitching method acting, which De Niro had learned under Lee Strasberg, against Richard's more traditional style, which had been learned at RADA and was all about learning your lines and sticking to your cues. That said, Richard did try his best to embrace the method, as during filming his retina had detached from his left eye, which had rendered him temporarily blind in one eye. On visiting him in hospital, Lucy had asked her father if he had indeed gone 'method'. 'Looking back, it was so bizarre, him losing his eyesight temporarily like that,' she says.

By the time they were ready to go for a take, Richard was still slightly confused but when Branagh shouted action he went ahead and did his best. 'I had no idea what to do,' said Richard, 'so I just said my lines. "Hello, hello, won't you come on in?" Nothing happened.'

Kenneth Branagh's rendition of what happened next, which he recalled in the television show *A Good Life* in 2000, is particularly amusing.

'Dickie said to me, "I can't even see if he's there or not, love. I don't know if you've noticed, Mr Director, but I'm supposed to be blind in this. I've got contact lenses in and I can't see a bloody thing."

'"OK," I said. "Let's just try again, shall we, Dickie?"

'"OK," said Dickie. "Let's try again. Do you want me to swear this time? Robert De Niro swears in his films."

'"No, Dickie!" I pleaded. "Please don't swear. Let's just go again. OK, action!"

'"Hello, hello. Don't be afraid. Come on in, come along, matey."

'"MATEY?! You can't say matey, Dick. It's Robert De Niro!"

'This went on for some time, and in the end, Robert ditched the method, came over to me and said, "I'll tell you what, Ken, I'll just come in. Don't worry about it, I'll just come in. Dick, it's fine, OK? I'm coming in. Don't say anything, Dick, I'm coming in. Keep the eyes closed."

'Afterwards Dickie said to me, "He keeps you on your toes, doesn't he, love? He keeps you on your toes!"'

Another mismatch took place during Branagh's 1996 film adaptation of *Hamlet*, in which Richard played Polonius. This one took Richard completely by surprise, and instead of not being able to see his famous co-star, this time, he couldn't understand them.

'When I played Polonius for Ken,' said Richard, 'I rang him about six weeks before the shoot and I said, "You've got this lovely scene which is normally cut of Polonius and his servant, Reynaldo. I'd really like to keep it in, if that's OK, but it'll mean you having to cast Reynaldo." The problem I thought Ken would have is that because it was such a small part nobody would want to do it.'

About a week later Richard received a telephone call. 'It was Ken. "I've found somebody to play Reynaldo," he said. "The problem is, he's French and doesn't speak a word of English." I thought, *oh my God, who's he got?* Then he said, "Do you mind if Gérard Depardieu plays him?" I almost dropped the bloody phone! "Oh well, that's done it," I moaned. "I'll be completely intimidated now. I mean, the man's a genius. This is the second time you've done this to me, Ken! First it was De Niro when I was blind, and now it's Depardieu and he doesn't speak English!"'

After flying Gérard Depardieu in from his vineyard, which he would be returning to at the end of the day, they had just a few precious hours to both rehearse and shoot the scene success-fully, and this took its toll on Richard. 'I must have lost several pounds that day. I had the responsibility of delivering most of the lines and all Gérard had to do was say, "Yes, my lord." It was terribly daunting. Who'd have thought I'd be appearing in a scene in *Hamlet* with the greatest living French actor?'

If Richard's portrayal of Malvolio is considered to be his greatest triumph for Kenneth Branagh, his performance as Polonius can't be too far behind. Once again, the word 'revelation' was much used when describing Richard's performance, with more than one critic noting that as opposed to portraying the King's chief counsellor as a foolish old man who is well out of his depth, Richard had created a clever and manipulative Polonius who had, as one critic put it, a 'conspiratorial edge'.

Two more film appearances followed for Kenneth Branagh: *Love's Labour's Lost* (2000), in which Richard played Sir Nathaniel, and *As You Like It* (2006), in which he played Adam. Neither did particularly well at the box office, alas, but they were the exception and not the rule.

It's hard to overestimate the effect that Kenneth Branagh, and his visit to see John Sessions at Chichester back in 1986, had on Richard's life and career. Without Branagh's influence Richard's career would probably have continued in the vein of light comedy. Had that been the case, we would probably be celebrating the king of sitcom within these pages as opposed to, as Michael Billington rightly put it, one of the most versatile actors of the twentieth century. 'Would Simon McBurney have cast Richard in *The Chairs* had he not seen him in something by Kenneth Branagh?' asks Billington. 'I doubt it. It wasn't just audiences who saw Richard differently. I think everybody did.'

Even if Kenneth Branagh hadn't approached Richard and, instead, the RSC had extended an invitation, it probably wouldn't have amounted to more than a couple of appearances and would only have been witnessed by a few thousand theatregoers. A challenge and an honour, yes. A career changer, almost definitely not.

Richard often claimed that he and Kenneth Branagh had a father and son relationship. 'Ken's the father,' he joked. 'And I'm the son.'

Although said in jest, there's obviously an element of truth in that. After all, it was Branagh who basically discovered Richard as a potential force in classical theatre and then proceeded to help him unlock all that latent talent. He offered him parts, he directed him and he gave him a senior role in his company. The difference, however, between this and other pupil/mentor relationships, which is what Richard was referring to when he said they were like father and son, is twofold, and is what made the union exceptional.

For a start, the mentorship was reciprocated to a certain extent, with Branagh often calling on Richard's vast experience. Richard had been the senior actor in a brand-new theatre company and had obviously been treated as a resource. And a very willing one, at that. Branagh was still steering the ship, of course, which was something for which Richard was always grateful. He was a company man, not a manager, and could never have done it himself. That said, he was an ideal lieutenant for Branagh and looked on him almost like a son.

'They really did love each other,' says Judi Dench. 'It was an extraordinary relationship. Unique, I think.'

In a way, Kenneth Branagh was Richard's very own Henry Irving; a working-class theatrical firebrand who inspired people and who changed the face of modern theatre. To even be on speaking terms with somebody like that would have been a huge thrill for Richard. But to be associated with one long-term and work with them on project after project was something else. Especially as the relationship also produced some of his best work.

When asked to describe what it was like working with one another, Richard was succinct in his description. 'Working with Ken is like having your very own football coach,' he said. 'He sits on the side-lines and tells you the important things you need to do to get you through the next ninety minutes. To an actor who likes to be directed, that's invaluable.'

Branagh, who was asked the same question after Richard had died, said, 'It was a sort of delicious agony appearing with Dickie. I had mouth ulcers because I had to bite the inside of my mouth so much trying to keep a straight face. In the meantime, he would be stealing the scene. In his back pocket, thank you very much!'

CHAPTER TWENTY-FIVE

'Tickets, please.'

When Richard was in his sixties he made the observation that all his friends had started dying off. 'I stopped being invited to weddings years ago,' he said. 'So now it's all funerals. I must go to at least one a month.'

Although not an especially sentimental person – the war had seen to that – he sometimes found these occasions difficult; none more so than when his good friend Paul Eddington passed away in November 1995. He and Paul had known each other since 1972 when both had sat on the council for the actors' union, Equity. Since then, as well as appearing in *The Good Life*, they had starred together in Roger Hall's hit comedy, *Middle Age Spread*, which had enjoyed a successful run at the Lyric Theatre in 1979 and 1980. But what transcended their success as actors was undoubtedly their friendship and, although neither was ever short of advocates or supporters, they championed each other's work constantly.

In an interview with *The Independent* after Paul's death, his widow Trish confirmed that Paul greatly admired Richard's work. 'He thought he'd taken a huge step forward when we saw him in Hammersmith in *The Wild Duck*,' she said. 'He surprised everyone. We usually think of him as a great comedian and his performance was very touching. Dickie is a considerable actor with a marvellous voice. He's a much "bigger" actor than most people imagine because he hides under his jokey personality. Dickie's opinion of himself as an actor and as a person is engagingly low, and quite unfounded. I'm constantly surprised by him; Paul was, too.'

In reply, Richard said, 'Although Paul was always in work – until *The Good Life* brought TV celebrity status – he was more of a jobbing actor. At times, he and Trish and their growing family were not at all well off. The huge success came late, but when it did the work doubled and then tripled. I was thrilled for him, but not at all surprised. I don't think I've known a more smashing bloke in all my years in showbusiness.'

About eighteen months before Paul's death, he and Richard had been approached about starring in a revival of David Storey's play, *Home*. Paul was already being treated for skin cancer at the time, which is something he had been suffering with for over forty years, and although his doctors had advised against it, Paul was adamant he wanted to do it. 'Dickie knew how ill Paul was,' said Trish, 'as did the producer and director. But everyone was very keen to do it. Dickie could just fit it in before he took on yet another project. He very much wanted to do it and Annie backed him up.'

At times the schedule was quite punishing for Paul, especially as he had to fit the rehearsals around his treatment. 'It exhausted him,' continued Trish, 'so Dickie – being Dickie – took away all the stress of the publicity and interviews. "Look," he said, "I'll do it. If they've got one of us they don't need both of us." That meant Paul could conserve all his energies for the stage. There were nights when Paul was undoubtedly feeling very ill, but the minute he had to appear, something extraordinary happened. He got up, did the play and was fine. I think Dickie knew how serious Paul's illness was, but I don't think he wanted to believe it.'

Home, which had been written in the late 1960s and originally starred John Gielgud and Ralph Richardson, centres on the interactions between four eccentric characters: two old men and two old women. Gradually, it is revealed that these people are living in an asylum, but the audience is also made to realise how similar their preoccupations and pretensions are to those of us living 'normal' lives. This was the first time the play had been revived in the West End since its original run and as well as receiving rave reviews it ran to packed houses at London's Wyndham's Theatre. It was a perfect swansong.

When Paul died Trish called Richard and asked him if he would like to do a reading at the funeral. 'I asked Dickie to read from *Cymbeline*, "Fear no more the Heat of the Sun . . .", at Paul's funeral. At the Thanksgiving Service, Dickie also read some P. G. Wodehouse, which Paul always loved. As a boy at boarding school, where he was frequently cold and undernourished, Paul would sneak off to the airing cupboard to read P. G. Wodehouse by torchlight under the blankets. He thought Dickie was the finest exponent of P. G. Wodehouse we have.'

Richard's final opportunity to pay tribute to his old friend happened when he was asked to read extracts from Paul's posthumously published autobiography on Radio 4. 'When Dickie rang to ask how I felt about him reading Paul's book for Radio 4, I told him that of course I'd love him to do it,' said Trish. 'He had no need to ask me, but it would have been out of character for him if he hadn't. He's a person who inspires friendships in people, and I love him.'

★   ★   ★

Always a little bit of a home bird, by the mid-1990s Richard had become almost addicted to the district of Chiswick and, although he was still gregarious, he preferred to do his socialising close to home. In the early 1980s he'd been persuaded to join the Garrick Club, and, after filling in all the appropriate forms and sorting out a sponsor, he had readied himself for a life of long lunches and bonhomie. Unfortunately, for Richard, the election system at the Garrick Club seemed to flow like a Pinter play rather than a farce and by the time he was finally elected in 1990, that initial enthusiasm had waned. Griff Rhys Jones remembers Richard telling him he had been accepted at the Garrick Club, but at the time he had no plans to go. 'I can't be bothered with all that now, Griff,' he said. 'I'm too old. I just want to go home to Annie.'

Over time Richard gradually became quite an enthusiastic member of the Garrick Club, partly because many of his oldest friends were members, but also because it had an extensive theatrical library that satisfied the passion he still held for the history of his craft. Even so, the Garrick was one of a decreasing number of places beyond Chiswick that Richard was happy visiting. In fact, the only time he was ever truly comfortable in that situation was when he and Annie went to East Sussex to visit Kate and their two grandchildren – Harry, who had been born in 1994, and Rachael, who had been born in 1996. Since their arrival they had been the focus of much of Richard's attention and he adored being a grandparent. Forget Polonius or Martin Bryce. This was his favourite role, and it would remain so for the rest of his life. 'Dad was so pleased when I first told him I was pregnant,' remembers Kate. 'He'd never really talked about being a grandparent before and I hadn't talked about having kids, so it was a surprise, I suppose, but obviously a nice one.'

Because he had been away so much when Kate and Lucy were young, Richard was determined to spend more time with Harry and Rachael than he had been able to with his daughters.

'I think Dad probably suffered more than we did by him being away so much,' says Kate. 'After all, he was the one sitting in a hotel room on tour or coming back to a sleeping house at midnight. Me, Mum and Lucy were all together living a relatively normal life. I think Dad wanted things to be different with Harry and Rachael and as often as was possible he and Mum would come to us, or we'd go to them. We used to have this little bike at home in Chiswick and Harry and Rachael would wheel it around the kitchen table. As they did this, Dad would have to stop them and ask for a ticket. "Tickets, please," he'd say, and they'd either slap his hand or hand him a piece of paper. It sounds really simple, but they used to play it for hours.'

Whenever it was time for Kate, Harry and Rachael to return home to East Sussex, Richard would bid them all an amusingly less-than-fond farewell. 'I'd say, "Right, we're going now," and Dad would jump up and say "Yaaaaaay! About time!" Then he'd say, "Have you got enough petrol?" That was always his last question. Dad's style of grandparenting was all about jokes, stories and tickling. He was a brilliant grandad. The kids just adored him.'

Harry says, 'My grandpa was just that, my grandpa. The room would light up when he entered, often with a comic for me and my sister behind his back. He would fill my days with laughter, proving that, no matter how bleak the situation, there was a release in roaring like a drain.'

Richard's quest for the title of west London's most contented grandparent may well have been earnest, but he was still a jobbing actor and, by the end of the millennium, he had reached yet another professional impasse. The Renaissance Theatre Company had long since disbanded and, with Kenneth Branagh now diversifying by taking more roles in other people's films, Richard was having to start again. That may sound a lot worse than it was as he was still incredibly busy. What was playing on Richard's mind at this time, however, was the fact that it was now well over a decade since he had been involved in a successful television series. Shakespeare had been fun, but television is where he had made his name and the financial security that a successful series provided – not to mention the recognition – was something he both craved and missed.

'I think Dad had become slightly bored,' says Lucy. 'He was still getting plenty of work, but nothing lasted more than a few days. He wanted some security.'

The opportunity for Richard to become part of a long-running television series again was just around the corner, but it would come at a cost. Not a financial cost, but a geographical one. 'My agent called me one day and asked if I'd like to go and read for a new television series,' he said. 'Of course, I was over the moon. It was the BBC, with whom I'd had most of my success, so I thought, great, let's go!'

For the past twenty years – on and off – the writer Michael Chaplin had been working on a series of scripts based loosely on what are known as the 'Highland Novels' by Compton Mackenzie, the first of which is entitled *The Monarch of the Glen*. By 1999 Michael had turned them into a series under the same name and, after being commissioned by the BBC, they went immediately into production.

Monarch of the Glen, which ran from 2000 to 2005, had seven series and sixty-four episodes. In the initial story, Archie MacDonald is called back from trying to make a living as a restaurateur in London to his Highland home and the bed of his dying father, Hector. When he arrives, however, Archie discovers that the news of his dying father was just a ploy by his mother to get him to Scotland, so they can tell him face-to-face that he has inherited, and will be responsible for, his father's large estate.

As is often the way, the writer was invited to participate in some of the casting interviews for the series, and one of the roles Michael was particularly interested in was Hector, the irascible Laird.

'When I heard that Richard Briers was up for the role of Hector I was very excited,' says Michael. 'I was hoping we'd get a big name for the role but hadn't bargained on somebody as well-known and respected as Richard. The producer invited me in for the interview and after having a chat we asked Richard if he'd mind reading the part. He was amazing. He took Hector off the page and turned him into flesh. It was as if I'd written the role for him.'

A few days later Richard was officially offered the role of Hector MacDonald in *Monarch of the Glen*, which would be the BBC's new flagship Sunday-night series. The pluses were obvious: he was back on primetime television and, as well as receiving a regular pay cheque – with more to follow, should it be repeated – he would be part of a new company. It was also a comedy drama, as opposed to a sitcom, which was something different. Unfortunately, the downsides to the new series were just as apparent, although fewer in number. 'There was just one, really,' says Annie. 'He'd be spending six to eight months in the Highlands of Scotland. As beautiful as the Highlands are, it was a long, long way from Chiswick.'

This didn't really hit home with Richard until the day he was due to leave to start filming the first series. 'Richard was in a total state of denial about going away,' says Annie. 'I remember seeing him clutching a carrier bag on the front doorstep when his car arrived. I think the carrier bag made him believe he wasn't going away for very long, but of course he was.'

Chiswick notwithstanding, it was Annie he was going to miss most. 'When he did *King Lear*, Mum had been with him,' says Kate, 'so that had been OK. As much as he loved Chiswick, she was the main reason he wanted to be there as her presence allowed him to relax and enjoy his surroundings. She didn't have to be by his side all the time, but as long as she wasn't far away, Dad was happy. Unfortunately, Mum wasn't able to be with him in Scotland all the time and I think he was really nervous. He was in his sixties now and was starting to slow down a bit.'

The last time Richard had been separated from Annie over a prolonged period of time was when he filmed *Fathom* in the 1960s, and even then, he had written to her almost every day. She had been the foundation stone on which he had built his career, and she had been as vital to his success as dogged determination or even talent. Why? Because Richard functioned best in the knowledge that he and his family were safe and secure, and although the work financed that environment, it was Annie who had created and maintained it. For want of a less hackneyed phrase, Annie was Richard's rock, and, as somebody who practised the same profession as he did, which also happened to be his passion, there wasn't much he couldn't discuss with her.

Bernard Cribbins, who has been married to his wife Gillian since 1955, is one of the few actors in the country whose career has been as prolific as that of Richard. He, as much as anyone, appreciates the advantages of having a happy homelife and cites Richard and Annie's marriage as being one of the happiest he has known. 'I think they got together about the same time as Gillian and me,' says Bernard. 'I first met Richard in the sixties, and even then, he was useless without Annie! Everybody knew that. How he managed during *Monarch of the Glen* I'll never know.'

The only things that were going to save Richard from a life of purgatory were the people he would be working with, and a telephone, of course. Providing they were all in good working order he might just get through it alive. Luckily, there were telephones everywhere in the Highlands and, despite the cast and crew being mainly unfamiliar to him, there would be plenty of opportunities to get acquainted.

The majority of the central cast, which included Susan Hampshire, Alexander 'Sandy' Morton and Julian Fellowes, had already met in London prior to filming and, if early signs had been anything to go by, he had nothing at all to worry about. The actor playing his son, Archie, was a twenty-nine-year-old unknown named Alastair Mackenzie. He had been as nervous as hell on meeting Richard, for the simple reason he was a fan.

'I'd grown up watching Richard on television,' says Alastair, 'and I felt an immediate connection. I thought I knew him. After the meeting he and I went outside and had a fag together, and I'd given up smoking! I had to pinch one from him and it was a rollie made with a liquorice paper. Not only did I become hooked on liquorice rollies, but I became hooked on him. That was all it took. I fell in love with him straight away.'

Home in Scotland was going to be an old shooting lodge in the village of Newtonmore, which was one of the locations. Richard would be sharing the lodge with Alastair and Susan Hampshire, so there was no chance of him being lonely.

'All of us had a suite of rooms each,' remembers Alastair, 'and downstairs there was a living room with a full-size snooker table in it, an open fire, some lovely comfy chairs and an honesty bar. Cash was never handed over. We just wrote everything down. Can you imagine it from my perspective? I was twenty-nine years old, this was my first big job, and there I was working and living with Richard Briers and Susan Hampshire. It was an absolute joy.'

Once settled, and with the first day of filming looming, Richard started getting to grips with his new character. Some of Hector's characteristics will have been familiar to Richard, such as a ribald sense of humour, but there was another side to his character that he hadn't had the opportunity to play yet; one that people had been accusing him of – and one that he had played up to – for decades: that of a cantankerous old curmudgeon. 'Richard could be a proper curmudgeon,' says his co-star, Sandy Morton. 'The thing is, he was also a mischievous little bugger and would use it either to make people laugh or wind people up. That's why he was so good at playing Hector. Hector was him!'

Yet again, one of the most important things Richard brought to the character of Hector, and one that wasn't necessarily obvious from the script, was vulnerability. 'There's a lot of humour in Hector's character,' says Michael Chaplin. 'But there's also a good deal of vulnerability, so he's quite a complex character, particularly at the beginning when Archie first comes home. Hector's a complete bastard then, but there's an explanation for that a few episodes in, which is all to do with his eldest son, Archie's elder brother, dying in an accident. That set the dynamic for their relationship going forward, as well as the fact that Archie was the opposite of Hector in that he was considered and business-like. As I said, the character of Hector was complex, and so Richard had to be humorous, angry and vulnerable. Over time, Archie and Hector become fond of each other which is one of the great joys of the first two series. That said, their love is never vocalised, which, on several occasions, leaves the audience crying, "Go on, just tell him!"'

Richard's talent for amalgamating comedy and vulnerability came as a big surprise to Alastair Mackenzie and would often leave him in tears. '*Monarch* was classed as being a comedy drama,' explains Alastair. 'There was slapstick, but there was also a lot of sadness, and that's where Richard was so amazing. He had this incredible skill where he could play tragedy and comedy in the same breath and he could make me weep openly. But Richard also had an extraordinary gravitas that was mostly masked by an ability to play inexplicably disempowering comedy. He could raise his eyebrow by a millimetre and I would be in bits. I could barely work with him for laughing, and he knew it. That was my Achilles heel and he found it within seconds. This happened every single day we were together!'

Something Richard was afforded more of with *Monarch of the*

Glen – more than he had been used to, at least – were rehearsals. 'Richard loved rehearsing,' remembers Alastair. 'In theatre, they're a necessity, but in television, they're a luxury, and as a perfectionist with a background in theatre Richard was never happier than when honing his craft with the rest of the company.'

Naturally, everyone was a little bit nervous prior to filming. After all, it doesn't matter how many hours you rehearse for, or how well you think you know a character, bringing it all to life is a very different proposition. From the moment filming began, however, everybody knew that the casting in particular had been absolutely spot on, not least Michael Chaplin.

'Richard may not have been very physically commanding, but that voice of his and the way he moved made him quite imposing. I have a vivid memory of one of the first scenes Hector has with Archie. He's coming down the stairs, so Archie is looking up at him, and he says, "Ah, so the prodigal son returns!" I remember thinking, *Wow!* He was so powerful. You see, regardless of what else was going on in a scene, your attention was always drawn to the fact that Richard Briers was speaking. That's testament to the uniqueness of his voice, of course – not to mention his verbal dexterity – but also to his standing as an actor. When Richard Briers spoke, everybody listened. To have that kind of influence over an audience must be incredible, and Richard knew exactly how to use it.'

Back at the shooting lodge, life had become quite enjoyable for Richard, and this was mainly down to the company he was keeping.

'Richard and I had a chair either side of the fire,' remembers Alastair, 'and we'd sit there night after night with a bottle of chardonnay, or two, and he'd tell me stories and give me advice. I encouraged him, of course, because I hung on his every word. Can you imagine that though, being stuck with Richard Briers in a shooting lodge for six months with two comfy chairs and a fully stocked bar? I know people who would give their right arm for that. In fact, I think most people would. When I wasn't working with him, I really missed him. It's hardly surprising.'

Such was the success of the first series of *Monarch of the Glen*, and the strength of the friendships he had made with the cast and crew, that when Richard was asked to do a second series he agreed. 'We had to make sure he came home every so often,' says Annie. 'And I went up to see him whenever I could. Had he not got on so well with the cast and crew he'd never have done it. They were the difference and he adored all of them.'

Not long after they had finished filming series two, Richard made the decision to do just one more. 'One more and that's it,' he told Annie. 'Three will be enough. I'm not going back, though, so I want them to kill me off.' The reason Richard wanted to be killed off was to avoid the temptation to go back. 'I know what I'm like,' he said. 'A little bit of gentle persuasion and I'll be on that blasted Caledonian Sleeper again!'

The Caledonian Sleeper is the overnight train that goes from Euston to the Highlands and was how Richard and Alastair were transported there prior to filming. When setting off to film series three, Richard ended up changing jobs for a few hours. 'We set off from Euston, as usual,' remembers Alastair. 'And, after dumping our stuff, we made our way to the bar. As we walked in, there was this large group of American tourists and when they saw Dickie and I they seemed visibly flabber-gasted. *Aww, how sweet*, I thought. Anyway, it transpired that these Americans were on a *Monarch of the Glen* tour and they thought that Dickie and I were part of it! Dickie absolutely loved this and as soon as he cottoned on he went into full-on tour-guide mode. He was in a bar, on a train, and with a captive audience of about twenty people. It was their lucky day!'

Before setting off for the Highlands, Alastair had made a conscious decision to cut down on the convivial side of life and devote more time to learning his lines. Somebody, however, had other ideas. 'I was trying to be quite disciplined about getting back after the day's shoot, learning my lines and having an early night,' says Alastair. 'After all, if you're not firing on all cylinders the days can seem very, very long. I remember being in my room after work on the first day and, as planned, instead of going downstairs I stayed in my room to learn my lines. I think I'd been there about ten minutes when suddenly the phone went. It was Richard. "Hello, love. Are you coming down? Come on! Get a move on." I was down there in about ten seconds! In those days you could smoke inside so within about a minute I had a rollie in one hand, a glass in the other, and was listening to one of the most amazing people I'd ever met tell me a story about Raquel Welch. I can't tell you how much I loved that man.

'The crew all loved Richard because he made them laugh,' remembers Sandy Morton. 'In fact, his motto was, "The weather's miserable, so let's make them laugh!" After he announced that he was leaving, the two props boys, John and Bob, got the art department to make some special wrapping paper for a present they were going to buy him. I think it was an Al Bowlly CD. Anyway, at his leaving party, everybody came up and gave Richard a card or a present and when John and Bob handed theirs over Richard immediately started studying the wrapping paper very carefully. "There's some phrase written on it over and over again," he said. "Aye, that's right," replied John and Bob. The writing was very, very small so Richard had to look hard. Eventually, he started to make out what it said and as he did tears of laughter began running down his face. This caused a ripple effect and within seconds the whole room was in bits, although only Richard, John and Bob knew why. "What does it say?" somebody asked. "It says," said Richard, taking a deep breath, "Get to fuck you miserable old bastard!" You can only do that with somebody you're very fond of.'

Several years later, Sandy, who became one of Richard's closest friends, suffered a heart attack and one of his many visitors while in hospital was Richard. 'Richard was an old-fashioned Tory,' says Sandy, 'and I'm the complete opposite. But every time he came to see me in hospital he brought me a copy of the *Daily Telegraph*. He'd just leave it at the bottom of my bed like a kind of calling card. Mischievous old bugger!'

Richard and Sandy's relationship was similar to that of Jimmy Stewart and Henry Fonda, in that the actors sat at opposite ends of the political spectrum yet always remained the best of friends. 'Their friendship was far bigger than their politics,' says Sandy, 'and Richard and I were the same. We didn't discuss it, we just laughed about it. Later on, I used to bring him copies of the *Morning Star* and as soon as he saw them he'd wet himself laughing. I could tell what he was thinking, *How can I get that bugger back?* He was like a giant elf.'

CHAPTER TWENTY-SIX

The Sunny Side of the Street

I n the spring of 2002, roughly a year after he had finished filming *Monarch of the Glen* (although he did appear in one further episode as a ghost), Richard was asked to appear as Smee in a big-budget production of *Peter Pan*. The director, P. J. Hogan, who directed *Muriel's Wedding* and the Julia Roberts hit, *My Best Friend's Wedding*, had already worked with Richard on a film called *Unconditional Love*. Rather refreshingly, the reason he had cast Richard in the first place had had nothing to do with *The Good Life*, *Ever Decreasing Circles* or the Kenneth Branagh films. 'It was all because of his association with Alan Ayckbourn,' explains P. J. 'I love Alan Ayckbourn, especially his early works, and I'd seen Richard in the TV version of *The Norman Conquests*. Ayckbourn didn't write gags, he wrote character comedy, and Richard could make anything funny. In my opinion, he was to Alan Ayckbourn what Jason Robards became to Eugene O'Neill, and ever since seeing him in *The Norman Conquests* he'd been on my bucket list of actors I wanted to work with.'

When P. J. was casting *Unconditional Love*, he had decided to go for broke and offer Richard a role, not thinking for a moment he would say yes. 'It was only a small part. Three or four days shooting, maybe? Most of his scenes were going to be with

Lynn Redgrave, who was a friend of his, and Kathy Bates, who he was a fan of, and he said yes. To be honest, I don't think he was bothered about the role, it was more about the company he'd be keeping. I was thrilled, though, because we seemed to get on really well.'

Richard's biggest scene during his short spell on *Unconditional Love* was with Kathy Bates and was what is known in the movie industry as a 'walk and talk'. 'We were on location in a town in Shropshire,' explains P. J., 'and Richard and Kathy had to walk down the High Street of this place while having a conversation. As a director I hate walk and talks because there's very little you can do with them visually, and this particular one was going to last about two pages.'

At this point in the shoot, P. J. was about four days behind schedule and, in that situation, you have to get a move on. 'In the scene we had Richard and Kathy Bates, nobody else. And because of their backgrounds, i.e. the stage, I knew for a fact that they'd be word perfect. Because of this I was confident of getting it done in one shot, which would have gone a long way to making up some of the time we'd lost.'

After setting up the shot, P. J. went for an early take. 'Because Richard and Kathy had to walk across the main street of this town we had control of the entire road. We'd stopped the traffic, the pedestrians, everything! After shouting, "Action" for the first take they started walking and talking but about halfway through the scene Richard dried for some reason. "OK, let's go again," I said. This time, Richard dried even earlier, which was strange. On the third take, he almost got to the end of the scene, but then fluffed it right at the last second. Every time I called, "Cut," Richard shouted, "Oh fuck! I'm so sorry, P. J."'

As time went on things just got worse, and as P. J. saw his day disappear he asked himself one question: how could this be happening to Richard Briers? 'This man had done Ayckbourn, for heaven's sake,' says P. J. 'And on consecutive nights. I didn't know what was going on.'

By the time take fifteen came along everybody, including Kathy, had started looking at P. J. as if to say, *He's not going to be able to do this*. 'I was definitely starting to panic by this point,' says P. J. 'Richard was becoming more and more frustrated and my schedule was going to the dogs. I was at a loss.'

In the end, P. J. decided to call a break in filming and while he figured out what to do, Richard was sent to have a break and a chat with Lynn Redgrave. A few minutes later P. J. decided to walk the scene himself and got to a point where Richard was required to stop for a few moments. All of a sudden, P. J. could see exactly what Richard had seen while they had been filming. 'As far as the eye could see there was traffic backed up,' says P. J. 'Hundreds and hundreds of people all sitting there waiting for Richard Briers to remember his lines. That, I'm afraid, was the problem. He must have been thinking to himself, *If I don't deliver these lines quickly, these people will be late for work, and if they're late for work, some of them might get into trouble*. The catastrophic scenarios were endless. Kathy would have loved having traffic stopped for her! Richard was a very different kind of person. My God, I felt for him!'

When it came to *Peter Pan*, which was filmed in Queensland, Australia, on a budget of $100 million and starred Jason Isaacs, Olivia Williams and Geoffrey Palmer, Richard's language went down well with the cast, but not their relatives. 'Obviously we had a lot of children on set,' explains P. J., 'and in the end they decided to make Richard a swear box. Actually, it was probably meant for all of us, but Richard was the one who filled it up. Although the kids found it funny, the parents and the chaperones were less understanding and while the kids would be laughing their heads off at Richard saying fuck for the eight-hundredth time after missing a line, the adults would be tutting and shaking their heads. Not that Richard could give a . . .'

The one thing P. J. encouraged Richard to do during the shoot was improvise; something he had never been comfortable doing. 'It happened by accident really,' remembers P. J. 'I needed to break a scene up one day that felt like it was dragging on and so I said to Richard that after Jason Isaacs had shot the pirate for interrupting, I'd cut to him momentarily. "Think of something to say," I said. "OK, love," he replied. "Just you leave it to me." Richard had a radio mic on and when Jason Isaacs shot the pirate he turned, looked straight into the camera, and said straight down the barrel of the lens, "Two dead already. Very exciting!" And then he looked back. He literally addressed the bloody camera! I couldn't believe it. It was so funny, though, I decided to keep it in, and after that I kept on encouraging him to do things to camera.'

In truth, Richard's adventures in improvisation – on P. J.'s watch, at least – had started on *Unconditional Love*, although it hadn't been entirely comprehensible. 'Every time Richard's character said something rude or controversial, which was often, Richard would do this strange kind of laugh that wasn't in the script. He sounded like Mutley from *Wacky Races*! At first, I wondered what the hell he was doing, but I quickly realised that it fitted perfectly. I remember thinking to myself, *That's why he's Richard Briers! Nobody else would think of doing that*. He'd take a part – any part – and squeeze every drop of potential out of it.'

A few weeks after arriving back in the UK from Australia, Richard received a letter from Buckingham Palace informing him that he had been awarded a CBE in the 2003 Queen's Birthday Honours list. He had been awarded an OBE back in 1989 and although he had enjoyed the trip to Buckingham Palace, he later confessed to Lucy that he hadn't felt worthy. 'I think Dad felt incredibly proud when he was awarded his OBE,' she says. 'Mum, Kate and I went along to the ceremony, but I remember him saying afterwards that he felt like a bit of a prat among all those people who'd worked tirelessly for charity or had saved somebody's life. That was typically him. In the ceremony room itself, there were two banks of seats and to get to the Queen Dad had to walk right down the middle of them. He knew where we were sitting and as he walked past he gave us a look, smiled and did a quick comedy trip. It was brilliantly anarchic, considering where he was. As she awarded Dad his OBE, the Queen said to him, "I think you've got this for making people laugh." Quite right too.'

When he went to collect his CBE in June 2003, he was accompanied by Annie, Harry and Rachael. There were no comedy trips this time. Just lots of smiles and a few photo opportunities. The occasion of him accepting his CBE raised a question that has never been answered conclusively and is certainly not exclusive to him. 'When he was collecting his CBE the question being asked by most people was, where's the knighthood? It wasn't something we dwelled on, but for what he'd achieved I do think he was slightly short changed,' says

Kate. Indeed, since Richard's death there have been entire articles written about why he never received a knighthood. Then again, until quite recently, protagonists from the genres of comedy and light entertainment had always been overlooked in this department; the establishment tending to favour more 'respectable' individuals such as sportspeople, businesspeople or actors who had appeared with the RSC. Anyway, as Lucy says, the last person who would have complained about this would have been Richard.

One of the reasons Richard had decided to leave *Monarch of the Glen*, besides feeling homesick, was that his breathing had started to become quite laboured and he was getting tired very easily. By that time he had been smoking for over fifty years and by his own estimation had been through over half a million cigarettes. 'The first thing I remember hearing as a child when I woke up was Dad doing his "morning coughing",' says Lucy. 'But you never thought anything of it. Everybody used to smoke back then, and hacking coughs were commonplace.'

As time went on, the coughing and breathlessness became more of an issue for Richard and by 2007 he had become a regular visitor to his GP. 'Then, one day, he told Kate and I that he'd been diagnosed with emphysema,' says Lucy. 'I remember looking it up and, although it was terminal, his life expectancy could be anything up to five years and, in that situation, you tend to put it to the back of your mind.' Funnily enough, that's exactly what Richard did and, despite the bleak prognosis, he carried on with the two things that made him truly happy: working and being a grandparent. The frustration he had felt prior to *Monarch of the Glen* of not being attached to a television series had disappeared now; partly because he was contented, and partly because he knew he couldn't do it any more. That must have hurt Richard, but the truth is that he was as adept at accepting difficult situations as he had been interpreting Ayckbourn. He didn't do self-pity and if anybody tried to talk to him about his complaint he would either bat the enquiry away – 'I'm fine, love. Just got a bit of a cough' – or cut them off at the pass with some gallows humour – 'I'm completely buggered! Would be surprised if I last a week.'

'Dad didn't talk to anybody about what was happening,' says Kate. 'In fact, he only told Mum what she needed to know. Again, I think that was a generational thing, but it's also who Dad was. You didn't talk about your problems. You just got on with it. He used to moan about stuff all the time, but just trivial things. That was him being a professional curmudgeon! One thing he never, ever did, was feel sorry for himself, nor did he allow others to feel sorry for him. Not publicly, at least.'

He may not have done self-pity, but after being diagnosed with emphysema Richard did develop an unhealthy sense of self-loathing, which resulted in him refusing treatment. 'Dad had no interest in doing anything that would help him,' explains Lucy. 'There was this huge sense that he'd brought it on himself and so didn't deserve treatment. Mum told me that he'd say to her that he'd "ruined his life". It was incredibly sad. The way he dealt with it was not to talk about it and get on with his life until he couldn't.'

One thing Richard did find difficult to hide was his sense of frustration at not being able to function properly. 'It was awful to watch,' remembers Kate, 'because he'd always been so active. He'd always been so alive!'

Certain death notwithstanding, Richard managed to cram

quite a lot of work into his final years, and between 2008 and 2012 he appeared in episodes of *Kingdom*, with Stephen Fry, *Miss Marple* and *Torchwood*, and narrated dozens of cartoons, short films and adverts. His final stage appearance took place in 2010 when he was invited by the director, Nicholas Hytner, to appear as Adolphus Spanker in Dion Boucicault's comedy, *London Assurance*, at the National Theatre. Despite his worsening condition, Richard was desperate to accept the role as he wanted to tread the boards one final time and so he told Nicholas Hytner he would do it. It was only a cameo, after all, and because it would be performed as part of a repertory season, he wouldn't have to do eight shows a week. That said, there was still plenty of comic potential in Adolphus Spanker, and Richard went into rehearsals in full-on squeezing mode.

Annie and Lucy went to see a preview of *London Assurance* and, as good as the show itself undoubtedly was, it was the reaction to Richard's arrival on stage that had the biggest effect. 'Lucy and I were a bit worried about him, to tell the truth,' says Annie. 'He obviously wasn't very well, and it doesn't matter how small the role is, you've still got to get up there and do it. When he finally appeared, he got a round of applause, which was nice, and I could tell just by looking at him that he was absolutely fine. There was also this chap sitting in front of us, and when he saw Richard he leaned over to his wife, and went, "Awww, Richard Briers!" Lucy and I were beaming with pride!'

Also starring in *London Assurance* was the actor Simon Russell Beale, who played the ageing fop, Sir Harcourt Courtly. Simon became a big supporter of Richard's, and this was despite Richard making him do something he had never been able to tolerate.

'I'm very pompous when it comes to corpsing,' says Simon, 'and until *London Assurance* I don't think I'd ever laughed on stage unless I'd had to. Then, Richard Briers came along, and everything went out of the window!'

This wasn't just a quick covert chuckle, however. It was a full-on, company-wide meltdown.

'At the end of the play,' explains Simon, 'when everything's being sorted out and people are getting married, etc., Adolphus Spanker, who is this peculiar mixture of timidity and comical aggression, which was very Richard, says, "I married for love, and you see how happy it made me?" One evening, when he got to the line, Richard said instead, "I married for love, and you see how *funny* it made me." Now I know it doesn't sound very amusing now, but at the time, to the ten actors on stage, it was gut-wrenchingly hilarious and one by one we all started to corpse. God knows how long it went on but the following night when he got to the same line – which he did properly, incidentally – we did the same thing again. A two-day corpse! That's unheard of.'

Of Richard's performance in *London Assurance*, Simon refers to Nicholas Hytner's book, *Balancing Acts: Behind the Scenes at the National Theatre*, in which he talks about the production. 'It's very interesting, and I'm paraphrasing here, but Nick says that you can look at Fiona Shaw and learn this, and you can look at Simon Russell Beale and learn that, but you cannot learn what Richard Briers did in *London Assurance*. Funnily enough, I don't remember Nick really directing Richard at all, which is perhaps what he's also referring to.'

After *London Assurance* had ended, Richard, for as long as he was able, followed the career of Simon Russell Beale and became an ardent supporter of his. 'I received a medal from the National Theatre for long service,' says Simon, 'and Richard and Annie came along to the lunch. I was so moved by that. He wasn't in good health, but he insisted on registering his support. He also came to my next two shows and came by afterwards to say well done. He didn't have to do that. Dickie Briers was a very dear man.'

The last film Richard ever made was a horror-comedy entitled *Cockneys vs Zombies*, in which a group of cockneys attempt to rescue their grandfather and his friends from their retirement home while a zombie apocalypse takes place. Richard, who played one of the friends in the retirement home, was joined in the film by his old RADA colleague, Dudley Sutton, Tony Selby, who had played Sam, the rag-and-bone man, in two episodes of *The Good Life*, Alan Ford, from *Lock, Stock and Two Smoking Barrels*, Honor Blackman and Georgina Hale. The film premiered at the 2012 London FrightFest Film Festival and despite not becoming a box-office smash, it performed favourably overall and is well on its way to becoming a cult classic. Lucy remembers Richard receiving the script for the film and, although he liked it, Annie did not.

'When Dad got the script for *Cockneys vs Zombies,* he and Mum read it and then he sent it straight to me and asked me if I thought he should do it. Mum had told him not to as there was so much swearing in it, but I told him he had to. For a start, the script was hilarious, and I was sure it would become a cult classic. But there was also this one scene in the film which I thought would be fantastic. It's a chase scene involving Dad, who's on a Zimmer frame, and a very lethargic zombie. Both are going at the same speed and neither are making any ground. It's just brilliant.'

If that weren't enough to whet your appetite, Richard also kills several of the undead during the film using an AK-47, which he's had gaffer-taped to his Zimmer frame, and gets lifted on to a Routemaster bus – literally – by an eighty-seven-year-old Honor Blackman. The promise of Richard Briers killing zombies should be enough to entice anyone, though. Genius.

Although he found it hard work, Richard enjoyed every second of that shoot. In fact, the chances are, it may well have prolonged his life. 'Every time Richard came back from filming he looked ten years younger,' says Annie. 'He was back doing the thing he lived for.'

During its cinema release, which started in August 2012, Richard, Annie, Kate, Harry and Rachael all went to see the film at the Empire Leicester Square where it was playing on one of the smaller screens. 'The kids thought it was amazing,' remembers Kate. 'Grandad, killing zombies! What's not to like? Suddenly, he was the coolest man on earth. We had a fabulous afternoon.'

Unfortunately, that was to be one of the last enjoyable family get-togethers Richard ever had, as by the end of the year his condition had deteriorated to such a degree that he couldn't even talk without coughing. 'That was really tragic,' says Kate. 'And I think that's when he gave up.'

Two months prior to that, in October, he had recorded an episode of *Two Pipe Problems*, a radio series he had been starring in since 2007 alongside Stanley Baxter. What had always been a source of great enjoyment to Richard had now turned into quite a harrowing chore and, with two episodes of the seventh series still to record, he returned home and announced to Annie that he was finished. 'I can't work any more,' he said. 'I'm done.' From then on, his decline was rapid, and by Christmas he had simply lost interest in life. 'He just wanted to go,' says Annie. 'He couldn't talk, which meant he couldn't work. And if he couldn't work, he didn't want to live. It was that simple.'

Richard died of a cardiac arrest at home on 17 February 2013, aged seventy-nine. Had his illness gone on any longer, the chances are he would have died in a hospice, so it was a happy release. 'Richard would have hated that,' says Annie. 'He died at home with me, and while he was still able to walk.'

When Richard's agent, Christopher Farrar, went public with the news, the reaction on social media was both immediate and touching. He trended on Twitter for over a day, which would have amused and baffled him, and the tributes that were offered by friends, colleagues and admirers numbered in their thousand. Although sad, it was clear that people were just grateful for the fact that we'd had Richard Briers in the first place, which made the aftermath of his death almost celebratory; like skipping the funeral and going straight to the memorial service. As somebody who was both gregarious and unsentimental, that would have suited Richard down to the ground.

One of the warmest tributes came from his friend, Stephen Fry, who was asked to speak about Richard for a show on Radio 4 Extra. He said, 'Dickie wasn't a great Shakespearean actor; he was a fine Shakespearean actor. You don't usually mourn great Shakespearean actors; you put up a great statue for them and you make noble speeches about how extraordinary they were. But somebody like Dickie you mourn because he was in your home every week and because he had a character and likeability and you just adored him and you wanted to hug him. People like that are rare and they're the ones you mourn. They're the ones you really miss. When I heard that Dickie had died, I just felt diminished because he was just so much a part of my growing up, particularly for my generation. He was a part of the furniture, a part of England. And he was a sunny part of it.'

Unfortunately for the family, they obviously had to adhere to social convention and plan a funeral for Richard, although he hadn't helped matters much. 'Dad never left any instructions about a funeral,' says Lucy. 'There were no lists of readings or music. In the end I had to listen to his *Desert Island Discs* to get inspiration. About once a day I'd say out loud, "Bloody hell, Dad, you could have made this easier!"'

The funeral was held at St Michael and All Angels Church in Chiswick on 6 March 2013. Over two hundred people attended the service with many more waiting outside. As well as a heartfelt tribute from Kate, Harry and Rachael, Brian Murphy brought applause after reading John Betjeman's 'A Subaltern's Love Song' and Penelope Wilton read from 'The Death of Sir Henry Irving'. There had to be a few laughs, of course, and these came courtesy of the vicar, Father Kevin Morris. The last time he and Richard had met, he revealed, had been at a church fundraiser. ' I do enjoy these things even though I'm not religious,' he told Father Kevin. 'Well,' Father Kevin told the congregation as he looked at Richard's coffin, covered in flowers and surrounded by candles, 'you are now.' The congregation burst into laughter.

The hymns at the service included 'Lord of All Hopefulness' and 'Morning Has Broken', which were two of Richard's favourites, and his coffin was carried into the church to Mozart's Serenade No. 10 in B flat major, and out of the church to Louis Armstrong's 'On the Sunny Side of the Street'.

As sad as the occasion was, it brought to the fore a number of rather endearing character traits that, because of the protracted length of Richard's illness, his family had almost forgotten about. One of these was his fondness for meeting new people at their place of work; something he had always taken great pleasure in doing whether at home or on holiday.

'The reason this occurred to me,' says Kate, 'is because at the funeral I saw a wreath from the Capital Motor Company, which is where Dad used to get his car serviced. At first, I thought, *That's sweet, but why on earth have they sent a wreath?* And then I realised. Dad used to adore taking his car to them and, as soon as something went wrong with it, he'd be down there like a shot.'

Richard's propensity for making the acquaintance of people had started at school and was something his adult subjects of interest would find either impertinent or simply amiable. The attention was always genuine, however, and as Richard got older the vast majority of people would plump for the latter.

Paul Sahota is the co-owner of the Capital Motor Co. and he remembers Richard fondly. 'He'd been taking his cars here since the early 1970s and when I got involved in the 1980s he was very much part of the furniture. He used to walk in, hand over his keys, and then sit down and make everyone laugh.'

By the end of his life, Richard had made almost as many friends outside the acting profession as he had made inside.

'One of his favourite things was visiting the dump in Acton,' remembers Kate. 'He knew absolutely everybody down there and used to love finding rubbish that wouldn't fit in the bin. "Just popping down the dump, love," he'd say to Mum. "What – again?!" He'd spend hours down there, just chatting. He wanted to know everything about everyone.'

Because of Richard's commitment to his profession, many people believed that he was only truly happy in the company of actors. He wasn't.

'When he was with actors he liked talking about acting,' says Lucy. 'And when he was with Paul at the garage or a chap down at the dump, he liked talking about them. Acting was his life, there's no denying that, but he also needed an alternative and getting to know people outside the profession was almost as important to him. It fed his inquisitive nature – the one that had got him into trouble at school – and he genuinely cared about them.'

Paul Sahota agrees with Lucy's sentiments wholeheartedly. 'Whenever Richard arrived at the garage all he wanted to know was how we were getting on, how our wives were getting on, and how our children were getting on. He wasn't interested in what we were doing to his car or how much it was going to cost. He just wanted to know about us, but in a caring way. I think he actually worried about us.'

In 2010, when Paul and his colleagues were thinking about doing some advertising, Richard immediately offered his services.

'We wanted to make a video about the company to put on YouTube,' says Paul. 'And when Richard found out about it he came straight over and offered to appear in the video free of charge. He wasn't well at the time but that didn't matter. That was a big thing for us, having Richard in the video endorsing us.'

Kate remembers this as being part of her father's philosophy.

'Dad wasn't a great one for giving advice, but one of the few things he did tell me was to be nice to people no matter what. Unless they were horrible, of course!'

As well as receiving a wreath from his friends at Capital Motors, the family's window cleaner attended the funeral service, alongside various local shop owners.

As they left the service, the guests were invited to sign a book of remembrance that would be presented to the family afterwards. Emma Thompson wrote, 'I simply can't understand what all the fuss is about. Get a bloody haircut. Yours, God.'

'Dickie used to write letters to me, as God,' explains Emma. 'And I used to write to him, as God. His letters would come from Prompt Corner, which is what he called his house in Chiswick, and mine would come from Mount Olympus. I have an entire folder full of these letters at home and they're all about how utterly naff everything is. Some of them are so rude!'

About fourteen months after the funeral, a celebration of Richard's life was held at the Criterion Theatre, the venue of some of his biggest West End successes. Organised by the family, it took eight months to put together and featured dozens of different tributes as well as segments from some of Richard's best work. 'It was an out-and-out celebration,' says Lucy. 'Ken made the most amazing speech, Patrick Doyle played the piano. Everybody who knew Dad wanted to get involved. It was amazing. The funeral had been something we'd had to get through, whereas this was something we all *wanted* to do. Four hundred and twenty people, in a beautiful theatre, all remembering Dad and having a huge celebration.'

Had he been there, Richard would no doubt have accused his family of making a big fuss.

'That's exactly what he'd have done,' says Annie, 'before having a quick drink, of course. Then he and I would have waved goodbye to everyone, and gone back home to Chiswick.'

ACKNOWLEDGEMENTS

The enthusiasm shown towards my endeavours by Richard's friends and former colleagues (not to mention my own friends) has been unprecedented in my experience and, as well as acting as a barometer for how Richard was – and is – regarded, it has made the task of researching his life a joy. Those who have generously given their time are: Sir Alan Ayckbourn, Simon Beresford, Michael Billington OBE, Michael Blakemore OBE, Peter Bowles, Sir Kenneth Branagh, Ray Brooks, Nick Butterworth, Bernard Cribbins OBE, Nick Butterworth, Grange Calveley, Michael Chaplin, Ken Clark, Bernard Dandridge, Dame Judi Dench, Patrick Doyle, Peter Egan, Alan Ford, Michael Frayn, Lucy Gannon, Ricky Gervais, Sheila Hancock CBE, Matthias Hoene, P. J. Hogan, Nerys Hughes, Sir Nick Hytner, Marilyn Imrie, William Ingrey, Griff Rhys Jones, Dame Penelope Keith, Felicity Kendal CBE, Alex Lowe, Alastair Mackenzie, Bruce Montague, Brian Murphy, John Nettleton, Eric Paisley, Geoffrey Palmer CBE, Dame Siân Phillips, Simon Russell Beale CBE, Paul Sahota, Prunella Scales CBE, Adrian Scarborough, Elizabeth Seal, Robert Sellers, Dudley Sutton, Dame Emma Thompson, Sandy Morton, Denis Norden CBE, Martin Rosen, Kevin Whately, Sir Tom Stoppard, Tamar Thomas, Samuel West, Timothy West CBE, Olivia Williams, Dame Penelope Wilton and Jimmy Yuill. Thank you all very much.

I am also indebted to Andreas Campomar and Claire Chesser at Constable. They too have been incredibly supportive, as has my literary agent, Tim Bates at Peters Fraser + Dunlop. You're right. It's not proper work.

Also high up on the support and patience scale is my family. First I would like to thank my Uncle Jim and his wonderful wife Joyce for putting me up in Chiswick. I've never known hospitality like it. And secondly, I would like to thank my wife Indra and my children, Henry and Louie. Over the past year or so Mr Briers has never been far away and they have indulged me without question. Cheers, my dears.

Finally, I would like to thank Richard's family: his sister Jane, his daughters Kate and Lucy, and his widow Annie. From the moment they granted me permission to write this book their enthusiasm for the project has equalled my own and if it hadn't been for Lucy's twenty-four-hour biographer helpline, which is effectively what she ended up running when I was calling her twenty times a day, I don't know what I would have done. Thank you all very much. It's been a privilege.

Bibliography

My Word Is My Bond: The Autobiography by Roger Moore, Michael O'Mara, 2009.

A Celebration of The Good Life by Richard Webber with John Esmonde and Bob Larbey, Orion Books, 2002.

Richard Briers' Coward & Company by Richard Briers, Robson Books, 1998.

A Taste of the Good Life by Richard & Ann Briers, Pavilion Books, 1996.

English Country Churches by Richard Briers, Robson Books, 1998.

Index

INDEX

INDEX